The Found Vagabond

KRIS OLSON

The Found Vagabond

How to be Inspired, Driven and Fulfilled by Travel

KRIS OLSON

The Found Vagabond

By

Kris Olson

Special thanks to Michelle Madison-Dick who assisted with the editing and review work. Also, a big thank-you goes to Michael Swanson for the cover artwork.

****

This book is dedicated to my wife Ana.

She is my passion, my partner, my constant companion, and my best friend.

May we travel together for eternity.

****

Table of Contents

INTRODUCTION

What qualifies me to write a book about travel? Let me convince you.

At the age of 40 I consider myself to be a very happy, balanced person with a beautiful family, an exciting life and a passion for living. And, quite simply, the root of my well-being and source of my happiness all leads back to travel.

Travel has blessed me with a life packed with joy, excitement, learning, adventure, wonder, surprise, and infinite possibility. Travel has directly facilitated the development of my business career and allowed me to make and keep friends all over the world. It has taught me so much about the world and its people, and given me an appreciation for not just the similarities we all share, but more importantly, the differences between us, which make the world such an amazing place!

Because of travel, I met my beautiful wife, lover, soul mate and best friend Ana. We met while traveling, fell in love traveling together and have created two gorgeous children, Magnus and Stella, now eight and six years of age, both of whom have been traveling since they were born and are probably the best little travelers in the world. As a family, traveling is our passion and our life revolves around exploring not just the world, but also our own country, region and neighbourhood.

I have travelled to approximately 80 countries and lived for a period in 13 of those (Canada, Denmark, UK, Pakistan, Bahamas, El Salvador, Costa Rica, Suriname, Barbados, Dominican Republic, Puerto Rico, Netherlands, Kazakhstan). Within North America I have traveled through all the provinces of Canada and about half of the states in the USA, many of these extensively. As a youngster, I never imagined that I would have the opportunity to explore so many fantastic countries!

I was born and raised in Saskatoon, Saskatchewan, which is in the west central part of Canada and is one of the most sparsely populated provinces. It is often called the "breadbasket" of the country as the population is largely rural and agriculture drives the economy. Although it didn't occur to me at the time, growing up in Saskatoon was somewhat isolating, as the nearest city to us was 250 kilometres away, and the next closest one after that was over 600 kilometres. After completing high school, I embarked on a Bachelor of Commerce degree at the local university. I paid for it on my own and came out of the four year program debt free, ready to take on the world, and feeling like quite the educated and valuable commodity. Unfortunately, I graduated in the midst of a big recession so there were simply no jobs available, or perhaps I just wasn't as valuable as my university professors had led me to believe. After one year of floundering, I packed my bags and left Canada in search of something better.

My educational background is in Finance, but my career path would organically wind its way into the field of IT (Information Technology) and software implementation. I gradually became an expert with a particular piece of software called JD Edwards, which is used by thousands of companies worldwide as the backbone of their financial information systems. Since the usage of this software is global in nature, my expertise would serve as the ideal springboard for securing international work on business improvement projects across a range of different industries, which involved installing, modifying or enhancing this software and improving the business processes it supported.

During this time of international work and travel, I would meet my future wife Ana and together we worked and traveled internationally for several more years, spanning dozens of countries and even learning Spanish along the way. Her marketing and web skills made her a natural fit for project work and we even worked together on some of the same projects. After a time we decided that we would start a family and wanted our children to have a childhood home and grow up with their cousins, aunts, uncles and grandparents. We made the decision to give up our nomadic existence and return to Canada. But before making this life transition, we took a year off and did a round the world backpacking trip that took us through 11 countries in the Southern Hemisphere and provided a lifetime worth of memories.

The first three years in Canada were spent in Calgary, Alberta, which was close to my family and where both of our children were born. Although we expected our traveling days would be somewhat curtailed, we both ended up working for an airline called WestJet so were able to travel more than ever, and did dozens of trips throughout North America. Of course, the kids always traveled with us and each of them experienced their first flight before they were one month old.

We made some great friends in Calgary and spent many, many fantastic moments with my family. But after Stella was born, we decided that we wanted to be closer to Ana's parents, who were approaching retirement, so I quit my job, sold our house and we moved to Paris, Ontario, which is in the south-eastern part of Canada. Here, we settled in quickly, but our traveling days were far from over, as Ana was able to retain her position with WestJet for three years, which meant continued access to inexpensive flights and many more trips. As her job with the airline came to a close, it was the perfect time to get back into our shared passion for sailing. We bought a sailboat and moored it on Lake Erie, which is a 45 minute drive from home, giving us access to the Great Lakes and the world. Our frequency of travel has not changed, but our primary method of travel has switched from airplane to car and boat, and we continue to explore as a family, making travel an integral part of our children's lives. And yes, they too are very happy little people and have already done more traveling than most people will in their entire lives.

This book is divided into two parts. Part One is comprised of ten chapters, each discussing a particular aspect of travel. It does not have to be read from start to finish and some chapters may be more relevant to you than others, so feel free to jump around, read the chapters that grab your attention first, then move on to the others. My goal is to provide useful and practical information that has helped me in my travels and may also help you. There is no such thing as "executing the perfect trip", but there are many precautions you can take that will remove some of the unnecessary stress from the travel experience, as well as things you can do along the way to really get the most out of your travels. These range from the methods of travel, how to plan and fund it, how to travel with children, how to be safe, and even ideas on how to find international work and live in a different country.

Part Two is a collection of ten true travel stories I have written over the years, many of which illustrate the concepts presented in the first half of the book, others which are simply fun stories. My hope is these stories will inspire you to take a chance and get out there traveling and experience some of the joy, passion, and wonder that travel has to offer. Or, if already a seasoned traveler, offer you some new ideas and perhaps allow you to view travel in a different way.

Finally, throughout the book I will relate many stories and events that have turned me into the person I am today and influenced my philosophy and outlook on life. As a result of my travels, I see the world and my life much differently now than I did before I began traveling, and am an infinitely happier person for it.

Are you convinced?

****

Part One – How to Be Inspired, Driven & Fulfilled by Travel

Chapter 1 – Why

Those who rarely travel may ask, "Why bother?" It is easier to stay home, follow your regular routine, spend your weekends relaxing, and generally try to avoid any unpredictable or uncertain situations. This may provide for a trouble-free and predictable lifestyle that, for many people, may be exactly what they want. But for those who crave challenge, variation, knowledge, adventure, and surprises, there is no better way to enhance your life than to travel!

My university graduation was an exciting time – finally the end to all those years of studying, writing stressful exams, riding the big green bus to school, being constantly broke and feeling like it was never going to end. Graduating in the midst of a severe recession did not bode well for job prospects, and after months of fruitless job searching, I took a job with a local newspaper selling advertising and doing a bit of writing. It was not exactly my dream job and a very depressing start to my working life. I ground through that misery for nearly a year, hating every minute of it, yet seeing no other obvious options. One morning in February, on a blisteringly cold day, I was sitting in my beaten-up 1968 Dodge Dart, chilled to the bone, because the car heater simply could not compete with the minus 34 degree temperature outside. I was parked in front of a local business, and should have been inside making a sales call, but was simply frozen with apathy. I was thinking to myself, *What the hell am I doing here? Is this the kind of life I want? Is this what I've worked so hard for? There has to be something better out there.* I decided right then that I simply was not going to accept my unhappy situation anymore

The next day I started looking for work and soon found a job as a fishing guide at Wollaston Lake, in the far north of Saskatchewan, which would enable me to save money for a backpacking trip to Europe. I quit my newspaper job and spent the next four months taking guests out fishing, exploring the far reaches of an enormous, pristine lake in pursuit of trophy fish, loving every second of it, and saving every cent I earned. At the end of that summer, I had a pocket full of cash, a yearning to explore and, most importantly, a new outlook on the rest of my life. I bought an open ended ticket to London, England and was soon standing at the Saskatoon airport saying goodbye to my family. As I saw the tears welling up in my mom's eyes, I told her I would be back in two months.

It would be ten years later that I returned to live in Canada.

Why Travel?

I've learned that the benefit of traveling goes well beyond simply expanding your horizons and discovering new places. Travel forces you to question your beliefs. Travel takes you out of your comfort zone and brings you back to the basics, where you have to rely on your instincts and can no longer trust the societal rules you believe to be true. Travel brings a heightened sense of awareness as you abandon your everyday, monotonous rituals. Instead of living on perpetual auto-pilot, you actually think about what you are doing, and why you are doing it. Days are not predictable, and though you may know where they will start, you never know where they will end. Travel brings your senses to life – you notice the smells in the air, the textured flavours of the foods you eat, the sensations of the sun and wind on your face, and the tiniest details of the sights before you. You meet people and actually look at them, in their eyes, and listen to what they say. And they listen to you. The conversations you have are significant, and interesting, and you rapidly develop strong bonds with others. Through travel, you get to know yourself, learn why you are the way you are, and sometimes understand what you would like to change about yourself. Travel brings you closer to nature, and gives you a fresh appreciation for the beauty and richness of the world. Travel leads you to appreciate every minute of life you have, to relish those minutes, and not waste them.

Travel changes you.

Reasons for Traveling

The decision to travel can be anything from a spontaneous, last minute adventure to a thoroughly planned journey, and everything in between. The reasons for traveling are many; below are some common examples.

Travel by Accident

I spent the summer after my first year of university living and working in North Battleford, a town located 150 kilometres away from my hometown. Towards the end of this summer job I received an unusual phone call from my grandfather. He told me a friend of the family, named Keith Graham, who I actually shared some university classes with, had booked a return air ticket from Saskatoon to Toronto but was unable to use it and it was not refundable. Keith wanted to know if anybody in the family could use the ticket. After pushing back my initial thoughts of *I can't leave my job, I still have one week to go* and *I don't want to spend all the money I've saved for school*, I got Keith's number, spoke with him and arranged everything, then immediately packed my stuff, got rid of my apartment, hauled my junk back to Saskatoon and, before I knew it, was on the plane headed for Toronto.

It would be my first trip to eastern Canada and one that I will never forget. In fact, this was one of the most important trips of my life as it really stoked my sense of adventure, curiosity, independence and, for the first time in my life, made me realize what a small town, non-worldly, cow shit between the toes, prairie hoser I really was.

I spent a week with my uncle Michael in Oakville, where he was working as a sous-chef at a local restaurant called Navy Blue. He put me up at his house in Oakville and that week I spent with him was truly eye-opening. I ate gourmet food, drank premium wine, raced a sailboat on Lake Ontario, went night clubbing in Toronto, visited wineries, orchards and greenhouses, ate a goat cheese pizza (you can make cheese from goats?), sampled my first fresh fig, and met dozens of interesting and fun people. Up until this point, my passions in life had been Rye & Cokes, cheesy 80's hair bands, hamburgers, and hanging out at the lake. After that trip…those were still my passions, but at least I learned that you're not supposed to pronounce the "t" in the word Merlot.

I have often thought of Keith and the remarkable opportunity he gave to me, and sometimes wonder if I would have developed this passion to travel if I had passed up that ticket. Fortunately, I took a chance, made the trip, had an incredible adventure, and look back on that as one of those pivotal moments in my life that made a real impact and changed me, very much for the better. That trip kindled my passion for travel, but would make the following three years of university nearly unbearable, as I yearned to travel more.

Traveling by accident can be the best way to travel, as your destination may not be your choice, you will have no expectations, and everything will be a surprise. These opportunities will come up from time to time and if you don't grab it….well, I guess you'll never know.

Travel for School

School can present all sorts of opportunities for travel. Back in high school, there was an Easter tour that students could attend if they had enough cash to pay for it, and these programs still exist in many schools. There were also many exchange programs available, such as Rotary exchanges, which were readily available if you were willing to put the required work and preparation into it.

Once you embark on post secondary school, there will also be travel opportunities available. The ability to travel as part of your studies is a very worthwhile add-on to your education, and like most things in life, learning seems to be most profound when achieved by actively experiencing and doing, as opposed to reading and writing.

Travel for Altruism

The thought of packing up and moving to Sub-Saharan Africa to help build a school in a poor village is romantic, charitable, inspiring, and appealing to the soul. Many people take this option and there are thousands of programs to help facilitate this. However, you do need to be very careful as many of these are for-profit organizations taking advantage of good natured people to squeeze money out of them, and then leave them high and dry with no support or organization to help them along. As usual, the internet is your friend so make sure you do your research and due diligence.

If you are involved with a church, most parishes have links with other churches for missionary work, where you are likely to have a good support system to assist you.

I will admit that I have never done this sort of traveling, though I have certainly thought about it over the years. It is likely something I would consider doing when I am a bit older, as I believe it would be an enriching, and quite likely, more satisfying experience than traveling for other, less benevolent reasons.

Travel for Work

Of all the ways to travel, traveling for work is the only way to travel on somebody else's budget, unless of course your parents are rich and set you up with a nice trust fund. Traveling for work is the primary way I have been able to do much of my traveling, and there are truly thousands of opportunities out there to do this. Many jobs today will offer possibilities for travel, whether it's a conference or workshop in your field, a short business trip to visit another facility, a short term project assignment in a different location or a longer term position sponsored by your company. Of course, the trick is to tack on a few days before or after these trips for personal time to do some exploring, and most companies are usually okay with this.

Some jobs are obviously more conducive to travel than others, such as sales jobs, working for an airline, some training jobs or any other position where travel is a fundamental requirement of the position. These are fantastic jobs when you are young, mobile, and have fewer responsibilities, such as a home and family to support, so you usually don't want to wait to do this type of job later in your career. When I was younger, I took every single work travel opportunity I could, but now I rarely travel for work, which was part of the appeal of the job when I took it. It's pretty boring being faced with an empty hotel room when you have a family at home, though perhaps that's just me. Many business travelers enjoy having a short break from the family chaos.

Mike Schaaf is one of my best buddies, and has been a road warrior for two decades. He has travelled to dozens of countries for project work, ranging in duration from a day to over a year. He maintains a home in Chicago, but for many years has spent only a small fraction of this time there. Despite being a tireless working machine, he still manages to get out and do some exploring while on the road.

Travel for Glory

Traveling for glory means visiting as many countries as possible, going to places nobody else has been, and experiencing things few others have. Some travel not just for glory, but also to outdo their other worldly friends in an ongoing international pissing contest. Whether this labels you a wanker or not depends entirely on how consistently you post evidence of each spectacular moment on Facebook, thereby increasing your personal inventory of social capital. Traveling for glory has always been cool, but it's just recently that you have been able to brag to every person you know, and many you don't know, with the push of a button. Sure, I've done it, and will admit it is cruelly enjoyable to torture your working friends with tales of your exploits. But it is also a bit tacky. I always find it interesting when you've known a person for a while, then one day they say something that leads you to discover they have traveled to some neat places you would not have expected. Maybe I just like surprises.

If you are going to travel for glory and hit as many countries as possible, you are going to need some rules. I'd like to claim these as my own, but they come from my friends Mark and Sarah, two English types who have lived all over the world, raised a family in various countries, been everywhere, seen everything, and are real fun to hang out with. I'm not sure what their country count is at, but last time I saw them it was well over 100 and that was ten years ago so I'm sure they've added on another couple dozen by now.

Mark and Sarah's rules for being able to "count" a country are:

- You must leave the airport
- You must have at least one meal

So, in other words, these touchdowns in airports where you open the door from the transit lounge, step outside, have a smoke, smell the wind, feel the heat, or even do a status update with the social media tool of your choice, DO NOT COUNT. This is a competitive sport and you cannot be saying you have been to fifty countries when ten of those were airport stops only.

There is an organization called the Traveler's Century Club, which is a non profit group dedicated to pursuing peace through travel. In order to join, you must have traveled to at least 100 of their official list of "Countries & Territories," which totals 319 and includes not just official UN recognized countries, but also territories, geographically separated portions of countries and autonomous regions, a few of which include Easter Island, Faroe Islands and Tibet. Their definition of a country visit is much more lenient and allows one to count a simple airplane touch down. If you qualify for membership in this club, chances are you are already well familiar with the concept of traveling for glory, so go ahead and fill out a membership form then start rubbing elbows and trading tales with the privileged.

Where to Travel To

Start With Your Backyard

In the span of only a few decades, the idea of travel has certainly changed a lot. Air travel is now incredibly cheap and thanks to 24 hour travel channels and the internet, information about the countries of our world is accessible and available anytime. As kids, the first flight for me and my brothers Marty and Curtis was to Los Angeles to visit Disneyland. I'm sure my parents saved for years to be able to afford that trip for us and it is one that is permanently stamped on my memory. Today, it is common for families to take annual winter vacations to all-inclusive resorts in the Caribbean. In fact, it seems many people can't live without it! And these are regular, middle class people, not upper crust. But it makes me wonder if some people have forgotten about their own backyards? I was lucky as a young fellow to find summer jobs that allowed me to travel all over my own province and really explore where I came from. Now, living in southern Ontario gives me a brand new, enormous backyard to explore, and what a backyard it is! In this highly populated region the only problem is narrowing down where to go, as the towns and sights are plentiful and the possibilities endless. Showing up at a town parade or fall harvest festival, in a town you've never visited, meeting people you otherwise never would have connected with, nearly always produces some interesting experiences.

No matter where you live, there are always new and interesting places to explore not far from your home. Often, when my family and I have a few hours to spare we will jump in the car and go for a drive nowhere in particular to see what we find, and we are rarely disappointed. For example, have you visited all the museums and public spaces in your own town or city? Take a day, pretend you are a tourist and look around for things to do to help you understand what your town is all about. You can probably learn more about your town and its history in a day than you have during your entire lifetime. If you live in a larger town or city, seek out a travel guide that a typical tourist would use and check out some of the recommendations. When a person travels, they try to see and do as much as possible in a short amount of time. But when they are at home, time seems unlimited and there is no urgency to explore, which usually means they never get around to doing it. Making a conscious decision to learn more about your local surroundings can be a fascinating experience.

So why invest time in local traveling? If you do plan to visit the world and explore hidden treasures in obscure parts of the globe, it's good to first get some experience in a more familiar environment. This helps you to develop some of the skills you will need as an independent traveler, such as asking strangers for help or information, using maps, developing a sense of direction, paying more attention to your environment, and making the best use of limited time when faced with unlimited options. These skills become even more important when faced with a different language in a foreign country.

Explore Your Country

I feel very fortunate to be Canadian. Ours is a huge, diverse, safe, modern, and easily explored country. And with a population density of 3.5 people per square mile, it is one of the most sparsely populated countries in the world. It goes without saying that Canada offers an incredibly wide range of travel opportunities, and most Canadians first trip away from home will likely be a visit to a neighbouring province. Travel in Canada, though, is far from cheap. The vast distances, limited options for public transport and less than competitive domestic air travel market, means that getting from place to place can be pricey. Because of this, some people may have traveled extensively internationally, yet may have explored only the smallest areas of their own country. Is this a mistake? Well, not really. There are no rules as to the order in which you need to travel, but I think it's important to explore your own country, first to understand your fellow countrymen better, but also to be able to speak intelligently about your home when you yourself are a visitor in another country and somebody asks you what your country is like. It's nice to be able to give them an informed, personal opinion.

What if your country is not so large, for instance, if you are from the Netherlands? Well, that is not a problem, as I've learned that small countries pack a lot of punch. The math works out like this. Canada is 216 times the size of the Netherlands, but in the Netherlands, there are 216 times the amount things to explore per square kilometre. Small countries are much more efficient to explore and usually have just as much diversity in its customs and traditions as large countries do, and in many cases even more. The best part is you can explore the whole country by foot or bike.

In the case of Canada, the cost of travel can certainly impact your decision. For example, today I can book a flight to England, Miami, Los

Angeles or the Bahamas for less than what it would cost me to fly to Saskatoon, which has seriously impacted the number of trips that we have been able to return home to see my parents. Traveling in Canada requires one to either keep a sharp lookout for airline sales or be willing to drive very long distances. We did a lot of our traveling in Canada when Ana worked for an airline, which offered absurdly low fares for employees, and therefore allowed us to explore Canada widely while keeping to a budget.

I have been fortunate enough to visit all ten Canadian provinces, but have not yet traveled to any of the three northern territories, though they are still on my list and I'm sure the opportunity to visit will present itself one day. How much of your own country have you explored? If your answer embarrasses you, consider planning a trip.

Regions of the World

As a young, green, naïve, and inexperienced prairie boy, my first trip overseas was the adventure of a lifetime. I bought a backpack, stuffed it with the coolest clothes I had, said goodbye to my folks and took off to London, England. The plan was to visit some university buddies who had been living in London for a year or so, then do a whirlwind backpacking tour of the continent. In the span of a month, I would visit a dozen countries in Europe, meet hundreds of fellow backpackers, experience some glorious architectural sights, and even manage to get laid once or twice. After four hard years of university, this was to be the beginning of a new, exciting life for me, and one that simply not would have happened without the magic of travel.

There are 196 countries in the world, give or take one or two depending on how one defines the word "country". Assuming you live to be 196, don't have to work for a living, and have an unlimited budget, if you start now, you will be able to spend a year in most of them, which should give you a pretty good idea of what's out there. For the rest of you, there are some decisions to be made. What follows is my brief description of the main regions of the world. No, I have certainly not visited all the countries of each region, far from it, but I hope I have traveled to enough of them to offer at least a humble opinion on the region. Of course, this book is not meant to be a world travel guide; there are plenty of excellent resources out there for that. It is simply one person's personal opinions, experiences, and recommendations, all of which may be completely different from what you experience when you travel to the same places. That is the beauty and wonder of travel; the only way to really know is to experience it yourself.

Europe

As a first international trip for a young guy like me, the European continent was the perfect destination. English is widely spoken, public transportation is plentiful and easy to use, distances are short, there is a single currency, cultures are diverse, borders are practically non-existent, and countries are generally very safe. As a backpacker on a budget it's possible to travel fairly cheaply, but if you want any moderate level of class or comfort, it will cost you. It is no wonder that Europe is the destination of choice for many travelers and it really shows during peak travel season when everything gets jammed, from public transport to shows to museums to simple sidewalk space. So if you are looking for some quality time alone with your thoughts and the earth, you may want to try elsewhere. If you want to see as much variety as possible in a short time, then there is simply no better region to visit.

United States and Canada

My home continent is expansive, cheap and safe, but difficult to cover. English is spoken everywhere, except most of Quebec, the far north of Canada and some parts of the southern US border with Mexico, where Spanish is a better bet. From the density of New York City, the isolation of Newfoundland, the flat, bald and never-ending prairies, the mountain ranges of British Columbia and California, the deserts in the southern US, and the forests throughout, the sights are diverse and the distances massive. Public transport in these countries is generally terrible and having a car is, in many ways, the only sensible option if you want to explore.

The two countries are quite safe, though like anywhere, you need to be careful in the larger cities where you get a lot of petty crime. If you are traveling on a budget, you will find that compared with many other regions of the world, you can get a lot of value for your money if you are careful. The cost of the basics such as food, accommodation and gasoline are actually fairly cheap compared to many other countries.

Mexico, Central and South America

Spanish is the name of the game, so if you don't know any then you are going to miss out on a lot this region has to offer. The best part of this region are its people – they are generally "muy simpatico", which sort of means kind, except of course for the ones who rob or kidnap you. Yes, they are not the safest countries, and if you spend any significant amount of time there you are likely be stolen from in some fashion. That said, some of the most memorable places I have visited are in these countries – from the Amazon jungle, to the temples in Mexico and Guatemala, Machu Picchu in Peru, the Atacama Desert in Chile, the beautiful beaches of Brazil and the Tierra del Fuego region of southern Argentina. Public transport can be spotty, but it's generally okay, and taxis and long haul busses are usually quite cheap. The food is delicious, especially if you have a fondness for beans and rice. If you are a meat lover, then you will find no better steaks in the world than in Argentina. In fact, I have never looked at a steak the same way again after gorging myself on tenderloins and strips in Bariloche for two weeks straight.

Traveling in these countries takes patience, persistence and, most importantly, a good sense of humour. Stuff doesn't work, schedules aren't adhered to, people often say "yes" when they really mean "no", and the bureaucracy can be infuriating. But if you can get past that, then you will discover a land of wonderful places and people.

The Caribbean

Emerald blue waters, outstanding beaches, gourmet restaurants, opulence, attitude, and overpriced everything is what you will find in the Caribbean. Exploring the Caribbean is only possible two ways; with an incredibly large wallet or with your own boat, which requires an incredibly large wallet. The Caribbean will always be the most cherished region of the world for me because that is where I met and fell in love with my wife Ana, and together we have explored over half of the countries of the Caribbean and plan to explore the other half before we are done. This reminds me of a third way to travel the Caribbean – work for a company located there who will fly you around on business trips, pay for your food and accommodation and give you spending money. It worked for me!

Africa

Believe it or not, there are plenty of people who think that Africa is a single country – it is not. Instead, it is a giant continent consisting of 54 crazy countries, a billion people, and some of the fastest growing populations in the world. These are not typically the first countries that new travelers choose to tackle, but it's said that once you've really visited Africa, it infects your soul, becomes a part of you and never lets you go.

I have not explored Africa extensively, visiting only Egypt and South Africa, Lesotho and Swaziland, but even that small sample gave me a glimpse into the incredible diversity of this region. Considering South Africa was one of the most fascinating and diverse countries I've ever visited, I plan to return one day soon to explore many other countries of this continent.

Middle East

While only a small region of the world, these countries pack a punch as it is geopolitically the hottest area of the world. What immediately comes to mind when one thinks of the Middle East are religious wars, veiled women, tankers of crude, scorching hot deserts, and incredibly wealthy sheiks. It is, without a doubt, the region that is the least accessible to tourists and probably the least well understood. But places that are hard to get to usually pay the greatest dividends and offer the possibility of real adventure, though real risks as well.

Asia

The countries of Asia boast an explosion of colour, smells, people, single cylinder motor vehicles, foods, natural wonders, and are home to the most chaotic drivers in the world. Long a favoured region for backpackers on a tight budget, it also has plenty to offer for travelers looking for luxurious accommodation and top restaurants. The countries of Asia include most of Russia, the ex-Soviet family of "Stans", Pakistan, India, China, Japan, the Koreas, Cambodia, Thailand, Indonesia, Malaysia, and many others. It covers a huge section of the earth and is probably the most diverse continent and certainly the most populated. For me, Asia immediately brings to mind the delicious foods, likely because of my palate for spicy cuisine, and many countries of this region offer dishes that will blow your sinuses to smithereens and give you ring sting for a week. What is the top tip for traveling Asia? Keep a toilet paper roll in the freezer. You will thank me.

Oceania

Oceania is the regional name for Australia, New Zealand and the islands of the Pacific and is home to over 30 countries and territories, many of which you have probably never heard of, but are some of the most beautiful islands in the world. Any way you slice it, if you want to travel extensively in Oceania, you are going to need plenty of money. The islands are expensive to get to and you won't find much for budget accommodation or restaurants once you arrive. Sadly, I have not traveled to any of the Pacific Islands, but have been to Australia and New Zealand, both of which are incredible, safe countries with amazing sights and people and so similar to Canada as to be uncanny. As a sailor, it's my dream to one day sail through the region and explore at my leisure on my own boat, but until then, I'll keep saving my pennies!

****

Kris Olson

Chapter 2 – Method

Travel can be as frugal or as luxurious as you choose to make it, but your travel budget rarely has any bearing on the depth of experiences you bring home with you. Sure, you will have to decide where to scrimp and where to splurge, which will ultimately depend on what is important to you. There are many different ways to travel, and things you can do along the way to make the most of your limited time and funds. The best travelers learn to use their imaginations to make the most of their available resources.

Ana and I were working on a project in Puerto Rico and decided to take a trip to the nearby US Virgin Islands for an extravagant little weekend getaway. After a short, easy flight to St. Thomas we found ourselves at a classy inn, sitting on the balcony of our room and enjoying a glass of red wine while admiring the million dollar view overlooking the harbour full of high priced yachts and high priced people. As these were the days before children, we had nobody else to worry about besides each other and were able to relax, forget about work, and really appreciate the admirable situation we found ourselves in. We enjoyed dinner at a nice local restaurant, went for a couple drinks at a bar then got back to the room relatively early for a crazy sex session, followed up with a beautiful sleep, awash in the sweet, salty, warm ocean breeze blowing through the wooden slats of the open window.

I awoke early, grabbed my book, crept out of the room and went to the common breakfast area of the inn to enjoy a strong coffee and more of the tremendous view. As I watched the boats and people coming and going, from off in the distance I saw an airplane approaching. As it came closer, I could see that it was a float plane, and within a few minutes it was skimming across the water, finally coming to rest almost directly in front of our hotel. A number of people disembarked with very little luggage, new people boarded, and then in no time at all the props were spinning, water was blowing everywhere and the plane was back up in the air, off to its unknown destination. I asked the waiter about this airplane and was told that it was a commuter plane that flew back and forth between St. Thomas and St. Croix, a sister island no more than 80 kilometres to the south.

Within 15 minutes I had two tickets in my hand, and when Ana arrived to the breakfast area she found her boyfriend sitting there with the most mischievous grin she had ever seen and knew something was up. After a typical Caribbean breakfast of fresh papaya, pineapple, bread, and cheese omelette, we strolled down to the docks and waited for the float plane to return, which it soon did. We crammed ourselves into the plane, along with a few others, and after a very fast safety demo, we were in the air and on our way to St. Croix – an island we knew absolutely nothing about. The plane barely got up to altitude when it started descending, and soon floated into the docks. We stepped foot onto a new island and started with a long, slow, romantic walk along the ocean paths and town streets. Just in time for lunch, we found a busy, brightly coloured ocean-side restaurant, ordered two pints of Blackbeard Ale, and once again found ourselves looking over the ocean, admiring the beauty of it all. The red snapper we enjoyed for lunch was delicious and after a latte and some people-watching, we returned to our wanderings then eventually made our way back to the docks, jumped on the waiting float plane and were back in St. Thomas to enjoy the rest of the afternoon. Fortunately, this was just the start to a magnificent, irreplaceable, and unbelievably expensive weekend, which also included chartering a sailboat, dining at a Michelin starred restaurant and smoked big Cuban cigars while soaking in a hot tub.

Yes, that lunch flight to St. Croix was decadent. It doubled the cost of the weekend and was not really necessary. But let me tell you that we think about that weekend trip very often and have never once regretted the amount of money we spent on it. We are now amongst the very few privileged people in the world who have flown to St. Croix for lunch!

Budget versus Luxury

I have traveled on a shoestring, I have traveled with unlimited funds, and I have traveled on every possible budget between those two extremes. I can honestly say that most of the best and worst experiences I have experienced while traveling had almost nothing to do with the sort of budget I was on, so you can never assume that an expensive trip will be more enjoyable than a frugal one.

As a home grown prairie boy, frugality was driven into me from a young age, as it was with my family and many of my friends. The majority of prairie folk are resourceful, handy, practical, thrifty and economically modest, which is just a nice way of saying they are cheap and prone to reusing dryer sheets and margarine containers. They know that a single tea bag can produce at least 18 cups of drinkable tea, disposable cups are not really disposable, potato peelings when baked and topped with cheese are perfectly edible, what lies beneath that thick layer of mould is perfectly good sour cream and throwing away socks is just not right. So for me, budget travel comes naturally, although as I have aged and my available resources have increased, I will admit the thought of sleeping in bus stations no longer appeals to me much.

When it comes to travel, our family approach is to spend as little as possible on the unimportant aspects of the trip, but splurge on the small or large extravagances that are unique to the place we are visiting, or on things that we know we will really enjoy and remember. During an extended trip to New Zealand we kept our expenditures to a minimum, but when we were looking for options for transport on the South island, we happened to walk by a motorcycle dealership and within the hour we had rented a beautiful Harley Davidson Heritage Softail Classic and were headed out on the highway with the heavy metal thunder roaring in our ears. I think we spent four hundred bucks to rent that bike, but what an experience! It was one of the highlights of the trip, and if we had not rented that motorcycle, I would have regretted it and that would have stuck with me forever. There have been times on other trips when we've considered similar extravagances, but our thriftiness has taken over, and we later wished we had. Regret is a terrible feeling so you need to make decisions carefully, but at the same time you cannot partake in every extravagance, so you must know yourself, know what you really value, what really matters versus what doesn't, and evaluate your options accordingly.

Knowing where to scrimp and where to splurge can only be learned over time. Below are a few of the areas where we typically try to minimize expenditures:

Transportation

If we can save a hundred bucks by taking an overnight flight we will take it. If we can buy cheap, economy train or bus tickets we do. If we can pack into a small rental car to save some money on rental charges and gas, we always do. These minor discomforts can save you a lot of money, and we've found that the transportation itself is rarely an integral part of the trip – the scenery you pass looks the same when viewed from a sub compact, a luxury sedan, a bike, or a camel.

Food

Nothing grinds me more than paying twelve dollars for a shitty egg salad sandwich and a weak coffee in an airport. Being careful with food expenses while traveling can save you big money. Overspending on food is primarily due to poor planning, and dining out can be the single biggest discretionary expense of a trip, so we try our best to minimize it. Before going to the airport, pack a lunch and snacks for the time you'll spend waiting at the gate and during the flight. Many airlines no longer provide free meals on board but they will happily sell you a dried up sandwich for the price of a rib eye steak. Why not eat great food for a fraction of the price? On driving trips, we always pack a cooler with food and make most of our own smaller meals. Eating out while traveling usually results in consuming a lot of unhealthy fried or processed foods. This is especially bad for kids, as most restaurants have virtually identical kid's menus – chicken fingers, burgers, macaroni and cheese, hot dogs, and always accompanied by fries. While traveling, we usually try to eat one restaurant meal per day, and then prepare the rest ourselves.

Drinks

Hitting the supermarket, stocking up on drinks and ice, and packing them in a cooler is a whole lot cheaper then buying them one by one as you go. Instead of bringing a cooler along from home, we will often buy a disposable Styrofoam cooler once we get to our destination and load it up.

Accommodation

We always try to find a great deal on accommodation, in particular, we try to rent private residences as opposed to hotels, which can be extremely expensive. Our choice of accommodation usually depends on the kind of traveling we are doing. For example, if we are on a road trip and only staying for a single night at each location, then we don't get anything fancy as our time there is limited. If we are staying in the same spot for a week, then we look for something nicer as we will likely be spending more time in the room itself. We would rather spend less on accommodation and use the savings to fund day trips or excursions. But we never cheap out on accommodation to the point of staying somewhere that is not safe or not clean.

The American Style Power Weekend

While living in Pakistan, I met Philippe Bovay, who is now married to one of my best buddies Trudy Taylor and is the coolest dude around. Philippe introduced me to proper Swiss fondue and the rituals and ceremony surrounding the consumption of said meal, the never-ending glass of champagne, and the wonders of Wilderness, South Africa. Together, Trudy and Philippe represent the epitome of a global, well traveled, fun loving power couple and are the only pair I have ever met who worked in very senior positions in their respective companies, but also know how to enjoy life, relish adventure and keep their priorities straight.

They are the masters of what Philippe calls "The American Style Power Weekend" and since learning this term, I have embraced it, practiced it, loved it and passed the concept on for others to enjoy too. To most people, a weekend is a time to catch up on sleep, relax, hang around the house and basically fend off Monday as long as possible. Not for Philippe – he squeezes every last drop of juice from a weekend, then sucks out a bit more with a big smile on his face. The idea is simple: you can pack as much into a weekend as you can a week if you approach it at 300 kilometres per hour, refuse to waste a second and consider nothing as impossible. Suppose you get away from work early on Friday, say at 3pm and don't have to report back until 8am Monday morning. That gives you 65 hours to do with as you please. That's right, 65 hours! If you really think about that number, and the possibilities of what you can do with 65 hours, you start to realize how much time one typically and painlessly lets pass by during these precious weekends. When you match this concept with Trudy's long standing policy of never, ever letting a single work vacation day go unused at the end of the year, you can imagine how much they usually pack into a year.

We have had some brilliant power weekends, in fact some have been so amazing that when I return to work on Monday and a colleague asks me how my weekend was, I'm actually embarrassed to tell them, because I think I'll make them feel lame…so I usually keep it to myself. One of our favourite tricks, on a power weekend or holiday, is to book our returning flight for late Sunday evening so that we don't waste that day, and can instead fly home during the night and still get back in time for work on Monday morning. Sure, we're a bit tired for the workday, but who cares? Get a great sleep on Monday night and you're back to normal, and can look back knowing proudly that you kicked ass all weekend long.

Here is something you can try. It's Thursday evening, you have no weekend plans, no commitments and some extra money you don't know what to do with. Go online and see what cheap, discounted weekend flights are available to somewhere you have never been. Book it, pack a small bag, don't tell anybody where you are going, don't do any cocky social media updates and focus on seeing and doing everything you possibly can in that location. If you can't find a cheap flight, pick a location you can drive to, grab some great tunes and hit the road. Don't waste a second. Talk to people, ask them about their town. Explore. Take pictures. Buy a souvenir. Surprise yourself. Grab a newspaper and see what's going on. Visit the local attractions. Stay up late and get up early. Assume you will never be back to that place so leave no stone unturned. Laugh, smile and don't think too much about it, just make it your goal to use every minute to expand your knowledge and experiences. By the time you return to your normal life on Monday morning, you will feel like a different person and be overwhelmed with a sense of accomplishment and adventure. No matter what happens during that weekend, you will never forget it. And Philippe will be proud of you.

Travel by Herd

For beginner travelers, people on a budget, or if you are just plain lazy, traveling by herd can be an excellent option. Many species of animals travel in herds for safety, comfort, companionship, and the knowledge that if you get attacked you can always squeeze out the weakest member and sacrifice him to save your own skin. Humans operate in much the same way. For instance, let's take a typical bus load of Chinese tourists visiting Niagara Falls. For safety, each member of the pack dresses in a similar fashion so that it's hard for a predator, such as a skinny, long haired white dude selling coupon books, to pick out any one individual. To the coupon flogger, it looks like one large mass of brightly coloured clothing and it confuses him. The pack is large enough to be able to charter its own bus, with its own television, stereo, adjustable seats and, most importantly, a Chinese speaking tour guide, thereby markedly increasing the comfort of each individual member of the pack. The herd system also works well for encouraging companionship, although often the entire herd originates from the same town or city, and may know each other already or even be related to each other. This way, there is no need to invite strangers to the pack, who may disrupt the natural ebb and flow of the group's travel culture. Let's suppose the coupon flogger does approach the group waving his coupon book speaking some broken Chinese, as a way to build rapport and fool the group into buying his useless product. Herd mentality takes over and the flight or fight decision is made immediately, resulting in either a massive rush of brightly coloured people racing down the sidewalk, in full sprint, with cameras and guidebooks flying everywhere, or the sacrifice of the intellectually weakest member, who will be elbowed and pushed towards the coupon flogger to do commercial battle. Even if the sacrificial member falls to the predator, the herd is better off as they may now all get a discount ride on the giant Ferris wheel or half price entry to the Haunted House Nightmares Fear Factory.

I'm not trying to pick on Chinese people – most other cultures are great herd travelers too and equally conspicuous when moving as a group in a foreign country. In fact, traveling by herd is something my family and I have taken up in recent years, beginning with the moment the kids reached the age at which a full price air ticket was required. We have found that buying an all-inclusive trip to the Caribbean for the mid winter getaway is usually the most affordable option, and if you want to do multiple trips per year then you really need to watch what you spend.

Another key advantage of traveling by herd is the simplicity – it really does remove much of the stress of traveling, and with kids this can make a big difference to your overall enjoyment of the trip.

Traveling by herd takes all sorts of forms, from all-inclusive resorts in tropical locations, to cruises, to package trips in Europe, to adventure safaris in Africa. Because you are stuck with the same people for the duration of the trip, this can result in lifelong friendships, but could also result in a lot of aggravation if you get stuck with an arsehole in the group. But even in the second case, it is sure to be memorable.

The Three Golden Rules of Travel

Over the years Ana and I have developed three ideas that we have found enhance the travel experience. I don't know if they are rules, per se, but they are concepts we try to stick to and have found them to be very effective.

Rule Number One– Always Have Two Trips in the Pipeline

Having one trip planned is nice as it gives you something to plan for, look forward to, anticipate and talk about. But what happens when you get home from that trip? You've got nothing. Why come home to that sort of terrible letdown? This is why you must always have two trips in the pipeline – so you can be planning actively for the first one, but still thinking about the second one, and anticipating that too. Having no trip to look forward to is a dreary state of affairs.

Rule Number Two – Stay with Friends

Staying with friends in foreign countries gives you a huge advantage over facing a new country on your own. Most people know somebody or another who has moved away from their home to another country or province for work, school or any other reason. Coming from someone who has spent a lot of time living in other countries, believe me when I tell you that having friends or family members visit is a special pleasure. It is fun to be able to show off your new home and I always went out of my way to entice visitors. Once they arrived they were not allowed to leave until they were completely exhausted and broke, which meant that I too was constantly exhausted and broke, but you just get used to it after a while.

Having a local contact that knows the lay of the land and, more importantly, knows some interesting places to visit that you would not find otherwise is a huge help on a trip. The other benefit is cost – staying with somebody saves you a fortune on accommodation and food, and can allow you to extend the length of your visit, or use the savings on other aspects of the trip. Another important aspect of staying with friends is that they are likely to have made local friendships and will have access to social events that an independent traveler wouldn't, such as attending a dinner party with locals or, if you are especially lucky, going to a local wedding. Being able to spend time with locals in this way will give you much more insight into the country then looking in from the outside as a regular tourist with a guide book.

As a frequent host of traveling friends, I have made myself famous with my "Welcome to Bahamas" packs. Whenever I was expecting visitors to arrive in a country in which I was living, I would pre-assemble a welcome pack, which was presented to them immediately upon arrival. Of course the contents changed, depending on who was visiting and where I was living, but here were the contents of the kits I made up for my brothers and friends who visited me in the Bahamas:

- Map of the island
- Tourist brochures highlighted with interesting things to do
- Tylenol, three packages of
- Small cards with my phone number, address, and some coins for the payphone
- Voucher for a free Kalik beer at my house, usually assumed to be "all the beer you can drink"
- Pack of condoms
- Name tags, in case of total memory loss at the end of a big casino night
- Schedules of happy hour times at local watering holes

These are only suggested items and the contents of the pack will depend entirely on the how degenerate your visitors are.

Rule Number Three – Take a Trip within the Trip

This is a crafty trick we have developed that can double the perceived time spent away on vacation. We always plan a trip within the trip, especially crucial for week long winter vacations at all-inclusive resorts in the Caribbean, where the days are so lazy and monotonous (in a good way) that they can become indistinguishable and before you know it the trip is over and you can't remember what happened. Here's how it works. As soon are you arrive in a location, you need to look around for an overnight, or at least a full day trip somewhere that you can do about halfway through your vacation. This does two things; first, it gives you something to look forward to during the trip itself. Second, it forces you to get out and explore things you probably would not have seen otherwise. We've found that you need to think about this right at the start of your trip, or even before you leave home. If you wait until halfway through the trip to start exploring options, you will be sure to run out of time. Here are two examples of the "trip within the trip" we have done recently:

- During a week long all-inclusive resort vacation in Cuba, we rented a car for two days and did day trips first to Havana, then to some small towns deep within the interior of the country, along the way getting completely lost several times, having our hubcaps stolen, and being pulled over by the Cuban cops four times in one day for various traffic infractions
- During a two week visit to the Azores, where we stayed with family, we did a two day trip to an adjacent island called Terceira, traveling there by ferry and spending the time speeding around the island at a blistering pace, seeing all that we could possibly see in the short time that we had

Visit Big, Visit Small

Visiting a new country provides an unlimited set of possibilities, but it can sometimes be overwhelming deciding what places you will visit and how you will spend your time. One thing I've always tried to do is to visit the big, important, must-see things, but also to explore the smaller or less well known attractions, where the real surprises are often found. This "big/small" approach can be applied to almost anything.

Cities and Towns

In every country I've ever visited, there is always a huge difference between life and culture in big cities versus the rural areas, and to get to know a country, you must experience both. When planning a trip, be sure to spend some time in the capital city, usually your first or last days are the best because this is where the airports are usually located. Cities are the nerve centres of countries while rural areas are the heart. Rural areas are usually more difficult to explore, often requiring a car or infrequent public transportation, but once you get there, the rewards will nearly always justify the extra effort required.

Festivals

Most countries have nationwide festivals at some point during the year, which are often draws for tourists. But also try to find local festivals or celebrations in smaller places, which will be less grandiose, but probably less crowded too and more easily enjoyed at a slower pace. While leafing through a tourist magazine I picked up recently in Erie, Pennsylvania, I noticed a small add at the end of the booklet, advertising an upcoming Polish festival that featured Polka Masses at a local church. I have no idea what a "Polka Mass" is, but it sure sounds cool to me!

Museums and Galleries

The grandest museums and galleries are usually found in the larger cities of any country and are on the must-see list of most travelers. For example, who has visited Paris and not seen the Louvre, or the National Gallery in London or the Prado in Madrid? These galleries must be seen to be believed, but in any country there are hundreds or thousands of smaller galleries and museums spread across the country. In fact, any small town you visit is likely to have some sort of public gallery and your experience there is sure to be much different.

Sights

The must-see sights in any location are usually well documented, easy to find and not to be missed. Be sure to also ask the locals for ideas and suggestions on lesser known places of interest to visit, which may not be found in travel books, but well worth a look. Remember that most locals will assume that as a tourist, you will only be interested in the big, touristy sights, so push for other suggestions that may lead you to some real gems.

****

Chapter 3 – People

The people you meet while on the road will be the highlight of your travels. Travelers often form special bonds with each other and locals, and friendships made while traveling can be intense and life-changing. You may find that the personal connections you make along the way will change you in immeasurable ways and you may return home as a much different person than when you left.

We met Fraser and Rebecca on an overnight train in Bolivia and immediately bonded over a bottle of cheap red wine and an onboard movie about foreigners being kidnapped in a dodgy South American country. From this initial meeting, we would end up spending nearly a month together, during which time we chased flamingos in Bolivia, had our passports and luggage stolen in Argentina, and gorged ourselves on cheap beer and seafood in Brazil. There was not one thing in particular that we had in common, we just enjoyed each other's company tremendously, whether it was playing cards over coffee and papaya in the morning, horseback riding in the mountains, or partying it up in the bars at night. It is quite a challenge finding people you are able to travel with for more than a few days at a time, but when you do, it is very special.

Friendships developed on the road are almost always akin to passionate, crazy, unbridled love affairs and, much like the real world of relationships, rarely blossom into a long term, "till death do us part" true love marriage. One thing great travelers have in common is they live for the moment and take nothing for granted. It is all about enjoying the sights, sounds, smells and feelings of the present and not dwelling on the past or being overly concerned about the future. This is what gives travelers such a completely different mentality than those in their regular, everyday routines.

The Annoying Tourist

Once you have some independent travel experience under your belt, it's hard not to be disappointed with how most tourists behave whilst on vacation. Many tourists go to other countries to see, conquer and buy the t-shirt and their interest in local culture is limited to pointing out how much better things work at home. They don't try to blend into their local environment and typically have the attitude, "This is me, if you don't like it then too bad for you." They don't make any effort to keep a low profile and tend to use their mouths much more readily than their ears. Good travelers are not afraid to take a chance on something new, something different or something foreign; in fact, to them this is the whole point of traveling. Annoying tourists spend much of their time expressing how incompetent the locals seem to be. They are often found racing around the country at a breakneck pace to hit all the must-see destinations they read about in the guide book, instead of discovering the real joys of a country, which are usually its people and culture. To really experience these, you need to slow down, be patient, listen and become absorbed in your surroundings.

By my condescending attitude you may think I consider myself to be the consummate traveler. I try my best but also sometimes fall back to behaving like a spoiled tourist, which can be very easy to do. As humans, it seems one's natural instinct is to complain about the negative aspects of a situation rather than appreciate the positive features of it, but this is where experience comes into play. After you've been through enough of the above situations as a tourist you eventually realize that the complaints and negativity really do nothing but get you down and diminish your enjoyment.

One of the first trips Ana and I took as a couple was to Cat Island, Bahamas. As I had been living in the Bahamas for a year, I had already visited most of the more popular "Family Islands", as they are called, so I wanted to take her to one of the lesser known ones. We found a place called Little Bay Resort which was owned by a fellow named John, a man who, we would learn, had fathered 23 children with the same wife. He ran a small, clean looking inn that was quiet, isolated, and much cheaper than the available alternatives. In other words, pretty much exactly what we were looking for. The big surprise came the morning after our first night when we woke up to discover we had been ravaged by bed bugs! Ana was attacked much worse than me and the outside of her left leg, completely covered in bites, would become violently itchy over the next several days. The natural tourist reaction was to storm down to the owner, scold him for the insect infestation and demand our money back. We resisted and instead politely told him what happened and asked for his help in clearing the room, which he happily did with the help of a very large can of insecticide. In the end, we learned two valuable lessons; first, in tropical countries always check a bed thoroughly for bed bugs before you sleep in it. Second, always carry an antihistamine drug with you to help relieve extreme itching. Although the experience at the time was far from enjoyable, these lessons would serve us well on future trips as we did come across bed bugs many more times and were better prepared.

One of my overriding maxims in travel and in life is this:

You cannot control the things that happen to you but you can control your reaction to them.

If we let our emotions completely take over when something unpleasant happens to us we usually wind up with nothing but regrets and missed opportunities to learn. A good traveler will expect mishaps and strive to draw wisdom from the unpleasant experiences. Annoying tourists instead attempt to avoid uncomfortable situations altogether in the hopes of steering clear of anything that is not familiar or within their control. And in the process they miss out on experiences that could have made them a better traveler. Take package holidays for instance – many companies offer all-inclusive travel packages where they take care of everything, from transport to accommodation to food, then charge you a single, high price for the entire holiday. This is the best option for a person who wants to minimize the number of unexpected occurrences during their vacation. Want to know what happens today? Open your travel itinerary to page 14.

Eastern European Adventure Holiday – Day 8

Today we begin with a hearty breakfast in the hotel restaurant at 8:15 am (note: Bloody Mary cocktails are not included in your package – please pay the server directly for these), followed up by the bus pickup at 9:45 where we will be dropped at the Museum of Antiquities. The bus will collect us from the museum at 11:30 and we will take a short driving tour through the city centre after which, at approximately 12:15 we will be taken to a charming local restaurant for some regional delights (note: when we arrive please find a table immediately as most of the other tour busses arrive at 12:30 and the restaurant fills up fast). After lunch, you will have 30 minutes of free time to wander around the lovely gardens behind the restaurant. By 2:00 pm you must be on the tour bus (remember, your bus number is #145, please don't get on the wrong bus!), as we will be departing for an afternoon tour of the charming countryside. Your tour guide will take you through a thousand years of history of the region during an entertaining onboard monologue. We will arrive back at the hotel at 5:00 pm where you will be allowed one hour of free time. Please be back at the bus by 6:00 pm as we will be departing for an unforgettable meal at one of the city's top restaurant (Please see page 11 of your Meal Guide booklet – there are three meal options available so have your selection ready for your server). After dinner, sit back and relax as you enjoy a live show of one of the region's top vocal choirs (note: wine is included with dinner but any drinks after dinner are not included in your package – please pay the server directly for these.) The bus will be leaving the restaurant at 9:00 so please be waiting outside in the parking lot.

A tourist may well be delighted with such an organized, regimented travel schedule, which has surely been honed and perfected over hundreds of repetitions to produce an effortless and comprehensive travel holiday. What you will not get, though, for your all-inclusive price is the sheer panic and joy experienced from waking up in a strange place not knowing where you are going to sleep that night. For me, that's what it's all about – never knowing what surprises each new day on the road will bring.

One of the most expensive trips Ana and I ever took was to Iceland. It was somewhat of a journey of self discovery for me as my great grandparents on my dad's side immigrated to Canada from Iceland and many Icelandic traditions persist in my family, mainly limited to hard liquor and sweet pastries, but traditions nonetheless. As usual, we traveled backpacker style and discovered on our first night in Reykjavik that budget accommodation in the YMCA was around US$80 for a tiny room, just large enough for two single beds and a backpack. As expected, the price of rental cars was astronomical so we instead decided to take a guided day trip to see the countryside around Reykjavik. We showed up to the departure point and found that we were the youngest tourists there by a margin of about 30 years – it seems that only well-off retirees can afford trips to Iceland. This was the typical tourist bus trip, complete with scheduled stops to points of interest and the onboard tour guide, who had the incredible ability to speak hypnotic monotone in English, German and French simultaneously and proceeded to do so during the entire trip. At one point, as I was dreamily gazing out the window, suspended between consciousness and slumber, listening to the tour guide explaining tectonic plate geology, I cast my gaze over to the others on the bus and realized that the half whom were not completely asleep were very close to it, or perhaps sleeping with their eyes open. Like me, the tour guide's monotonous drone of "tectonic platessss, tectonic platesssss" had lulled them into a blissful hypnotic trance.

Curiously, it would seem that I have contradicted myself. A boring day on a tourist bus actually provided one of the more memorable moments of the trip, not because of an exceptional experience, but simply a brief, but somehow powerful, observation of the state of the world around me at the time. And to this day, every time I hear the words "tectonic plates" it immediately and delightfully yanks me out of the present and plops me back there on that bus cruising across the lava encrusted plains of Iceland listening to the tour guide.

You never really know what's going to do it for you. But that ever present opportunity of a unique and unforgettable moment is, in itself, the true beauty and power of travel.

The People You Meet

I honestly believe that every single other human being on the planet has something important to teach me. Almost without fail, whenever I've had a chance encounter with a stranger and put some extra effort into communicating with that person, I walk away with something unexpected, in some cases even something astonishing. This does not mean that you must grill each and every person you meet with intrusive questions, but it does mean that you should treat every person with respect and strive to become an outstanding listener. Most of the time we will walk away from an encounter without learning the lesson that person could have taught us, probably because we didn't have either the time or patience to discover it. Imagine the following scenario:

You are on a backpacking trip around South Africa and find yourself staying at a cool hostel in a beautiful town called St. Lucia. You decide to go out for an early evening stroll and along the way pass a young boy sitting by himself on the curb. You wonder to yourself, *what is he doing there? Why is he sitting alone? Is he waiting for somebody? Is he homeless? What's going on?* With these questions darting through your mind you unconsciously decide to mind your own business so you walk by the boy and go along your way. As you walk away you think to yourself, *He probably doesn't speak English anyway.*

A few minutes later a completely different person, in fact another traveler staying at the same hostel, is out for a similar walk and just so happens to come across this very same boy. Thinking it strange that this boy would be sitting all by himself out here she says, "Hi!" and motions for permission to sit beside him. He nods his head and she sits down. As she begins to ask him a question, he simply puts his finger to his lips and says, "Shhhhhh." Respecting his wish, she sits silently beside him, trying to figure out what exactly is happening. After a few minutes have passed there is a noise, and the little boy raises his arm and points to a spot in the bush a few metres away. She immediately hears the sound of crashing brush and like a dream, a 5000 pound hippopotamus emerges, stops and looks directly at her. Their eyes meet and an exhilarating human-versus-hippo stare down ensues. The hippo is so close she can count the hairs on its nose and feel the wind from its every breath. She has never been this close to such an enormous wild animal before. She does feel scared, but her fears are trumped by an overwhelming sense of awe and wonder at this magnificent animal. After what seems like hours, the hippo blinks, turns, and continues on its way across the road and into the bush on the other side. She strains to see the hippo through the brush but the beast is gone and the brush is now silent, almost as if the hippo had never been there. She then turns to the lad who returns her gaze with the largest, happiest smile she has ever seen in her life, and with that, the boy hops up and runs back down the road, jumping along the way.

Although this is not a true story (actually, it may very well be a true story – I would not be at all surprised if something like this has happened in the beautiful town of St. Lucia in South Africa) these serendipitous events happen all the time. Many call it good luck or fortune but I don't believe it to be luck at all. It has much more to do with constantly putting yourself in situations where the unexpected is more likely to happen, and this is often where you are not comfortable and not confident. When you are unsure of yourself and your surroundings, the body's natural senses come alive in anticipation of the unexpected, and you experience a heightened state of awareness. A task as simple as talking to a stranger is one that many people are not at all comfortable doing. If your plan is to become a better traveler, and to travel like you mean it, then this is something you must learn and practice.

At the beginning of my first trip overseas I had just arrived in London, England and was staying with my university friends Earl and Colin. The first full day after I had arrived was a weekday and they both had to go to work. Before Earl left in the morning, I asked him what he thought I should do that day. He said, "Go out and practice talking to people". Being a fellow small town prairie boy, he knew that I was not used to being in a new place and around people I didn't know. During his overseas experience he had learned how important it was to quickly get comfortable with asking questions, approaching people, and not being afraid to look or sound stupid. It was a lesson I took to heart, learned quickly and has since served me with many wonderful experiences.

Locals

What is a "local" exactly? Well, when you are not traveling, and are at home living your everyday life with everyday routines doing what you normally do to make a living, YOU are a local. Imagine you are out in your front yard on a Saturday afternoon in your suburban neighbourhood hurriedly cutting the grass since you have to meet up with some friends in an hour. As you're working up a sweat pushing the heavy lawnmower, out of the corner of your eye you notice somebody standing on the sidewalk motioning at you. You shut off the lawnmower and suspiciously eye this stranger as he walks across the grass towards you. He says, "Hi!" and you notice right away that he has a strong accent and is obviously not from here. He asks you for directions to a street he is looking for, which you give him, then he immediately subjects you to an intense interrogation. Does everybody own an expensive lawnmower? How often do you have to cut the grass? Do you have a garden? What do you grow there? What do you do for a living? Why does everybody look so busy on a Saturday? And so on.

How would you feel towards this person? Chances are, you would tell him to get lost and mind his own business. If you were particularly tolerant you might hear him out and answer the questions but would certainly consider him to be an exceedingly rude and pushy person and wouldn't have too much respect for him. You certainly wouldn't ask those kinds of questions to a neighbourhood person you had not met before.

This may sound extreme, but I've seen tourists do this to locals in other countries many times and am always ashamed to see it. Quite often tourists look upon locals as oddities and as something to be investigated, studied, and understood so that they can log in their travel journal exactly how this country and its people "work". Not only is this inconsiderate, but any information you may glean from such an inquisition probably wouldn't be anything you couldn't find from doing a search on the internet. Knowing facts about a country is not the same as truly having knowledge about a place. Becoming knowledgeable takes time, patience, luck and experience.

Ana and I spent five weeks in Australia during a round the world backpacking trip. We split our time between staying with our Australian friends, Karen and Jamie, in a small city called Busselton in Western Australia, and traveling the east coast from Cairns to Sydney. The time we spent on the east coast was fantastic and we did such diverse things as spending a week sailing a tall ship, drove a 4x4 around Fraser Island, did a canoe trip, and spend hours exploring some of the most beautiful beaches in the world. But nearly the entire area was overrun with tourists and once you were on the tourist circuit, you just went with the flow and did what everybody else was doing. Although we participated in many tours where the guides delivered a stream of facts and figures about Australia, I don't remember a single moment during that phase of the trip where I had a decent conversation with a local Australian…and I certainly don't remember any of the facts or figures. It was on the west coast where we really learned about Australians. In this area there was much less tourism and we had the advantage of staying with locals, which makes all the difference. We weren't racing from spot to spot, desperate to squeeze as much time as possible from our schedule to see all the attractions. Instead, we spent hours with Karen and Jamie walking around the city, going to pubs, going crabbing and squidding, visiting wineries and enjoying great meals at home. We had lots of long, interesting conversations and, though it wasn't a conscious goal to learn as much about Australia as possible, this certainly happened throughout the course of these chats. During this time I realized why Canadians and Australians get along so well – our countries are very similar in many respects. If we had based our opinion of Australia on what we experienced on the east coast, I would have left thinking our countries had almost nothing in common.

How to Meet Locals

Waking up one morning on the road thinking, "Today, I'm going to make a local friend" is sort of like saying, "Today, I'm going to meet the woman of my dreams." It's not the sort of thing you can just go out and do. Trying to force things to happen can make one appear desperate, and there's nothing more off-putting than that. Making friends while traveling takes time, patience and effort and, quite often, involves taking a risk. One of the biggest hurdles in making local friends is the language barrier that may exist, which is why learning other languages is one of the most rewarding aspects of travel. It not only opens the door to a whole new culture, it also allows you to communicate with people in their own language, which obviously makes it much easier to befriend locals.

Locals are not found in the same places as travelers. In fact, if you stick close to the tourist infrastructure that inevitably exists in every country, you can usually insulate yourself completely from locals. If you want to know about this tourist infrastructure for any country, just pick up any of the hundreds of travel guide books out there. The majority of travelers plan their entire journeys based on these guide books; they stay at the recommended accommodations, eat at the recommended restaurants, visit the recommended sights, and even travel to the same "Off the Beaten Track" destinations that most guides offer. The explosive growth of the travel industry in the past two decades has produced an enormous volume of tourists, all looking to explore new places and see the sights, making it very lucrative for every country in the world to cash in on these travel dollars being spent. Guidebooks are a very useful tool for navigating this infrastructure, but to meet locals, you must spend time in places that are not in the guidebooks. Think of your normal routine. How often do you take one of your free days and go out to see the sights in your local area? How often do you visit local museums, places of interest, and any other location that may be mentioned in a travel guide for your country? My guess is that your answer is "rarely". With that in mind, here are a few non-typical places to visit when you're traveling in a new country.

Libraries

This is probably my favourite place to visit in any country – what better way to learn about a country than to visit the place where they store all their information! People you find in libraries are usually inquisitive and eager to learn and are often intrigued to find foreigners there. Libraries are nearly always peaceful, quiet, pleasant and most importantly, provide an environment where nobody is in a rush, making it an ideal place to strike up a conversation with a local. The added bonus with libraries is that they are free! For a traveler on a budget, this is one place that offers a temporary refuge from the incessant budget drain. Librarians always have plenty of information on local happenings and interesting places to visit that the guidebooks have missed. I often travel with a notebook computer, and one of my favourite tricks is to raid the music section of the library and rip a pile of local cds to my computer hard drive. It is a great way to build up my library of world music.

Local Cafes

Skip the Hard Rock Café and Planet Hollywood and find a good local café. It's where regular people, especially younger people, spend much of their free time. Don't look for the flashiest café on the main street, try to find one this is a little harder to get to and a bit run down – usually an indicator of lower prices, which is a great magnet for young locals. The added benefit of visiting cafés is you get to try out the local drinks and eats, which may not be available in the tourist restaurants.

Social Club Meetings

There are hundreds of social clubs with chapters worldwide, some of which include Rotary, Toastmasters, Lions, running clubs, sports clubs and hobbyist clubs of all varieties. A great way to prepare for this is to be involved with some of these social clubs in your hometown, which gives you an automatic in with the locals where a chapter of your club exists. If you've ever had a foreigner show up to one of your local social club events or meetings you'll know that members will go out of their way to help this person make the most of their visit to their community.

Church

Regardless of your religious beliefs, churches are a great place to visit as they are never hard to find, usually have very welcoming people and offer a glimpse into the local culture and beliefs. Attending a church from your own faith can be very interesting as the services can be very different from country to country. Churches often have social events after the service, which is an excellent opportunity to meet people.

Shopping Complex

At home, where do you find yourself nearly every Saturday? Likely at the shopping mall picking up groceries, clothes and other things you need. It works the same in other countries, which makes shopping malls, complexes, markets or any such commercial area a good place to see and meet locals.

Festivals

Every city, town and region has local festivals that do not show up on the radar of the travel guides. Look through local newspapers, magazines or even regional websites that showcase local events or festival. Larger towns may have a tourist office or if not, the local town hall or library is another place to find such information on these. Alternatively, stop at a hotel and raid their brochure rack, or ask the front desk staff about information on local events.

Sports Arenas

Local sports events are a great way to experience a country's culture and you can be sure that mainstream tourists rarely attend these. These can range from specialized sports that are not widely available elsewhere (bullfighting in Portugal, cockfighting in Dominican Republic, kickboxing in Thailand, cricket in Pakistan) to more common and familiar sports such as soccer, baseball and rugby. The love of sports is something that all cultures share and this passion manifests itself in different ways from country to country. Attending a local event may expose you to cultural differences you otherwise would not have noticed as a tourist and it's a great opportunity to befriend a local, fellow sports enthusiast.

Friends in New Places

If you have the luxury of being able to spend enough time in a country that you are able to make some local friends, there's one thing I've found that holds true: don't expect the friendship to last very long after you have left. Enjoy every moment and savour the time you spend with them because those memories will be the most valuable thing you take with you from your travels. The old adage, "out of sight, out of mind" tends to hold true, but it is hard to accept when you are in the midst of a passionate friendship. This is also precisely the reason it can be difficult to make local friends during your travels. It is understandably tough for a person to commit themselves to a friendship when they know the other person will be gone in a few weeks or months, off to another adventure with many new people and new experiences. The local person is the one left with their same life, except now there will be a sad void since their friend is gone.

When I was in my final year of high school in Saskatoon, Saskatchewan, I met a traveler who would change my life. His name was Martin Olsen and he was from Denmark but living with his uncle Johnny in Saskatoon for a year. He was one year older than me and had been in all sorts of trouble back in his hometown of Odense, so his mom had dispatched him to a frozen wasteland to cool off – Saskatoon in the winter being a perfect such place to whip the spirit out of a rowdy Scandinavian teenager. He was crazy, out of control, intensely fascinating and so much different than everybody else I knew. We struck up a friendship and ended up spending a lot of time together, hanging out with my other friends, going to parties, spending time at my house with my family and basically doing what teenagers do. The time eventually came for him to return to Denmark and I remember it like it was yesterday. It was January and the weather was bitterly cold, probably below -30 Celsius, which is common at that time of year. I borrowed my dad's Mercury Sable and collected Marten at his uncle's place, then drove him to the bus station downtown where he would travel to Calgary for his flight home. I promised him that I would come for a visit, probably after I finished university, which would be four years hence, then gave him a hug and watched him step onto the bus. As I drove away from the bus station I felt like my heart had been ripped out. My new, interesting friend was gone and I was probably never going see him again. To make things worse, I had been completely neglecting my other friends during the time Marten had been there so I probably had a whole lot of relationship mending to do. That drive home was the coldest and loneliest of my life.

Although the above story seems to have a sad ending, it actually doesn't. This was one of the rare times that a short intense friendship is strong enough to last a lifetime. Marten and I kept in contact by mail for five years, sometimes one letter per year, sometimes several, but the year after I finished university I strapped on a backpack and embarked on my first overseas trip. The two month trip to visit Marten and see Europe would turn into a ten year adventure where I would travel to over 80 countries, find the love of my life Ana, and make friends all over the world. To this day I believe much of my luck and good fortune in life stems from this unlikely friendship with a bad boy Dane.

Since that time, I have made friends with hundreds of locals in other countries but very few of these friendships have developed into a real long term relationship, even though at the time I was sure that many of them would. It takes an incredible amount of effort to keep friendships going when you are not in the same place and do not see each other regularly.

This does not mean that I recommend avoiding local friendships – far from it. I think that when you find a person that you love spending time with you should devote yourself entirely to the friendship. Life is all about passion, devotion and learning, so if you hold yourself back and are reluctant to become emotionally connected with others, then you are not living the full life you could be. The only caution is to work hard on these friendships but don't expect every one to last for the long term because they will not. But you can be sure that the friends you make in the places you visit will teach you more about the world than you could ever hope to learn any other way.

Travelers

Above all, traveling puts you into contact with fellow travelers. Other travelers are nearly always anxious to meet new people and swap travel stories, especially if your past destinations include some of their future ones. Communication is usually less of an issue with fellow travelers since many are multi-lingual and it's not often you meet a traveler who doesn't know at least enough basic English to have a simple conversation.

Ana and I spent some time living with a host family in Monteverde, Costa Rica as part of an intensive Spanish course. There were a large number of foreigners in this particular town whose enthusiasm for learning Spanish was matched only by their passion for drinking beer in the local taverns. One night, which happened to be Christmas Eve, we found ourselves joining the merrymakers in a small pub that, unfortunately, sealed up the taps and closed its doors at around 2 am. With a few hours of darkness still left to enjoy, we followed the horde of mainly foreigners up a muddy hill to a hostel where a few of them were staying. Amidst giggles, outright laughter and the sounds of a half dozen different languages being spoken, we poured into the common area of the hostel and made ourselves comfortable while one of our new friends went to fetch beer and weed for all from his private emergency stash. A single American was part of the scrum and decided that now would be a perfect time for a group drinking game, so he took the head of the table and began explaining, in English, the rules of the game. I looked around the room to see some people who appeared to be listening to him, others who were half asleep, and others still who were happily puffing away on sweet smelling joints. After what seemed like ten minutes of detailed instructions on the game, the American said, "OK, ready? Let's play!" When nobody moved he repeated, "Right, you guys ready to play or what?" After no response he continued with, "Do you have any questions on the rules?" Finally taking a cue from the obvious lack of response he bellowed, "DOES ANYBODY HERE SPEAK ENGLISH??" It turned out that we were the only English speakers in the crowd.

After you have done some traveling, and met people from all over the world, you cannot help but develop stereotypes about people based on the country they are from. I have always found it to be a great source of entertainment when I meet a new person who perfectly fits the stereotype I hold for them. By the same token, I've met people from one country who I would swear must be from a different country based on their personality, accent and demeanour. I love people like this because they always keep you guessing, but when a person fits their stereotype perfectly their actions can be quite predictable...which is simply boring. One attribute that devoted travelers of all nations have in common is that they can be very different than their countrymen who do not travel, therefore stereotypes of travelers don't always hold for all their countrymen. I'd like to share a few of my country-specific stereotypes, which will probably say more about me than about the citizens of these countries!

Australian

You can spot an Australian right away because they will be wearing sunglasses and be smeared with sunscreen. But don't make the mistake of asking them if they are English because they will cuss you out since you're too dumb to know the difference in the accents. Australians love drinking beer and partying but hate tourist attractions. They are the hardest people to impress but that shouldn't bother you because they are not out to impress anybody either — that's just a waste of effort. With an Australian, what you see is what you get and if they don't feel like doing something they will tell you as much. Australian English is laced with slang, jargon and colloquialisms that only a fellow Australian will fully comprehend. Aussies are seemingly unaware of this aspect of their speech and refuse to tone down the jargon when speaking to non-Australians, rendering much of what they say a curious mystery. But when it comes to being a great friend, Aussies will never let you down.

Brits

All male Brits have cropped hair, large foreheads and love nothing more than watching football. Female Brits are animal lovers and passionate environmentalists. Both sexes love beer equally and turn crazy after they've been drinking excessively, which is most of the time. The British have a wicked sense of humour and are fun to be around, especially when they are making fun of Germans or the French. They do tend to whine a fair bit and their phoney elitist accents can drive you crazy after a while, but most of the Brits I have met are intelligent, well spoken and know more about world history than anybody. Brits are fun to be around and the best to party with, but beware of the British Black Panther….if you tell a story about a black cat, he'll have an even better story about a black panther.

South Africans

South Africans are a hard group to peg. They have this weird accent that is absolutely impossible to imitate, no matter how long you've been hanging around them and how much you practice. The South Africans I have met (incidentally, I've only ever met white South Africans while traveling and had to go to South Africa to meet black ones) have all been so different, from off-the-wall party monsters to quiet, unassuming and meek. Generally, South Africans are well off financially, a little spoiled, a little sad, quite mysterious and are a hell of a lot of fun to chum around with. They prefer to hang around other South Africans, more so than nationals of most other countries. South Africans hold a lot of interest, likely due to their country's extraordinary history and the changes it has gone through in recent decades. If you want to impress a

South African, just tell them you love Castle beer and Pinotage wine, and then watch their eyes light up.

Americans

Americans are one group that I've found to be relatively homogeneous. They are large in all respects, from their physical size to their generosity to their expectations. They are indeed loud, sometimes obnoxious, always determined and strong willed and see no good reason why limits should exist, which is why they are often financially successful. They live by their own rules, have strong beliefs, are not easily shaken and are never afraid or ashamed to be who they are. Above all, they are political animals – you should never discuss politics with an American unless you are prepared to lose a friend or change your views. Most have a zany sense of humour and can usually find it in difficult situations, except for those that explode at the slightest inconvenience. Americans will befriend you instantly and are likely to pour their heart out on a whim. If you have known an American for five minutes and you haven't already been told of her two divorces, successful business, notable life achievements, and what her therapist recommended at their last appointment, then you might actually be talking to a Canadian. It is hard for a Canadian like me to have a neutral opinion of Americans as there seems to be this one way love/hate relationship between our countries, running from north to south. Personally, I love Americans and some of my best friends are from there.

Canadians

Canadians are best described as "American Light" but don't tell them that because living next to the US gives them an unshakable identify crisis. In most respects they are similar, from looks to language to volume, but have less of an edge. Canadian men are tall, stocky, have no fashion sense and sport the same haircut they had in high school (or am I just talking about me?) Canadian women are independent feminists on the outside but deep down they are beer drinking, hockey-loving hosers, just like the men. Canadians usually define themselves in terms of Americans, except those from Quebec who know they are the best and don't bother traveling since everywhere else in the world sucks. Canadians are inquisitive, adventurous, have lots of friends and always looking for more. They think of themselves as big drinkers but actually know absolutely nothing about beer, which is why most young, first time travelers go to Europe for beer training.

Japanese

You'll meet plenty of Japanese travelers but never get to know a single one. The difference between Japanese tourists and travelers is more extreme than for any other nationality. It's very easy to see a group of Japanese tourists approaching as it will be a mashup of bright tacky clothing, flashing cameras, and genuine smiles. Independent Japanese travelers are very different – usually reclusive, shy and always have very strange hair. Ana and I met a Japanese guy in South Africa who was traveling through 75 countries in eight months. We met him in the common kitchen of a hostel where he was having a single sliced, fried potato for supper, and judging by his physique and complexion, that was all that his travel budget allowed for. I wish I could write more about the Japanese but I've just found them to be very hard to get to know.

Germans

Wherever you go, you will meet Germans. It seems to be the result of living in a country where most people make very good money and everybody gets at least six weeks of holidays per year. Let's face it – some Germans can be pretty cold, which is the most common stereotype of a German, but it is not always true as many are warm, friendly and easy to get to know. A common habit of Germans while traveling is getting up very early in the morning to be the first at the beach so they can claim the best beach chair by throwing their towel on it. After staking their claim they immediately return to bed and by the time you get down there all the good chairs have towels draped over them and no people. I have found that some Germans speak extraordinary English while others hardly speak a word, and all of them love exploring, seeing new things and enjoying fine beer and wine. One thing for sure, Germans are very good at what they do and do not appreciate incompetence.

New Zealanders

New Zealanders, or "Kiwis", as they call themselves, love to have fun and don't seem to have hang-ups about anything, even being called Australian. All Kiwis go through this seemingly mandatory rite of passage where they leave New Zealand and go wandering around the world for a few years before returning home and staying there. They have a love/hate relationship with Australians that is actually quite fun and not at all toxic like it often is between some other neighbouring countries. Kiwis are often pudgy, love to drink beer, say "sex" when they mean "six" and are the kindest, craziest and funniest people you will meet when traveling.

Dutch

I have a special place in my heart for the Dutch or "Cloggies" as they are sometimes called. I worked for the Anglo-Dutch company Shell for many years and met and worked with dozens of people from the Netherlands. They are proud, funny, competent, self-effacing, down to earth and so easy to peg it is comical. The Dutch, both men and women, are always tall, speak perfect English, love chocolate and black licorice and turn orange after being in the sun for a couple of days. Once you know it, their accent is unmistakable, but don't get too close to them when they are speaking Dutch as the spit will fly when they say words like "Scheveningen". They can be rude, demanding, tactless and impatient, but at least you always know where you stand with a Dutchman. If you really want to know how you look in those pants you are wearing, then ask a Cloggie. They won't tell you the pants you're wearing make you look fat – they will tell you it's all the ice cream and chocolate you eat that makes you look fat!

The Permanent Traveler

Stillman Bradish is the one person I know who has been traveling since I met him and continues to do so. I first met Stillman during my first year at the University of Saskatchewan, when we had both volunteered for some duty that involved standing out in the parking lot directing people to go somewhere. Back then he was known as Earl and only began going by his middle name Stillman sometime in his late 20's, after what I expect was some sort of premature middle age crisis that likely involved a Brazilian, Canadian whiskey, a remote beach and perhaps a bar fight. But in those early days, he was simply a small town prairie boy destined for greater things. How small town was he? Well, his grandparents were farmers, his dad owned a Chrysler dealership, they lived on a lake front acreage near a town called Moose Jaw and he had six siblings. We soon became close friends and spent a lot of time together as we were both in the Finance program in the College of Commerce. I also became acquainted with a friend of Stillman's, named Colin Spilak, and our careers would coincidentally all follow a similar trajectory later in life.

Upon graduation, Stillman and Colin moved to London, England, both on a UK Working Holiday visa. While Colin had taken an internship position through an international business students exchange organization, Stillman was working as an accounting temp on short term contracts. I kept in touch with them after we graduated and after spending a year working in a dead end job in Saskatoon, I too decided to go traveling and soon found myself sleeping on Stillman and Colin's living room floor, spending all my available income drinking with them and their three crazy Irish flatmates.

Stillman remained in the UK for the full two year term of his working visa, doing plenty of short trips around Europe, and then headed off to Australia for a year where he lived in Sydney, enjoyed the sunshine and learned to scuba dive. He then decided to move back to Canada and found himself in Vancouver, where he began focusing on IT technical work. He remained there for two years, learning how to sail and snowboard along the way. Thanks to Vancouver's unique geography, these two activities can actually be done on the same day!

After two years, Stillman became bored with Vancouver and moved to New York to begin working with Oracle Corporation as a business and technical consultant. He spent three years here, simultaneously building up an impressive resume of skills and doing an incredible amount of travel throughout the US, Europe and the Caribbean, along the way developing a love affair with Mexico, which he visited at least 15 times.

At the end of this phase Stillman decided it was time for a break and managed to secure a one year sabbatical from his employer. The Brits use the term "gap year" and it refers to taking a year off between secondary and post secondary school. This time is typically spent traveling, usually backpacker style, to countries of interest with the goal of becoming more worldly, expanding ones horizons, gaining maturity, learning empathy and a whole bunch of other crap they tell their parents who are funding their travels. In reality, most kids just want a year long vacation to drink, screw and smoke as much marijuana as possible before having to embark on their real life.

Stillman has taken this gap year concept, pluralized it, and simply calls it a "year off", which he takes every once in a while to regain his bearings and reset his life compass. I remember Stillman and I drinking Crown Royal whiskey, late one night in my apartment in Puerto Rico. We were discussing life philosophy, as one often does under the influence. At one point he said, "We're going to wake up one day and say 'Today is Wednesday...and I'm 50! What happened?'" He has done everything possible to ensure not a single moment is wasted.

Stillman bought a round the world ticket and spent a year exploring many countries, chasing women, learning Spanish and visiting his brothers who were now themselves scattered around the globe. This year off produced a lifetime of adventures, and he traveled through such diverse countries as New Zealand, Australia, Japan, Tahiti, Peru and Mexico. At the end of this year he returned to the US, but moved his base to Florida and would remain there for three years working on various projects. By the end of this stint he was again burned out and ready for a break so he quit his job and bought another round the world ticket, this time bringing a girlfriend with him, which would end up tripling his budget and teaching him that it is much more affordable to meet women along the way. During this trip he visited several countries in Europe, China, Hong Kong, Vietnam and Hawaii, and then returned to the US looking for something new.

Stillman has spent the past two years in Washington DC trying his hand at two internet start up companies and now has a US green card that enables him to work there permanently. His long term plan is to remain in the US, where the opportunities are plentiful, the weather is acceptable and the world is a simple flight away.

Stillman has incorporated travel and change into his life more than anybody else I know. He has never been scared to try something new and loves nothing better than arriving in a new country, finding a café, and waiting to see what happens. He has met thousands of people all around the world and feels that opening yourself up to other cultures, making personal connections, trying new things and taking chances is the best way to make the most of the limited time we have. In the end, you don't want to be 80 years old, looking back on your life thinking of all the great television series you have watched. The only thing Stillman hasn't tried yet is having children, but I certainly do look forward to calling him from my catamaran in the Caribbean as he's taking his kids to soccer practice. Now that will be funny!

The Friends You Make

The first time I met Todd Van Hees, I was so hung over I could barely see. I had gone to a three day music festival in Reading, England with my best buddy and constant companion, John Eyre-Walker. John and I lived in the same flat in London and he had often spoken of his friend Todd, who was a fellow Australian, and had wanted me to meet him for some time. Todd lived in Bracknell, which was quite close to Reading, so the plan was to meet up with him on the Saturday for a pint at his local pub. It seemed like a great idea when planning the weekend, but when Saturday morning arrived, it brought with it great pain and agony caused by the previous night's overindulgence of deadly toxins, head banging and loud music. I initially tried to excuse myself from the day trip, but Johnny would hear nothing of it as he flipped me some Tylenols, a warm can of beer and dragged my ass out of bed. My memories from our initial meeting are dim; all I recall is sitting at a table wearing my darkest sunglasses, slowly and painfully nursing my pint, trying to keep my eyes open and limiting my involvement in the conversation to the occasional nod. He must have thought I was quite the loser. Fortunately, our future encounters would be plentiful, spanning a dozen countries, thousands of beers, and resulting in Todd being one of my closest friends, even though we haven't lived in the same country for fifteen years.

After years of traveling I now find that my closest friends are people who are the furthest away from me. Fortunately, that doesn't seem to matter, as traveling seems to instil a greater sense of patience, purpose and eventuality in you, while also breaking down the barriers of physical distance and time. Before I began my travels, the idea of maintaining friendships with many people I rarely saw and who lived thousands of miles away seemed unlikely. But now I believe that, for travelers, it is not just unlikely, it is nearly inevitable. The bonds you develop with other travelers are like steel.

Why do travelers develop such strong bonds? First, when traveling you often find yourself in unfamiliar and potentially risky situations where you may not know the language, customs or local etiquette. The natural concept of safety in numbers comes into play and you instinctively look for others in a similar situation who can be your allies. Thus, your initial contact with other travelers can sometimes be based on pure survival, which is an immensely powerful way to begin a friendship. This may sound exaggerated, but I'm not necessarily talking about life and death situations, it could be as simple as this: you are in a train station in Latin America, late at night, trying to figure out which of the last trains for the day you need to take in order to get to the hostel which is located far out in the country. You see another foreigner, looking similarly anxious, reading through the train timetables. You walk over to them, ask if they speak English, and find out they do and are also trying to get to the same hostel. Together you use your smatterings of Spanish to piece together the information and successfully figure out which train will get you there. This immediately creates a strong bond between you because you have had to join forces and together figure your way out of a difficult situation. Individually, you may not have done so well and could have ended up on the wrong train destined for the middle of nowhere.

Second, travelers from all nations share some common characteristics – a sense of adventure, passion for learning and anticipation of the unknown. It makes it easy to get along with another person when you hold many of the same world views.

Lastly, the advances in information technology have reduced the cost and effort of maintaining friendships. When I first began to travel there was no widespread email or internet availability and communications were done the old fashioned way – by written correspondence or expensive telephone calls. Now, once you've made a new friend on the road, you have the ability to communicate with that person anytime you like for almost no cost via the multitude of social networking tools available. At the risk of dating this book, the popular ones are the moment are Facebook, Google Talk, Skype, Facetime, and plain old text messaging on the cell phone. There is hardly a doubt these technologies have made a huge impact on the proliferation of international friendships and the endurance of them. The advance of these technologies is mind boggling and so rapid that it's difficult to imagine how the world of social communication will be in ten years. I can't wait to find out!

****

Chapter 4 – Spirituality

Although traveling takes you away from home, it often brings you closer to yourself. The time you spend traveling will be much different than your regular routine; you will think more, consider more, and be more open to new ideas. Your perception of the passage of time may be different. You will experience startling coincidences along the way. And you will have the opportunity to visit spiritual sites that may stimulate deep thoughts on humanity and reflections on your soul.

It was a crispy, sunny, gorgeous Monday morning as I loaded a case of paint cans and supplies into the back of my work truck – a blue, battered, mid 80's GMC with the words "Trans Gas" stamped on the side. I was fortunate enough to find summer employment with the provincial gas company during my four year program at the University of Saskatchewan. It was an excellent balance, the opportunity to work my arse off for four months in the summer, save every cent I made, then be able to pay for my own schooling and have enough left over to serve as spending money throughout the entire school year. These summer months were really my first experience with independent travel, and one in which I learned many valuable lessons, the most important of which is always grabbing the opportunity to travel using somebody else's money.

My job was to clean and paint steel markers indicating buried, high pressure natural gas transmission lines. These markers were present at every junction where a gas line crossed a road, and the area we covered was huge, approximately 100,000 square kilometres. I was given a map of the province, a truck, a credit card, a whole bunch of paint, and a kick in the butt, catapulting me off to some obscure part of the province. There is something liberating about driving across the prairies, under the enormous clear skies of Saskatchewan, with no boss looking over your shoulder, a full mug of hot coffee, shitty AM radio and only yourself to keep you company. My adventures during those summers were plentiful and ranged from being chased by rabid farm dogs, getting hopelessly lost for hours, enduring the worst lunches in small town cafes, getting the truck stuck in mud so bad that all four tires were no longer visible, and having to negotiate land access with creepy, suicidal farmers. What those experiences gave me were a real sense of independence, self reliance, a yearning to explore, and a good sense of direction, all of which are useful skills for an independent traveler. Each summer I would rack up nearly 20,000 miles on that truck, taking me through many towns and places that few people will ever have the chance to visit, and most of which I will never return to. When I look back I know this was an invaluable experience where I really got to know myself and my home, and learned to trust my instincts.

During one hot, dry and dusty week in July, I had a profoundly spiritual experience. I was near the town of Duck Lake, driving my work truck down a violently bumpy back road, which was really more of a path and almost completely grown over with weeds. I was looking for a gas line signpost marker with the help of a map that was desperately trying to convince me the road I was traveling on did not exist. As I plowed down the road with branches whipping and scratching the sides of my truck, I turned a corner and was suddenly in a clearing and faced with a small tent and a very old Indian man standing nearby, seemingly awaiting my arrival. At such a surprising moment, the fight or flight part of my brain urged me to hit the accelerator and speed away from here, but my rational mind took control and I stopped the truck, turned it off and went out to say hello to the old man. He didn't seem surprised to see this young, hopelessly lost kid suddenly appear, and simply looked at me. The man was very old and I could sense the wrinkles and folds on his face reaching out to tell me a story, even before he said a word. Although I have long since forgotten his name, I remember he was wearing a red, half buttoned, checkered plaid shirt, a green ball cap and a pair of old jeans. As way of introduction, I told him that I worked for the gas utility and was looking for a road back onto the main highway. He told me to simply keep following this trail and it would lead to the main road. I couldn't help but ask him what he was doing there, to which he replied, "Watching over my friend," as he motioned towards the tent. Curiosity piqued, I probed further and the old man was happy to talk with me. He told me that the man in the tent had been fasting for three days and had a couple more to go. He had been in some sort of trouble with the law and had returned to his family home in Duck Lake to try and sort himself out, and the fasting was meant to clear all the rubbish from his mind and body and allow him a fresh start. I was told that the fasting would culminate with a sweat lodge ceremony in which he would be joined by several others in the community to help him through. I asked him if non-Indians were ever allowed to join in a sweat lodge ceremony. To my utter surprise, he told me that it was open to anybody and that I should return in two days to join in. After giving me directions to the sweat lodge he added, "Don't forget to wear shorts and bring a towel."

Two days later, after work, I drove to the sweat lodge and found the old man accompanied by six others, who were all speaking Cree together as I arrived, but switched to English after I introduced myself. They immediately included me in the conversation, which made me feel very welcome and not at all self-conscious. The old man was the elder of the group and obviously well respected by the others, who were all quite a bit younger, but at least ten years older than me. After speaking together with them for a few minutes I turned my attention to the lodge. A sweat lodge is a small, dirt floor, igloo shaped leather tent used for ceremonial purposes by many different Indian tribes. The interior of the lodge is simple and sparsely adorned with various native items such as beaded bracelets and braided sweet grass. The centerpiece of the lodge is a simple pit dug in the centre of the earthen floor. The extreme temperatures inside the lodge are generated by heating rocks in a large fire outside the tent, carefully transferring them into the pit inside the tent, then throwing water on them, which generates blistering steam.

I was included in two ceremonies that evening. The first sweat was lead by the old man while the second was lead by a younger man, perhaps one who was earmarked to become a leader, although I was never told exactly what role each of them played. Suffice to say that the younger man may have had something to prove – the temperature inside that lodge during the first sweat was unbearable, but the second sweat was of such excruciating heat, I felt as if my body was about to burst into flames, and before the leader reached the end of the ceremony, I couldn't help but bolt out of the lodge and escape to the heavenly chill of the outside air.

I must now, unfortunately, admit that I cannot relay exactly what happened inside the sweat lodge during the ceremonies. At the conclusion of the second ceremony, as I lay covered in sweat and dirt on the cool prairie ground, looking skyward, being devoured by mosquitoes and feeling as if my scorched skin was peeling off, I began telling one of the others what I had seen and experienced in the lodge. He stopped me mid sentence and with a grave expression and serious tone told me that whatever I saw and felt in there was for me and me alone. Since that moment, I have kept my experience to myself and will store this memory as one of the most precious and the most spiritual of my life.

During the short time I spent inside the sweat lodge, with the new friends I will probably never meet again, I felt more spiritual than I ever have and am eternally grateful to that old man.

What is Spirituality?

Although it's lovely to visit and explore grand European churches, Tibetan monasteries and elaborate Jewish temples, the spirituality of one's travels is about much more than religion. I consider spirituality to be very personal and defined by one's innermost reflections, hunches, thoughts, sense of purpose, equity, history, and sense of awe. For the vast majority of people, your fundamental religious beliefs are handed to you by your parents or taught to you by your teachers or religious leaders. For example, how many people do you know who have actually chosen their religion? Picture a young person researching each major world religion, interviewing members of these religions, perhaps visiting countries where these religions are practiced, then compiling a benefits and drawbacks list per religion, perhaps scoring each one on its relative attractiveness, then choosing one to believe in. Sounds a bit ridiculous? To me it certainly does. It is much more likely that such a person either was not brought up in a religious family or perhaps rejects the religion that was handed down to them for whatever reason. In either case, if they do embrace a formal religion, it is not a conscious choice; instead the particular religion somehow connects with this person, maybe through a friend or through an experience with a religious person.

Spirituality is something different – it is something organic that grows, develops, is unbound by rules and dogma, and is profoundly affected by the people you meet, the places you visit and the decisions you make. I would define a spiritual person as one who is introspective and thoughtful, one who naturally feels empathy for others instead of judging them outright, and one who is able to draw meaningful insights from simple occurrences, which many others would simply disregard. As we all know, there are many people who claim no particular religion yet are profoundly spiritual while others we know may be deeply religious and dogmatic but not at all spiritual. A clear example of the latter are religious terrorists – people who are so overpowered and controlled by religion that they are unable to make a spiritual connection with anybody who lives outside a rigid set of rules. Any person willing to kill others in the name of religion is clearly not a very spiritual person.

I've found that travelers are generally quite spiritual, which leads me to believe that putting yourself in new surroundings and in the company of new people causes one to become more reflective. Or maybe it's the difference of living a life of routine versus living a life of adventure. Routine is the mortal enemy of spirituality. Endless weeks, months and years of mind numbing routine does not allow much opportunity for spiritual growth. Since repatriating myself to Canada over ten years ago and becoming firmly entrenched in what most we consider a normal routine with jobs, kids and possessions, I find that my own sense of spirituality is at an all time low. It seems that all the other activity in my life has gobbled up that space and spirituality has been relocated to a lower and much smaller shelf. The worst part is that what we as a family think of as a routine is probably considered anything but routine by most others. Both Ana and I have flexible work hours and days so our schedule can be very different from one week to the next. We are also able to get away on vacations many times per year to destinations near and far. It is most often during these trips that my own sense of spirituality is re-ignited and this is probably one of the strongest reasons for my passion to travel.

Spiritual Sites

Every country, region, city, town and village in the world has locations that hold some spiritual value or quality, some obvious such as mosques, churches and temples and others not so obvious. No matter what your religious inclination is, it's hard to argue the spiritual impact of visiting places that hold religious and spiritual significance for others. For me, spiritual sites are places that simply cause you to stop and think, quite often about your own humanity, sense of worth, purpose of being and even your own infinite smallness in this large world.

Adam's Peak, or *Sri Pada*, is one of the most sacred sites in Sri Lanka and a destination for pilgrims of many religions including Buddhists, Muslims, Jews, and Christians. The 2,200 metre mountain is crested with a small rock formation that resembles a large footprint, thought to have been left by one of Shiva, Buddha or Adam, depending on which religious beliefs you subscribe to. The mountain itself can be scaled a number of ways, the most accessible of which is a very long set of staircases and hand rails, which eventually lead to the top. The goal is to begin the ascent sometime after midnight and reach the summit in time for sunrise where there are various rituals performed in honor of the sun.

I made a trip to Sri Lanka in 1998 with a good friend of mine named Trudy Taylor, who was also my boss at the time at Shell Pakistan. It was a last minute sanity trip done to escape the heat, filth and limited alcohol supplies of Karachi. During this trip I heard about Adam's Peak from a German man (whose name completely escapes me) I met on a diving trip. He was planning on doing a pilgrimage to this holy site so I invited myself along and after a bumpy eight hour taxi ride, we found ourselves at the base of the mountain shortly before midnight. There were hundreds of fellow pilgrims around, ranging in age from infant to ancient and seemingly representing every social class in Sri Lanka. As we set out, the climb seemed easy as there were stairs and railings for the most difficult parts, but after climbing stairs for two hours my legs decided otherwise and the rest of the climb was punishing.

In fact, at times I was close to giving up and taking a rest, but then I would see a young Sri Lankan helping their 90 year old grandmother climb the same stairs as me, which forced me to man up, take a breath and continue. As I finally achieved the summit, an hour or two before dawn, I was overwhelmed by my surroundings – there were hundreds of people clamoring for a place to sit or sleep, exhausted from the climb, elated by the surroundings and enchanted by the spirituality of the peak, patiently awaiting the sunrise. All faiths were present that morning, making it an extraordinary, inter-denominational religious experience, one that I will never forget. And yes, the sunrise was spectacular.

There are spiritual sites in any country you visit and I've always made it a priority to find these and visit them. This has become even more important to me since having children because we want to raise them as spiritual people with an appreciation for the various religions and beliefs of people all over the world. Finding a church service is always easy and accessible, so we sometimes do this, but we also look for spiritual sites or landmarks to visit. During a recent trip to the Azores, while her mom and brother were shopping, Stella and I did a hike up a large cliff via an ancient looking grass pathway with stone walls and steps. I fully expected her to run out of energy but she surprised me and kept up the whole way, and before long we had reached the summit, where there was a giant obelisk topped with a statue of the Virgin Mary and an indescribably beautiful view over the ocean harbor and town. For me this was a very spiritual experience, almost like a mini-pilgrimage, and having my daughter there with me at my side was emotional and wonderful and at that moment I felt very happy, blessed and fortunate to be alive.

Maximize Coincidence

It was in a small hostel in Betty's Bay, South Africa where we met a young lady and her mom, who were also backpacking through the country. At first, we weren't sure if they were Canadian or American, as it can be difficult to hear the difference in accents, especially for Americans from the western states. We struck up a conversation and learned that they were from Canmore, Alberta and had chosen South Africa for a mother/daughter bonding experience, mainly because the girl had been on a Rotary exchange to South Africa during one of her high school years. I wondered to myself if it could be possible that she was there the same time as my cousin Talia who had also been on a Rotary exchange to South Africa. I assumed it was a long shot but when

I mentioned Talia's name the girls eyes widened and a huge, excited smile spread across her face. Talia had been her closest friend during their time in South Africa.

Coincidences such as this are an absolute delight and happen much more frequently than you would ever guess when you are traveling. Over the years I have shifted from being amazed when these coincidences happen to practically expecting them at every turn. But why do they seem to happen so frequently? After an unlikely coincidence takes place, one's natural reaction is to question the chance of that exact occurrence happening. But the right question is not what the chance is of a single particular coincidence happening but, rather, what is the chance of *any* sort of coincidence happening. And the answer is "very high". Think about it. How many people do you know, know of, have heard of, or have even just briefly met over the years? The answer is thousands. If you then consider how frequently people travel, then you can safely assume that the vast majority of these people will have traveled throughout their own country or to other countries many times during their lives. Because tourists tend to frequent the same 1% of locations within any particular country, it is quite likely that any two travelers visiting a country will have gone to some of the same places. If the two travelers had been in the same country during the same time then it is not unlikely that they would have crossed paths.

Coincidences add a special significance to a traveler's experience. They show how intimate the world really is and can easily affect your perception of fate and destiny. For example, in the story above, a lot of events had to line up for us to meet these people – we chose that particular hostel on that particular day, we were assigned to the same common room as them, we talked to them and the subject of student exchanges came up, and so on. Of this series of events, which did we have control over? The answer is we chose to talk to them. Everything else was due to chance and therein is the secret to maximizing coincidences: you must talk to people. You could be standing right next to your long lost pen pal, but if you choose not to speak to each other, you will forgo an amazing coincidence and a personal connection that may have changed the significance of your trip. I've found that you can almost always find a connection with a new person you meet

Coincidences can range from being life changing experiences to slapstick comedy. My friend Ian Lavoie was in the midst of a European backpacking trip and stayed with me in London, England for a few days.

He was on the UK segment of his travels and had just come from Ireland, Scotland and Wales. I was doing my best to give him a taste of what living in London was like, which for us, was mainly limited to avoiding sleep, drinking ridiculous quantities of beer and chasing women. One afternoon we were riding the London Underground and ended up sitting across from three young, good looking girls. Ian, unfamiliar with the unwritten but socially mandated decree of "Don't talk to anybody on the Tube", naively struck up a conversation with the girls. They noticed he had a downhill skiing lift ticket attached to his jacket and asked if he was a skier. He told them he was a ski instructor (which was actually the truth) then casually mentioned that he had brought an excellent ski magazine with him from Canada, which had this particularly interesting article, but that he had unfortunately left it in some hostel in Scotland. At that moment, this strange expression came over the face of one of the girls as she slowly reached into her day pack, pulled out a ski magazine and told us that she had found it in a hostel in Scotland. Of course, it was Ian's magazine! We all had a laugh and just as Ian and I were telepathically thrashing out the decision to either pursue these girls or to continue to the pub, the doors of the train opened, they waved goodbye and scurried off to their own futures. We continued to the pub.

I experienced a more profound coincidence sitting in a hot tub with Ana and another couple at a small, out of the way, hotel in Costa Rica. We were living in the capital, San Jose at the time and had taken a weekend trip away to the Manuel Antonio area, which is in the Central Pacific region. A month prior to this I had received the terrible news that my grandfather had suddenly passed away, which came as a shock as he had been perfectly healthy and there were no warning signs of any illness. Fortunately, he lived a long, happy and healthy life.

The other couple in the hot tub was older than us by perhaps 15 or 20 years and we were having a nice chat as we blanched ourselves in the overheated waters. We knew immediately they were Canadians, and from the accent I suspected they were from the prairies. The husband soon revealed that he was from Wynyard, Saskatchewan, which is less than 50 kilometers from my parents' hometown of Foam Lake, Saskatchewan. When I told him my name and where my family was from he asked, "Is Max Olson your grandfather?" After I confirmed this, he told me that, as a kid, he used to accompany his father to Foam Lake and they would always stop at my grandfather's hardware store where he would have great fun running around the aisles, playing with the toys. He was sad to hear that he had passed away but it was heartwarming for me to see the happy twinkle in his eye when he remembered my grandpa.

Expect them, enjoy them, feel amazed and share your coincidences with others, as they will be one of the most fascinating aspects of your travel.

Making the Time Last

Why do some days seem to last so much longer than others? Imagine a typical busy work day where you wake up at the same time, fly into your morning routine, think about what to pack for lunch, mentally review what's on your list of things to get done for the day and evaluate what's happening the rest of the week. Your mind is constantly racing, planning, remembering and reviewing. You can barely find a moment to stop and think about anything besides what you need to do to get through the week. The days at work are usually filled with inconsequential, shallow conversations and the time is consumed by busyness and multi-tasking, with few moments dedicated to the present moment. Sometimes a week can go by and you can't remember any significant event happening, nor stopping even once to really look at what was going on around you or to look into the eyes of your partner or kids and have a real, significant conversation. At the end of the week, you may have accomplished much, but really experienced nothing, and the time will have passed quickly. In fact, you may feel that the time flew by so fast that entire days have been obliterated from your memory, or the days have blended and mashed into one other so completely that they have become indistinguishable. Sound familiar?

The reason why time seems to pass so quickly during a typical week is because we are rarely in the moment, considering the moment. Our mind is focused on upcoming tasks, checking off tasks we have recently completed, speaking on the phone, reviewing our friends' Facebook status, planning, rehashing and so on. When our attention is focused on the present, it is usually focused on several things at once in an effort to multi-task ourselves to a productive, yet gutless day. When we do feel like we've had a successful, productive day, there is rarely time to reflect on it, as there will be a whole new round of challenges to face tomorrow so we don't often stop long enough to really consider what we are doing.

Now imagine you are away from your regular life and job, by yourself, on a beautiful day and you are standing on the banks of the Amazon

River, or at the edge of the Grand Canyon, or in the Valley of the Kings or at Ayers Rock. You have three hours to yourself to explore the area with no interruptions, no commitments, nothing to fix, nothing to review, no phone calls, no email and nobody else to think about besides yourself. You can bet those few hours only reluctantly pass as you stand in awe at the wonders before you, noticing the fine details of the objects you see, the textures of things you touch, the smell of the air you breathe and the sensation of the sun on your face. Nothing else in your life is more important than that exact moment and you become truly aware of where you are, who you are and what you are. Your normally racing mind will slow down and focus on one thing at a time, and in the process, slowing down your perception of the passing of time. You might decide to sit down on a rock for a while, pick up a leaf and look at the shape of it, noticing the veins running through in such an organized pattern and wonder how it is possible for a leaf to be so perfect. You may wonder why you've never taken the time to pick up a leaf before and really look at it.

Those three hours will last forever.

The sense of awe you feel when experiencing something vast, overwhelming, spiritual or breathtakingly beautiful can and does alter your perception of time. Fixing your mind on the present moment slows the passage of time to a crawl - just ask anybody who practices yoga or meditation and they will tell you the same. Moments like this are as frequent while traveling as they are rare during your normal day to day routine, and memories made during these moments of reflection can be everlasting.

****

Chapter 5 – Favourites

A book on travel would not be complete without mentioning a few of my favourite places. These are sites which had a special significance for me or which I found particularly interesting or inspiring. Travelers may experience the same place very differently so, while I can recommend places for you to consider visiting, the experience you have will be yours and yours alone, and may be very much different than mine. Falling in love with a particular place sometimes says more about the traveler than the place itself.

I knew we were in for something special when the last remaining employee at the Paramaribo airport in Suriname shut all the lights off the second Ana and I stepped out of the airport doors and into the moist, jungle air. With the airport and runway lights doused, we stood amazed under a blanket of stars listening to the music of the jungle and its creatures. The flight crew and other passengers who joined us on the flight had already left the airport, leaving us alone with only a single taxi cab, waiting to drive us into the city. Paramaribo would become our new home for the next two months.

Ever heard of Suriname? Sure, it's in Africa. Or is it in Southeast Asia? Let's face it, you have no idea, and neither did I. At least not until I joined an intriguing Shell International project, which was based in El Salvador, but covered two dozen countries across the Caribbean. Suriname used to be called Dutch Guiana and is found on the South American continent, located north of Brazil, sandwiched between English speaking Guyana to the west and French Guiana to the east. It is difficult to get to as only three airlines fly there, and you must first get to either Amsterdam or the Caribbean to pick up one of the few flights. Like most little known countries, being one of the fortunate few to visit is a privilege indeed and often it feels like you may be the only tourist in town.

The country is a multi-cultural tapestry, with substantial representation from ethnic groups as diverse as the Dutch, Maroons (descendents of escaped African slaves), Jews, Javanese, Hindustani, Amerindians and Brazilian gold diggers. Dutch is the primary language spoken, but after that it's up for grabs as you will also hear the national Creole language

Sranan Tongo, Hindi, Chinese, Maroon languages, English, Spanish and Portuguese, making a national identify somewhat difficult, if not impossible to nail down. Paramaribo is the capital city with the unique privilege of featuring a Jewish synagogue and Islamic mosque located beside each other on the same street. Over 80% of the country is covered by Amazonian tropical rain forest and sparsely populated, providing for a pristine ecotourism destination. The Surinamese people are friendly, gentle, hospitable and very, very welcoming. Our experiences during the short time we lived there were unexpected and amazing.

When people ask me what my favourite country is, Suriname is the first one that comes to mind. But it is a difficult question, and in come cases a question that almost defies an answer, simply because so many countries are so special to me in their own unique ways. A more relevant question may be, "What is your favourite country for food?" or "What is your favourite country for scuba diving?" or "What country offers the best value for money?" These questions are much easier to answer, and probably provide more insight into the sorts of things I enjoy and what you might expect to experience in each.

Here are some examples of places or sites I have visited that have really left an impression on me and might be worthwhile adding to your places to visit list.

Beautiful Beaches

Stella Maris Resort, Long Island, Bahamas

I have visited many stunning beaches all around the world, but when I think about the best of them, the beaches around Stella Maris Resort in Long Island, Bahamas are at the top of the list. And yes, there is not just one, there are many, including the Love Beaches, Deal's Beach, The Rock Pools, Millerton's School Beach, Salt Pond, Guana Cay, Lochabar, Cabbage Beach and Turtle Cove. This was the first place that Ana and I visited as a new couple, and we spent one glorious afternoon on Deal's Beach, with two miles of pristine sand and ocean all to ourselves. It's a good thing I took her there first, because the next island I took her to in the Bahamas was Cat Island where she was consumed by bed bugs on the first night, but thankfully she was already madly in love with me by then.

Tar Bay, Exuma, Bahamas

Exuma is another of what they call the Family Islands of the Bahamas, which is pretty much everything outside of New Providence, home of more than half the population and the capital city Nassau. I rented a five bedroom beach house in an area called Tar Bay, which is six miles north of the main city Georgetown, and I spent four days there with my grandparents, mom and step dad back in 1998.

There were other houses there, but very few people and most days it was just us sitting on the beach chairs out in the sand. I spent hours with my grandpa chasing crabs around on the beach and swimming in the stunningly clear water looking for conch. The entire family had all pitched in money to help fund their trip and I can remember the tears welling up in my eyes one morning as I walked out on the patio and saw Grandma and Grandpa holding hands, walking slowly down the beach, enjoying life and each other. There wasn't much else there, just a pristine beach, shallow water full of sea life and lots of time to think about what is important in life.

Marshall Beach, Turks & Caicos

Our first international trip with our new baby Magnus, back in 2004, was to the island of Providenciales in the Turks & Caicos. We found a great little hotel called Turtle Cove Inn where we paid $120 per night, which was a terrific bargain considering the larger hotels on the main beaches were well over $300. Most days we took the local busses around to explore but one day we rented a car to do some adventuring on our own. We cruised around much of the island and eventually found ourselves on the west side where, after driving down a long, bumpy, twisty, gravel road, we came upon Marshall Beach and were the only ones there. We scavenged up some sticks and used them to build a frame, then topped it with a blanket and had ourselves a baby sun shelter. We plopped Magnus beneath it with a bottle of milk and a couple toys then we submerged ourselves into the smooth blue water. It felt like our own deserted island as there was not a person, building or any sign of humanity as far as the eye could see. After a while, one of us went back up the beach, whipped off Magnus's diaper, and brought him down for his first ocean swim!

Natural Wonders

Fraser Island, Australia

Smack in the middle of the main tourist route on Australia's east coast is Fraser Island. Before visiting Australia I had never even heard of it, but it turned out to be one of the highlights of the trip. Tours range from a single day to multi day trip, most of which originate from the nearby town of Hervey Bay. We decided on a two day trip and probably saw and experienced more unique, astonishing, and unforgettable moments than we ever have in such a short period of time. Fraser Island is formed completely out of sand, and because of some naturally occurring elements that are not common on other sand islands, vegetation grows wildly. The nearly 2000 square kilometres offer such diverse sights as rainforest, mangroves, expansive beaches, swamps, freshwater lakes and gigantic coloured sand dunes. There are also dingoes present on the island, and we were visited by some of them at night as we sat around the campfire. It was a thrilling moment for a few of our travel companions, but they just looked like mangy, dirty dogs to me.

Iceland

Iceland is the country from whence my paternal great grandparents originated and I have always had a desire to visit, since we still have some family connections there. Ana and I did a two week backpacking trip there in 2002 and found it to be a remarkable place in so many ways. After recovering from the initial shock of the astronomical prices, we threw budget concerns aside and tried to explore as much as we could in a short period of time. Most of the tourist propaganda you see describes Iceland as the "Land of Fire and Ice", mainly because of the frequency of volcanic activity and the glaciers that cover much of the interior of the island. We did several interesting day trips, one of which was on the Golden Circle – the most popular tourist route in the country. This bus tour leaves from the capital Reykjavik and stops at three sites; Geysir, the Gullfoss waterfall and Thingvellir (Þingvellir in Icelandic).

Thingvellir is the location of the founding of the Icelandic parliament, which happened in 930 and has played a central role in the history of the country. For two weeks each summer, all the chieftains of the island, as well as thousands of regular citizens, would meet here, and all the disputes that arose during the previous year would be presented and discussed, then legal actions would be initiated. The location itself is a large valley and plain, and is the meeting point of two tectonic plates, creating a great fault that traverses the region. The location itself is spectacular, but being able to stand on the Law Rock and imagine the thousands of people camped out across the plain listening to the speeches from the leaders, is almost overwhelming.

The Gulfoss Waterfall is another of Iceland's natural wonders. The river Hvita follows an erratic course then plunges into a deep crevice, almost making it appear as if the river has disappeared entirely into the earth.

The Haukadalur valley is where you will find the Great Geysir, a natural geyser that erupts hot water over 100 metres in the air. It was the first geyser discovered by Europeans and has been active for thousands of years, going from periods of frequent eruptions to sometime becoming almost completely dormant. The landscape itself is stark – a treeless plain with smoke rising from Geysir itself as well as the many other smaller geysers also located there.

Another site close to Reykjavik is the Blue Lagoon. Despite being man-made, it certainly appears to be a natural wonder, and is the most expansive hot springs you will ever experience. It is a huge open hot pool in the midst of a giant lava field, filled with tourists from all over the world. We spent a lovely few hours there soaking in the mineral rich, therapeutic hot water and enjoying the steam rooms that are built into the surrounding piles of lava rock.

Iguazu Falls, Brazil

Iguazu Falls is a massive set of waterfalls located at the junction of Brazil, Argentina and Paraguay and has the second greatest water flow of any waterfall after Niagara Falls. The area itself is very spread out and there are many walkways built where you can get very close to the falls, allowing you to experience the area one section at a time. When we visited, I was amazed at how accessible and natural the area was, especially compared to Niagara Falls, which is highly commercialized, paved, packaged and sanitized. At one point along one of the walkways you are almost completely surrounded by waterfalls and the moisture hangs on you like a blanket.

Uyuni Salt Flats, Bolivia

One of the strangest moments of my travels was when I found myself in a beaten up army truck speeding at 120 kilometres per hour across a completely flat, blindingly white salt flat with absolutely nothing else in sight. The Uyuni Salt Flats are the largest in the world at 10,000 square kilometres and are basically a huge, dried up lake with several metres of salt crust on top. It is one of the flattest places on earth, which in conjunction with its surface reflectivity, allows it to be used for calibrating orbiting satellites.

If that isn't strange enough for you, in the middle of the flats is Isla Incahuasi, a small island covered in giant cacti and interesting coral-like formations. Standing on top of this island, surrounded by cacti, sweating through your shirt because of the heat and looking out at the seemingly frozen and icy landscape is an odd sensation indeed. You have to experience it to believe it.

Arenal Volcano, Costa Rica

Less than 100 kilometres north-west of Costa Rica's capital city of San Jose is the Arenal Volcano which was, until recently, among the top ten most active volcanoes in the world. The only problem was you had to be pretty lucky to actually see anything, as the area surrounding the volcano and the district of La Fortuna is nearly always covered in a thick blanket of fog. We visited the area three times and didn't manage to actually see the volcano at all, but if you did happen to go on a clear day, then you were usually able to see lava running down the sides and sometimes see and hear small explosions. The real attraction for me were the numerous hot spring resorts located nearby that offer a gorgeous natural spa environment with a hot river originating from the volcano. One of my most vivid memories of my time in Costa Rica was sitting in a natural hot pool of the river, surrounded by beautiful, thick vegetation, joined by my wife and in-laws, and all of us enjoying a cold beer as we relaxed and soaked in the water.

In 2010 the volcanic activity from Arenal basically stopped and it is now no longer active. Fortunately, the hot springs still are so visitors can continue to enjoy the resorts and the multitude of tourist activities that are available in the area.

Unforgettable Sights

Sagrada Familia Cathedral, Barcelona, Spain

The time I've spent in the country of Spain, sadly, is limited to a single long weekend in Barcelona. While the tapas bars, restaurants, clubs and shops were all fantastic, what really blew me away were the architectural artworks of Antoni Gaudi. Born in 1852, Gaudi lived and worked as an architect in the Catalan region until his death at age 73, leaving behind an incredible legacy of twisty, unique, and visually stunning buildings, parks, statues, newsstands, houses and churches. His most ambitious project, left unfinished at his death, was the Sagrada Familia cathedral – a Roman Catholic church in Barcelona.

The original plan was of such a grand scale that construction was expected to last for several hundred years, and at the time of his death it was only 20% completed. Due to improved construction techniques, the church is now expected to be completed sometime before 2030. Interestingly, the ongoing construction is funded by neither the Spanish state nor the Roman Catholic Church – instead it is supported entirely by private donations and the proceeds of ticket sales to tourists.

The cathedral itself is overwhelming. Gaudi's style evolved into an organic approach to building, which means you see very few straight angles or flat surfaces. Instead, there are curves, rounded corners, elaborate spires, points, designs, spheres and many irregular, yet visually pleasing shapes. One of the facades, an elaborate collection of carvings and icons, was built in such as way that it appears to be in the process of melting and sliding down the edge of the building. It is possible to climb the towers and get a dizzying overhead view of the cathedral and the city of Barcelona. In truth, it is hard to describe the cathedral, and any description I may offer would simply not do justice to this incredible work of art. But suffice to say that it is the most visited location in Barcelona and draws millions of visitors every year.

Machu Picchu, Peru

I expect that anybody who has visited Machu Picchu will have it on their own amazing sights list, simply because even after seeing film documentaries and hundreds of images of it, you can never prepare yourself for actually being there in person and looking down on this incredible sight. And this is despite being only one in a swarm of thousands of people there for the same experience.

While it was possible to do a multi-day hike along the Inca Trail, which enabled you to arrive at Machu Picchu at dawn, before the crowds arrived, we took the easy and cheaper option, which is a day trip from Cusco. This involves a strange train ride, which slowly climbs a mountain by alternating directions up a series of switchbacks, then a hair-raising bus ride up a narrow road with tight corners, dangerous drop-offs and a worryingly steep grade. After paying our entrance fee, we joined one of the Spanish speaking tours and the guide led us to an area in the trees before the ruins were actually visible. He asked us to sit down, and then told a story of what life was like back in the Inca times. He slowly built up our anticipation, and then just when we couldn't stand it anymore he walked us over just a few steps and Machu Picchu came into view. It was so overwhelming that the group fell completely silent for a few moments. After the initial jolt we were allowed to freely explore the entire area so we spent a couple hours wandering around exploring the artefacts and structures. Because of the expansive area of the sight, it did not seem crowded at all and you had plenty of time and space to yourself.

Gadani Ship Breaking Yard, Pakistan

50 kilometres north-west of the city of Karachi, Pakistan, is a ten kilometre long beach, which is home to the Gadani ship breaking yard. This was once the largest ship breaking yard in the world, employing over 30,000 workers and ripping apart hundreds of ships per year. When a ship has reached the end of its useful life it is sailed to Gadani, and at high tide it is cranked up to full speed and driven right up onto the beach.

When I visited Gadani it was during the least busy phase of its history and there were only a couple ships there, but since then it has ramped back up so I can scarcely imagine what it is like now. The most shocking, but sad, sight was the workers, most of whom were not just lacking safety equipment, but were actually barefoot and gloveless, crawling all over these rusted monstrosities with cutting torches, ripping them apart piece by piece. I visited with a group of friends and we were lucky enough to speak with one of the foremen, who gave us a rundown of the operation and admitted that they have plenty of accidents. He told us that workers are regularly squashed to death by giant pieces of hull being cut away from the ships. The surprising part is we had no problem driving up to the beach and wandering up and down exploring the yards. There didn't seem to be any security or restrictions on visiting, though we did keep a safe distance away from the ships to avoid getting flattened.

Altos de Chavon, Dominican Republic

Yes, one of my unforgettable sights is a completely fabricated, inauthentic replication of a medieval village and Roman amphitheatre, located in La Romana, on the south cost of the Dominican Republic. Why? Well, I guess simply because you just don't expect it to be there.

Completed in the early 1980's and built on a high cliff overlooking the Chavon River, it has the feel of an actual village and features shops, galleries, a couple restaurants and a beautiful church. It is primarily a tourist destination but has been used for many other purposes over the years, including weddings, art school, film set and an unforgettable concert venue. In fact, my most memorable visit there was when Ana and I attended a sold out Duran Duran concert at the open air amphitheatre in 2001!

Lake Titicaca, Peru

Lake Titicaca is a high elevation and enormous body of water that straddles the border of Peru and Bolivia and is the largest lake in South America. Besides the many historical Inca ruins that dot the shoreline, it is notable for the few hundred Uros tribespeople, who build and live on approximately 40 reed islands that float in the shallows.

Tourists are invited to visit these islands and a boat and guide can be hired from the nearby Peruvian town of Puno. These same reeds, called totora reeds, are used to built boats and watchtowers and are also edible and used for medicinal purposes. They live a very traditional lifestyle, but also supplement their income by selling tourists handicrafts and souvenirs. It is interesting to see how they have used a single material to produce pretty much everything they need to live, and have been doing so for generations.

Cool Cities

Ponta Delgada, Azores, Portugal

The largest city in the Azores is Ponta Delgada, located on the shores of the island of San Miguel, also the largest of the nine island chain. The Azores is an autonomous region of Portugal and with its clean air, wonderful people, nautical history, delicious food and ridiculously inexpensive wine, is one of my favourite places to visit.

Ponta Delgada is on the south shore and protected by an enormous man made breakwater, which is also used to receive shipping container vessels. The city has recently completed a major infrastructure project called Portas do Mar, which is a long boardwalk extending into the harbour and is used for public events, a cruise ship and ferry terminal, a public swimming venue, and a marina. It features many shops, restaurants and bars and being in the city centre on a warm summer evening is one of the most pleasant experiences you can imagine. Walk down the promenade at 11 pm and you will find young couples in love walking hand in hand, families with small children enjoying an ice cream, partygoers priming for a club night, many older folks out for an evening stroll, and even the odd, stunned tourist looking like they just discovered paradise.

San Juan, Puerto Rico

For such an accessible, tourist friendly, easy to navigate and stable Caribbean island, it surprises me that more people have not visited Puerto Rico. Old San Juan, which is the well preserved city centre from Spanish colonial times, is the most visited area and for good reason. It is located on an island that is connected to the mainland by several bridges, and was originally enclosed by a giant wall, much of which still exists. The area is protected by a citadel called Morro Castle, dating from the 16th century, as well as two other Spanish forts. Old San Juan is clean, safe and always very full of both locals and tourists, enjoying the sights and the plentiful bars and restaurants. Beyond Old San Juan, you will find pretty much everything a typical large American city has to offer – shopping malls, museums, sports facilities and an unbelievable quantity of automobiles, which can make driving frustrating and slow, so you need to learn to enjoy the Spanish radio while spending hours in traffic jams. Ana and I spent several months living in a beautiful high rise condo right on the beach, only a short drive east of the main tourist areas, directly across from the airport, which was an ideal location. We found the Puerto Ricans to be delightful people and made friends there whom we have kept in contact with after all these years.

Havana, Cuba

While most tourists hit the all-inclusive resorts of Cuba and shelter themselves as much as possible from the local population, the first few times I visited Cuba was spent in Havana and I loved it from the start. The crumbling magnificence of this city is almost overwhelming, rife with possibility and an ever present reminder of what Havana was like before the Cuban Revolution.

Back in those days, Havana was the social and economic capital of the Caribbean and boasted luxury hotels, casinos, bars, gourmet restaurants and a huge tourist industry, primarily Americans. During the subsequent decades of socialism, much of Havana has been left to slowly rot away, though there have been recent programs to restore some of the grandiose buildings and monuments.

Havana is still the cultural capital of the country and within the city you can find hundreds of museums, art galleries, ballets, music venues and cultural events of all varieties. One of my favourite museums is the Museum of the Interior Ministry, located in the upscale Miramar area of the city. It is dedicated to the hundreds of failed CIA attempts to assassinate Fidel Castro and destabilize Cuba. Many spy gadgets are on display, some so ridiculous that it is hard to imagine the most powerful country in the world hatching such ludicrous schemes.

During one visit, Ana and I stayed at a bed and breakfast in Miramar, rented a scooter and spent three entire days cruising around Havana, exploring the sights, looking for restaurants, smoking fine cigars and enjoying everything this unique city had to offer.

Capetown, South Africa

Capetown must have the most majestic backdrop of any major city in the world, as it lies in a bowl surrounded by mountain peaks thousands of feet high, the most famous of which is Table Mountain. This city has everything – a diverse population, fantastic weather, dozens of beaches, impressive architecture and historical sights, a lengthy waterfront, marinas, and endless shops. It is certainly not the safest city in the world, but if you mind your manners and stay out of trouble, then it will be a very rewarding visit. There are many day trips within reach of Capetown, including wine tours, shark diving, whale watching, and the famous Cape of Good Hope where you can see penguins, monkeys and ostriches along the way. To top it all off, prices are cheap – you can buy a 24 pack of Castle beer for fifteen bucks or a nice bottle of wine for less than five.

Florianopolis, Brazil

Florianopolis is an ultra cool city on the island of Santa Catarina, located a thousand kilometres or so south-west of Rio de Janeiro. The island is home to 42 beaches, some of the most beautiful people in the world and is often called the best place to live in Brazil. Surfing is an extremely popular activity and there are spots perfect for newbies while others are regularly used for international competitions. When Ana and I visited, we stayed at a small hotel that was clean and inexpensive and run by a lovely couple who even invited us to a family barbeque. The island is large enough to visit a new beach every day, or if you get tired of that there are dozens of interesting small towns scattered throughout. This is also an adrenaline junkie paradise – you can find sand boarding, hang gliding, off-road driving, kite surfing, and paragliding. Be prepared to not exactly fit in with the standard Florianopolis beach crowd, unless you are muscled, lean, rich, six packed and extremely beautiful, in which case you will blend in perfectly.

The Ultimate Day Trip

22 Hour Houseboat Cruise – Bay of Islands, New Zealand

She is a giant houseboat called "The Rock" and this trip redefines what can be accomplished in less than 24 hours. She sleeps 36 people, sports a billiards table, fully stocked bar, and wood stove. The available activities are plentiful and include fishing, target shooting, kayaking, snorkelling for mussels, island hiking, rappelling, dolphin watching and night swimming with phosphorescence. The trip leaves from Paihia, located in the upper part of the North Island, and tours the beautiful Bay of Islands, which boast some of most gorgeous ocean and island sceneries in the country. The action is non-stop, the crowd is young, cool and groovy, and the pace is as fast or as slow as you like. Stepping off that boat as the end of the trip felt as if we had been gone for a week.

Felucca Journey on the Nile River, Egypt

Back in 1998, I spent a mind bending two weeks in Egypt with my two Aussie buddies Johnny and Todd where we stomped all over the country, backpacker style. The highlight of the trip was a three day, two night journey from the city of Aswan to Luxor on a traditional Egyptian sailing boat called a felucca, which is a simple, flat decked vessel with cotton sails and no engine. I imagine this boat style has been used for hundreds, if not thousands, of years and probably hasn't changed much, as it is suited perfectly for cruising the wide, slow moving waters of the Nile.

Our particular felucca was piloted by two Egyptian fellows named Captain Jack and Mister Weed (which, I assume, were stage names) and they treated us to three days of peace, relaxation, introspection and some stunning vistas along the banks of the Nile River. It may be a bit too rustic for some, as there is no toilet on board, which spawned a very interesting game we played throughout the journey called "How do I do a poo on a moving boat and retain my dignity?" The girls seemed to be fine, as women are somehow able to completely decommission their body's waste ejection for days at a time when social courtesy demands it. Not the lads, though, especially those of us who spent most of our time eating dodgy street food, drinking warm Heineken beer and testing local herbs. Sometimes you would get lucky and find an unpopulated piece of shrubbery during one of the infrequent stops we made on shore, which was a treat. When that didn't work out we were forced to test different methods of water releases. One lesson we learned immediately is that it's impossible to simultaneously tread water and move your bowels. And releasing anything directly by squatting over the side of the boat is socially awkward, not to mention frightening to watch. After several trials we discovered the best approach was to hang a long rope off the back of the moving boat and drag behind it, which allowed you just enough relaxation to be able to do the business. The only surprise we got was that sometimes the released objects would get caught in an eddy and somehow achieve a river velocity greater than that of the boat.

These floaters would actually pass you upstream and swarm the guy further up the rope. That was pretty funny.

Day Trip to Greenland

While visiting Iceland, Ana and I came across an opportunity we simply could not pass up – a day trip from Reykjavik to Kulusuk, Greenland. It was quite expensive, over $400 dollars, but was well worth it, especially considering it was quite likely the only time in our lives we'd have the opportunity to visit Greenland. After a two hour flight you arrive in the tiny village of Kulusuk and a guide takes you for a walk around the town where you get a glimpse of their everyday life and have a chance to buy some souvenirs. We were also taken on a short boat ride where we saw icebergs up close as well as an island where they keep their sled dogs, and periodically throw a few fish up there to let the animals fight it out and determine pecking order. Lunch was quite a treat as seal was on the menu. What is it like eating seal? Looks like meat, tastes like fish.

The highlight of the trip was actually the flight home. As it was a beautiful, sunny day, the pilot decided to take us for a sightseeing tour and he flew us up and down the coast where we saw bays, icebergs, and even saw a few kayaks in the water. At one point, the pilot started descending on a glacier, and got lower and lower until all sorts of lights and bells started going off in the cabin, which he ignored. We were so close to the ground that it felt as if you could step off the plane onto one of the ridges of the glacier and snap off a piece of ice.

Strange Bars

Bob Marley Bar, Sri Lanka

It was in Sri Lanka where my friend Trudy and I sat very late one night in awe, enjoying a cold alcoholic beverage and surveying the marvellously bizarre scene around us. The most apt, though potentially overused, Hollywood imagery for this bar was the *Star Wars* cantina. Remember when Luke Skywalker and Obi-Wan Kenobi walk into the local watering hole in Tatooine and find an eclectic assortment of intergalactic wasteoids? Blue elephant creatures playing saxophones, bubble headed crooners, long fanged hairy humanoids drinking shots of fluorescent liquids, green ant-head creatures covered in suction cups and scaly, yellow multi-eyed monsters? The beings that surrounded Trudy and I in the Bob Marley bar in southern Sri Lanka formed a similar menagerie of weird and wonderful creatures. There were the ever present white Rastafarians with the dreads, flip-flops and reefers, but also some less well known specimens, such as the Aging Hipster, the Quiet Germans, the Obnoxious Japanese (likely the rarest of all travelers) and even a string of buxom blonde backpackers who were being roundly ignored by every male in the bar – a most unusual situation to be sure. The most intelligent creature in the bar seemed to be the 15 year old dog who would find an unoccupied slab of floor, lay down for a rest, then move just in time to avoid being stomped on and find another momentarily tranquil piece of floor. He also seemed to be keeping a close watch on the patrons – at one point he barked and saved a half unconscious, completely drunken man from falling backwards off his chair. It's quite possible the dog was, in fact, the manager.

Peter's Café Sport, Azores, Portugal

In the town of Horta, on the island of Faial of the Azores, right in the middle of the Atlantic Ocean, is a legendary café which serves as a refuge and home away from home for sailors making the Atlantic crossing. Most sailors crossing between Europe and North America will make a stop in Horta to pick up supplies, do repairs and take a welcome break from the rolling waves to enjoy solid ground for a day or two. Peter's is a smoky, small, warm, welcoming and adorned with thousands of artefacts left by sailors from all over the world, from country flags to pennants to letters to photographs. It also serves as an information centre for sailors, offering help on securing marine services, weather information and currency exchange. It is the best location on the island to meet and socialize with other sailors. Surprisingly, Peter's is known for its gin & tonics and is credited for introducing the drink to the Azores, originally for the many English who worked for the underwater cable companies in Horta.

On the second floor of Peter's is a museum dedicated to the art of scrimshaw, which is a practice whereby artists take the teeth and jawbone pieces from sperm whales and use a pin or scribe to scratch in elaborate drawings, usually scenes from a whale hunt, but also portraits, island vistas, historical events and many others.

Sadly, my first visit to Peter's Café Sport was not part of an ocean crossing, but if fortune smiles on me, the next time will be.

Mojo Bar, Barbados

Across from a lovely beach, on a busy street in the Worthing parish of Barbados is the Mojo Bar. I discovered it while working on a project in Barbados and it immediately became my favourite hangout. It was, and still is, owned by a cool Bajan guy named Mark, who thought it might be fun to own a bar so that he and his friends could drink every weekend and make money while doing it. Well, I don't know if Mark made much money at Mojo, since every time I went there, he and the staff were drinking harder and faster than the customers! I was there so often that I came up with nicknames for the main characters. Mark was called Hockey Hair because he had a cool mullet that hung a few inches down his back. One staffer I called Hootie because he was a dead ringer for the singer from the band Hootie and the Blowfish. As for his other staff buddy, I simply called him Stoner because he looked permanently high. These guys could seriously drink. Besides the shots they had with customers every ten minutes, they also always had a beer to sip on, except Stoner who preferred a beverage of half coffee half vodka. The food at Mojo Bar was decent and the drinks were reasonably priced, but the main reason why it is one of the most memorable bars in the world is the music. Their motto is "Music for the People" and once you step in the doors, it doesn't take long to realize they play the best music on earth.

MacDuff's, Bahamas

On tiny Norman's Cay in the Exuma island chain of the Bahamas, legend has it there exists a bar, the only bar for miles around and a sacred place for sailors. On a 1999 sailing trip aboard *The Lost Shaker*, my 30 foot Hunter sloop, three of us including me, my friend Stillman and my dad, undertook a week long journey to the Exumas. The many adventures we had during that week included grounding the boat several times, narrowly avoiding being swept out to sea by a vicious ocean current, ripping our main sail, escaping a barracuda attack, breaking the drive shaft, exploding the toilet, blowing up the boat's alcohol stove (which set Stillman's forearm aflame), and nearly being run over by a booze cruise ship. Amidst the chaos, we found time to track down this legendary pub and prove its existence beyond a reasonable doubt.

To get to MacDuff's, fire up your personal jet and fly there. Sorry, there are no commercial airlines that go there, no public boats and no bridge. If you don't have an airplane, or if it's currently in the shop, then get in your boat and sail there - there's a nice anchorage on the south-east side of the island. Once you get anchored, jump in your dingy and paddle over to the beach, but beware the sometimes vicious tidal current. Stash your dingy in the bush then look around on the beach for an ancient wooden sign that says "MacDuff's – 2km." Follow the arrow that points to a slight trail, being sure to watch for iguanas along the way, and be especially careful of the last couple hundred meters as you have to scoot across the runway. Look left, look right, look up, cover your head, and then run.

MacDuff's may be the smallest bar you've ever seen. They serve delicious cheeseburgers, conch salad and fish sandwiches but you'll be so happy to have actually found a restaurant in the middle of nowhere that everything will taste twice as good as it actually is, and may be the best food you've ever eaten in your life. And they serve Kalik – the legendary beer of the Bahamas, which has its own magical properties and helps to enhance the MacDuff's experience. While you're there, ask about Carlos Lehder, the American cocaine dealer who previously owned the whole island and used it as a base to supply 75% of the cocaine to the US in the 1980's. He also used to host some wonderful orgies for his drug dealer friends like Pablo Escobar, but sadly they all eventually got either busted or murdered so now the island is back in the hands of the people.

If you do happen to drink too much Kalik and can't remember where you put your boat, then you can rent one of their lovely beach cabins for about $250/night. Don't feel bad, these things do happen from time to time.

****

Chapter 6 – Preparation

This chapter is dedicated to the reader interested in the nuts and bolts of travel. Yes, there have been volumes written on this topic, so the information presented here is focused on the key administrative aspects of travel that may make the difference between a trouble-free trip and a disaster. Saying that, some of the travel disasters that I have experienced throughout the years have provided for the most memorable experiences!

As a ten year old boy, my first airplane trip was planned by my parents through a travel agent. Of course it was – back then there was no internet, no direct booking and people just couldn't be expected to trust themselves to successfully organize something as complicated as an overseas trip. Travel agents were industry experts and insiders who had access to special information and insight into the world of travel.

Today, I can book every possible aspect of a trip with my two thumbs and a smart phone and can do so with the expectation that it will all work. This is nothing short of astonishing! The travel business was one of the first consumer industries to be transformed by the invention of the internet, and many of the traditional leaders have gone down in flames while internet-based travel companies such as Expedia, Travelocity, Orbitz, and a rash of others, have been successful in making a profit while reducing the cost of travel to end consumers and realizing efficiencies in all stages of the process.

Preparation & Planning

A long preparation and planning stage is not just important, it is also part of the fun of a big trip. The anticipation of an exciting trip and the time you invest into research and investigation is really the start of the adventure. Of course, not all trips are well planned and prepared; there are few things more exciting then embarking on an unplanned trip to a destination you know nothing about and flying by the seat of your pants. But having that lead time to plan and think about a trip just extends your enjoyment of it.

Naturally, the internet is the most comprehensive and easiest tool to use to research a destination. From personal travel blogs to country sponsored tourist sites to independent travel review sites, the resources are endless. Simply spending time on the internet browsing around will provide many sources of information, and the key is not to use only a single source, but instead look at many. The internet is full of trolls who like to criticize every place they visit, complaining about insignificant details and inventing things to bitch about. If you make it your mission in life to find things to complain about then you will find plenty. Also, many people can visit the same place and all come away with vastly different opinions, so who do you listen to? Thanks to the law of averages, reading a hundred reviews on a hotel is likely to give you a pretty good idea of what to expect.

A long planning cycle also gives you time to look for deals. Ana is the greatest bargain hunter in the world and she spends time on the computer, day after day looking for bargains on flights, hotels, cars and admission tickets. We like to stretch our dollars far beyond the point of natural elasticity, simply because it allows us to squeeze in one or two more trips per year and still keep within our travel budget.

While the internet is like a sugar rush, books are a meal. Before any big trip, I like to go to the library and pick up some books on the destination that go beyond simple travel guides, such as those that deal with the history, politics, culture or food of the country. Being familiar with a country's history allows you to better understand and appreciate what you see and experience during your visit. It can also sometimes help to explain why things and people are the way they are. Standing in the grand plaza of the Colonial Zone in Santo Domingo, Dominican Republic looking at the impressive Alcazar de Colon mansion is one thing, but knowing that it was originally twice the size and built by the son of Christopher Columbus as a family home in 1510, and served as a base for conquest and exploration in the New World certainly gives it much more significance than simply a grand, old building.

If history is not your thing, then try to find novels set in the country you plan to visit. For example, Ernest Hemmingway was not Cuban, but reading *The Old Man and the Sea* is an absolute prerequisite for visiting Cuba. Novels, especially ones written by local authors, will give you insights into the country that you will not find anywhere else and are sure to enhance your visit.

At the moment, my family and I are planning on taking a three month long trip next year during the summer months. Where to? Well, we're not sure yet, but the original idea was to spend the entire time on our sailboat, taking it across Lake Erie, all the way up Lake Huron and into Georgian Bay and the North Channel. Then, around the dinner table one night, we started talking about doing a backpacking trip, and sharing what countries we'd like to go to. I picked up a pile of guidebooks from the library, first a whole set of European guides, then a collection of ones on various Asian countries. When we opened up these possibilities, the ideas started to flow and the enthusiasm grew as we realized the whole world was fair game. Our current thinking is to spend the time in Southeast Asia, exploring Malaysia, Thailand, Cambodia and Laos, but by the time the trip actually happens, our destination could be somewhere completely different. When planning a trip of this magnitude, we never run out of things to discuss at the dinner table and having something this exciting to look forward to certainly keep one's spirits up.

Is it possible to over plan a trip? Of course it is. Planning a trip right down to the exact activities you want to do each day, and the sights you want to see is really not necessary. If you are on a guided trip or package holiday, then that will probably be done for you, but if you are on your own, you don't need to go that that level of detail. We like to make up a list of places or sites that look interesting, then decide on our exact itinerary once we are there and have a chance to feel the place out and talk to people. Having a flight booked, accommodation sorted (at least for the first couple days), and your vaccinations and visas arranged is really all the basic planning you need to do.

What to Pack

When Ana and I took a one year backpacking trip around the southern hemisphere, the first major challenge was packing. We were planning on spending a lot of time walking so everything we took was going to have to fit into one backpack that could be carried for long periods of time. For a fashion diva, this is not a trivial exercise, and for Ana it was even more difficult. Anybody who really knows me must be laughing right now, as my packing took about twenty minutes, and several days into the trip, I discovered that practically every item of clothing I had chosen was green. The situation only improved when I found an abandoned red wash cloth, ripped it in half and wore it as a headband, transforming me into a Green Beret, which was a huge confidence booster until Ana told me I looked like an idiot.

For an extended backpacking trip, the only really essential contents of our single bag each was one set of dressy clothes, one comfortable pair of walking shoes and our Pacsafe backpack protector, which is a wire mesh bag that holds your pack and can be chained to an immovable object – an essential piece of gear for overnight stays on trains, busses or dodgy hostels where you want to ensure nobody steals your stuff. The rest of the contents were simply comfortable, easily washable clothing, basic toiletries, a couple books and a notebook computer.

The days of traveling with a single, easily carried bag are long gone. Since having children, it now seems mandatory to take everything we own, jam it into multiple suitcases, and take the whole lot along with us, even if it's just a weekend trip. Since I have been completely and permanently excluded from the packing process, I just keep my mouth shut, carry the bags and can rest assured that we will have everything we could possibly need.

When it comes right down to it, there are essentially only three things that are absolutely mandatory to have when you are taking a trip. These are Passport, Tickets and Money. Every single time we drive away from our house, embarking on a trip, Ana and I look at each other and repeat the words, "Passports? Tickets? Money?" If you have those three things, then you will get by. Anything you've forgotten can be purchased at your destination, and if they can't, then you'll probably find that you get along just fine without them anyway. These days we often don't even have tickets anymore as they are emailed to our smart phones, but we say it anyway just to make sure we haven't forgotten our devices! Mobile phones these days are a miracle space saver for packing, as these electronic Swiss army knives can now serve as a camera, high definition video recorder, computer, binoculars, voice recorder, library, credit card, photo album, travel guide, music player, agenda, flashlight, video game machine, DVD player, scanner, map, gaps locator, and even a personal safety device, because the larger ones are so big they can be used to bludgeon an assailant. The only features they currently lack is the ability to fillet fish and clean your teeth, so you might want to throw in a knife and a toothbrush.

Flights, Passports, Visas

Much of this information is available elsewhere in excruciating detail, so I want to pass on only the aspects of this that I have found important. The first thing is checking your passport. All passports are only valid for a certain number of years and most countries will not allow you in if your passport expires in less than six months. The Canadian passport processing systems has improved tremendously in recent years and a passport can now be processed in 48 hours, but please give yourself more time than this. When I got my first passport, you had to have a guarantor who would validate that the photos you used were actually you, and this guarantor had to be in a certain class of professionals, which included dentist, doctor, high school principal or Member of Parliament. Yes, it was known as the "persons likely to be wankers" list and pretty much none of my associates at the time in Saskatoon fell into any of those categories. But the doughnut baker, unemployed, student, bartender, factory worker and musician groups were well represented. Thankfully our family dentist, cousin, and legend of a man Colin Bowerman, happily stood as guarantor for thousands. Every time I went to see him he would have a nice tidy pile of signed passport applications sitting on the front counter awaiting pickup, all done for free. I suspect he probably did pick up some dental business when these passport seekers realized how nasty their teeth were, and got a couple fillings done since they were in the dentist office anyway. The Canadian government has recently changed the rules, so now pretty much any valid passport holder can act as guarantor, which has been a terrible blow to the general dental health of Canadians.

Once you have a passport, you need to check the visa requirements for the countries you plan on traveling to. These requirements can change so you must check the latest requirements. The information is easy to find on the internet, just make sure you're looking at a valid and up to date government website. Getting visas can also take some time, and you need to send in your passport so won't be able to leave the country while you are having visas processed. Another option to consider is getting a passport with extra pages if you have a lot of travel planned in the coming years. This can be requested and might cost a bit more but will be well worth it. I remember during one visit back home, I was with my best buddy Darren and told him I was on my way to pick up my new passport, which was a replacement for my old one because it had run out of pages. He looked at me disgusted and told me I was a prick. If only all insults could feel that good.

If you are one of those fortunate folks who have citizenship in more than one country and hold two or more passports, then be very careful on which ones you use, and never let a border control agent see that you have more than one passport. Even though you may be perfectly entitled to two passports, border agents do not see this very often and it will simply arouse their suspicions and probably result in you getting yanked out of line and grilled with questions. Also, when you are leaving a country, be absolutely sure to use the same passport you came in with. If you used a different passport to enter, then there will be no record of you entering the country under the passport you are trying to leave with and that will cause you problems. Lastly, it is possible to gain citizenship in a country without ever having lived there, for example, because Ana has Portuguese citizenship, our children are automatically entitled for citizenship and are eligible for a passport. Certain countries in the world still have conscription, or mandatory military service, and if you are within the eligible age range, and identify yourself as a citizen by using that country's passport, then you are exposing yourself to the possibility that you could be conscripted. Of course the chance of this happening is highly unlikely, but there is no sense in taking an unnecessary risk, so use a different passport when traveling.

Oh my, how air travel has changed over the years. It is such a ruthlessly competitive industry with airlines scrambling to cut costs, increase margins and fill every seat on the airplane. A lot of the tricks we picked up over the years just don't work anymore. For example, it used to be nice to request the emergency exit seats to give you a bit of extra legroom, but now due to online seat selection, those are often taken up first, and some airlines even charge a premium for those seats. We use to try and pack our entire luggage into carry on sized bags to avoid the risk of lost luggage in transit or somebody grabbing your bag off the carousel. Having no checked luggage also saves you time at check-in and arrival. But since the terrorist attacks on September 11, 2001, it's very hard to do this because of the content restrictions on items such as larger bottles of liquids, razors and other so called dangerous items. In fact, the whole experience of traveling on an airplane has become quite miserable from start to finish. From the long check-in lead times, to giant queues at airports, to the virtual assault experienced at security checkpoints, the probing and accusatory questions by border guards, the astronomical prices charged for goods and services in airports, and the in-flight service, which offers nothing for free beyond a sack of chemically fabricated salted morsels and a glass of water to help choke it down. The only real improvement has been the introduction of seat back televisions, which are a fantastic way to kill the time on long flights, and an excellent excuse to avoid talking to your seatmates if you're not the chatty type.

Saying all that, I will happily admit that once you get through the check-in counter, past security, through the boarding gate and into your seat, there's nothing quite like that thrill of the airplane taxiing out to the runway, pausing, hearing the engines crank up, feeling that rapid acceleration, watching the scenery through the window pass by faster and faster until you finally feel the nose of the plane lift off the ground, then the whole plane begins to rise and it feels like the tail of the plane is going to skid across the ground, which it never does, then once you're up in the air and over the houses, that momentary dreadful feeling of panic expecting the engines to fail, which doesn't happen, then you finally sit back, settle in, get comfortable, and think about the adventure ahead.

Insurance

Before you leave your country you must check into your insurance requirements, in particular, health insurance. For Canadians this is particularly relevant, as our underappreciated social medical program stands in stark contrast to the private, for profit system in the United States. Many people have been caught with enormous medical bills after failing to have the proper health insurance and falling ill while visiting other countries. Health insurance can be purchased through insurance companies, banks, travel agencies, or even online and it pays to shop around, but always ensure you go with a well known provider. For young people, health insurance is cheap. But for older folks it can get pricey, and the older and sicker you get, the more expensive it becomes, up until the point it becomes prohibitively expensive and will be the key reason many people stop traveling.

While health insurance is what you will need to cover major medical bills, generic travel insurance is available to cover everything else. The term "travel insurance" can cover many areas and situations and there are hundreds of different sorts of plans. Generally, travel insurance can cover the following:

- Trip cancellation or interruption
- Emergency medical care
- Air flight accident
- Public transportation accident
- Baggage
- Theft

- Legal expenses
- Automobile
- Damage to rental properties
- Financial default of travel suppliers
- Accidental death or dismemberment
- Repatriation of remains
- Travel delays due to weather
- Adventure sports or risky activities
- Travel to high risk countries

Most packages will not cover pre-existing conditions, self inflicted damage (such as injury or illness caused by alcohol, drug use or suicide), war or terrorism, pregnancy within a certain number weeks of the delivery date, criminal acts or care or treatments for cosmetic procedures (yes, many people travel the world in search of a discount rhinoplasty or tummy tuck). The only way to truly know what is covered and what is not is to review the actual policy in detail and ensure you understand it. If not, then ask clarification from the policy provider before purchasing and try to get it in writing. Additionally, if you do have the misfortune of having an accident, call the insurer immediately and explain the situation, because there is usually a clause in the insurance contract that can revoke coverage if you do not immediately make the provider aware of potential claims. Keep the insurance provider's contact number handy, and make sure your travel companions also have this information in case you are incapacitated and not able to make the call yourself. It's good to travel with a paper copy of your policy as well as a digital copy on your mobile device.

Packages can be purchased for a single trip, multiple trips, or even a whole year of coverage. The geographical coverage can be from a single country or region to the entire world. They can be purchased for individuals or families. They can have different provisions for what constitutes a "cancelled trip", from being able to cancel your trip for any reason to only if the airline cancels the flight. The options are many and can be tailored to your exact needs.

When deciding on your insurance requirements, you must first think about what you are likely to be doing on your trip and where you are going. It is important to get coverage for what you think you will need, but equally important not to over-insure yourself, which simply drives up the cost. Your existing insurance policies may cover many of your requirements, for example your credit card or auto club membership may cover rental car accidents. Your state or provincial health insurer may cover medical incidents outside your country. Home insurance may cover theft. The airline should cover baggage loss. Your life insurance policy might cover accidental death or dismemberment while on vacation.

In general, use these steps for acquiring insurance

- Make a list of your existing insurance policies and what they cover
- Decide on where you are going and what you will be doing
- Fill whatever insurance gaps remain with a well researched travel insurance package from a reputable company
- Before you pay for the policy, read it in detail then read it again and get answers to any parts you do not understand. Do not leave this step to somebody else, such as a travel agent. Do it yourself to ensure you are satisfied with the coverage.

If disaster strikes and you need to file a claim, hopefully all goes smoothly and you are reimbursed, but there is always the possibility that your claim gets denied. Do not take no for an answer! An initial denial is not necessary the final answer and most insurance providers will have a formal appeals process for grievances. The more persistent you are, the higher the chances of getting reimbursed so do not give up until you have exhausted every possible avenue.

Handling Problems

Problems happen. The ones you experience in your everyday life are predictable – water heater breaks, car won't start, boss is getting you down, bakery is out of bread, kids spilled juice on the carpet, dog needs a root canal, and so on. When you are traveling, there will still be problems, but they will be much less predictable, the stakes will be higher and may require greater imagination to solve. The big difference is these problems will occur in an unfamiliar location within a different social and cultural environment, so the way you get through these issues may not be the same way you would approach them at home. For example, one of the first things you will likely need to do after arriving by air to a new country is take a taxi. Over the years I have learned that there is a 90% chance that you will get ripped off on this ride, since you are in a vulnerable position and really have no other option than to trust the cabby's decision on the route to take and what to charge. I call this the "tourist tax" and the sooner you get used to smiling, paying whatever the premium charge is, and getting on with your trip, the happier you will be. The only thing you can really do to avoid this, is to tell the cab driver where you are going, ask what the price will be, then when he or she tells you, stop for a moment, look extremely puzzled, then ask again, as if the price is so ridiculously high that you must have heard wrong. If you're lucky, you'll avoid giving the impression that you are a clueless tourists with no idea how far away the destination is or how much it should cost, and might get a better price. If not, then all you can really do is hop in, enjoy the ride and let the learning begin.

When these problems happen, whether they are big or small, it's easy to let your emotions take over and blow a fuse, but the fact is that this rarely helps, and can make it much more difficult to overcome the issue. When things go wrong, it's best to keep smiling, find some humour in the situation, and try to get through it while retaining your composure. Remember that the people you are dealing may have a much different way of handling disputes than what you are used to. As a traveler, there is nothing funnier than seeing an arrogant, rich tourist in a third world airport having it out with a desk agent and causing a huge scene. You know that they are going to get absolutely nowhere besides embarrassing themselves and their fellow countrymen, but yet they carry their first world expectations with them and assume that the squeaky wheel will get the grease, just like it does back home. Sadly, this technique just doesn't work very well in many places and may serve to get you further in trouble.

Leave your expectations at the door, treat every obstacle as a learning opportunity and be patient and open minded. If you want things to be like they are at home then why bother traveling? Expect inconveniences, problems, issues and annoyances, then they won't come as much of a shock when they happen. Remember too, that what you consider to be a major issue may be a regular occurrence for the locals and they will not give it a second thought and instead just get on with it. And in the end, after your trip is finished and you are back in your familiar world, you will find that over time the human brain has the remarkable ability to purge most of the insignificant bad memories and retain the good ones, so when you look back at a trip, you are likely to see it in a much more positive light than you experienced it at the time.

There are things you can do to mitigate the fallout from problems, at least the predictable ones. The most likely major problem you will encounter is the loss of your passport or wallet. In fact, it is better to assume that this will happen to you, because if you travel long enough, and to many places, it is practically inevitable. If you take one recommendation from this book, take this one; whether you travel frequently or not, make digital copies of the following documents for everybody in your family, and save them to a secure internet location that can be accessed anywhere:

- Passport, all pages
- Credit and debit cards, front and back
- Drivers licence, front and back
- Birth certificate, front and back
- Marriage certificate, front and back
- Health card, front and back
- List of necessary prescriptions
- Contact list
- Set of utility bills or other document proving your home address
- Student ID

Before any particular trip, make copies of these and save them to the same location:

- Air tickets
- Itinerary or locations and addresses of key locations you are visiting
- Recent bank statement showing an adequate balance to fund yourself during your travels
- Recent photograph of all members of your family
- Health or travel insurance policies
- Immunization records

If disaster strikes, having access to these documents can save your skin. Thanks to the internet, simply uploading these to a document storage site, secured ftp site, internet email, "the cloud", or any other secure service will allow you to access your important documents anywhere in the world. Replacing lost or stolen passports or credit cards will be infinitely easier with access to your personal documents.

Paying for Stuff

One of the most cleverly hidden costs of travel is currency exchange
fees. There is really no way to avoid them and they range from moderate
to criminally high and can take a real bite out of your budget. The rules
on what banks and other financial institutions can charge are constantly
changing and new methods of payment are cropping up all the time,
along with their associated fees and charges.

While traveling you will be paying for things every day and will need
access to your money. Historically, travelers would visit their main street
bank, pick up a wad of travellers cheques then cash them along the way
as required. Or they might buy the foreign currency of the country they
were planning to visit from their bank and carry cash with them. Today,
these are among the least efficient ways of using your money. First, there
are not many places these days who will accept travelers' cheques and
those that do often charge an exorbitant administration fee to cash
them. Second, exchanging currency at a bank can be a pricey option. I
recently exchanged Canadian dollars for Euro at my bank and was
charged over 5% on the transaction! I thought it must have been a
mistake but after doing some research I found this is the standard rate
charged by all Canadian banks, and some of them even charge more
than this, up to 8% in some cases.

The available methods of payment for travelers are plentiful, though
many of them are very expensive options. While in a different country,
here are some of the ways you can pay for things:

- Credit card
- Credit card cash advance
- Prepaid credit card
- Debit card
- Prepaid debit card
- Prepaid travel cards
- Foreign currency credit card
- Travelers cheques
- Bank draft
- Withdraw cash from a foreign ATM
- Use foreign currency cash purchased from home bank

Instead of going into an in-depth analysis of the various advantages and disadvantages of each, and their related fees, I will instead highlight what I have found to be the best and worst options.

When we travel, we typically like to have some foreign currency cash on hand for the initial few hours in the country, when you are paying for things like coffee, taxis, train or bus tickets and so forth. If possible, we'll try to save some currency from a previous trip to that country so we have it available for next time.

While on the trip, we pay for things two ways; first we use our regular Canadian dollar credit card for larger purchases as hotels, car rentals, excursions, restaurants, and any purchase from a reputable vendor where we feel the risk of having our credit card information stolen is minimal. Second, we make relatively large withdrawals from foreign ATMs, and keep most of the cash in our hotel safe or other secure location where we are staying, then carry what cash we need for the day. At times, we have also used our debit card, which seems to work well in Europe, but not as well in the US, as many of their point of sale machines do not have chip readers and won't accept them. The rate charged on debit card purchases is comparable to what you pay with credit cards.

I looked back at two trips we did last year to see how much we were charged for credit card purchases, ATM withdrawals, and foreign currency purchased from our local bank, comparing the exchange rate we were charged in each case with the official currency exchange rate. The worst rate we got was buying currency from our bank, which was a 5.43% premium. The ATM withdrawals and credit card purchases varied, but averaged about 3%. On a single day, we were charged 2.6% on one transaction and 3.1% on the other so you can see that you are truly at the mercy of the financial institutions, and you won't even know what rate you were charged until you get your statement, at which time it's probably too late to complain.

Most of the other payment options in the list above are going to be more expensive than using your credit card or withdrawing cash from foreign ATMs. The worst are those currency exchange kiosks you see in airports, credit card cash advances, prepaid travel cards and travellers cheques.

Here's a list of other tips:

- Get a debit card with the lowest foreign currency exchange and transaction fees, your bank should be able to provide a list of these rates
- Use ATMs within the network of your debit card to reduce transaction fees (the Plus network is owned by Visa and the Cirrus and Maestro networks are owned by MasterCard, you will see these symbols on your card and the ATM machine will identify the networks it supports)
- If there is a flat fee charge per withdrawal, and there probably will be, then make relatively large withdrawals, but not more than you are willing to lose in case of cash theft.
- Get credit card with best international terms, but make sure you're charged on local currency; a favourite trick of vendors is to offer to put the transaction through in US dollars, claiming it will save you money, when in fact they apply an atrocious exchange rate in their favour. Ensure they use local currency and let the bank apply the exchange rate
- Use credit card for larger purchases and be wary of unscrupulous merchants who may steal your credit card information
- Use travelers' cheques sparingly. There is hardly an airport in the world that doesn't have an ATM machine that will dispense local currency at a much lower rate than what you pay on travelers cheques (although we did manage to found one country that didn't have any ATMs – Suriname)

Before You Leave

When planning a vacation, don't forget to consider what happens at home while you are away. You don't want to have to spend your traveling time worried about loose ends you left dangling at home.

Home Safety

- Ask neighbours or friends to pick up your newspapers or flyers and do yard maintenance
- Install automatic timers on certain lights to simulate an occupied household

- Have a neighbour or friend periodically check inside your house for problems such as leaky plumbing, broken furnace, running toilets; most insurance companies require a vacant house to be checked regularly otherwise the insurance could become invalidated

Financial

- Arrange for a line of credit that you can access in case of an emergency or if you simply run out of money
- Prepay bills that will come due or set up automatic payments
- Complete any government returns, renewals or other paperwork that will due when you are expecting to be away
- Check your credit card expiry dates and renew if the expiry date is near
- Call your credit card company and tell them of your travel plans; often these companies will deactivate your card when they detect out of country transactions taking place, assuming the card number has been stolen

Before Walking Out the Door

- Shut off water main
- Unplug electronics that do not need to be on
- Adjust thermostat down in the winter or up in the summer to save money on home heating/cooling
- Run dishwasher
- Remove all garbage and recycling
- If you have a cold room or fruit cellar, remove any vegetables or food that could spoil; arriving home to the odour of rotting potatoes is not pleasant
- Remove any perishables from the refrigerator

****

Chapter 7 – Finances

Paying for travel can be done in some very creative ways. For people who like to travel many times per year, managing the finances is extremely important – not just during the trip, but before it too. I have discovered many useful ways to fund my own travels and seen how other travelers have done it. And yes, it is possible to travel for free – read on!

Ana and I were traveling through the Drakensburg mountain area of South Africa when we struck up a friendship with an American woman, several years older than us, likely in her mid 30's. She was a traveling fanatic, having visited and traveled through dozens of countries over the course of almost two decades. To fund her traveling she worked in the US as a waitress in high-end restaurants where she made very good cash money in tips, reducing her income tax burden considerably. She kept her day to day living expenses as low as possible by renting a modest apartment on short term leases, acquiring roommates, not owning a car and so on. Maintaining this modest lifestyle enabled her to save the vast majority of the money she earned and she would devote herself to this regimented saving for as long as it took to accumulate the sum she needed to pay for her next trip, which was usually about six months. This hard headed saving enabled her to live a second "adventurer" lifestyle for nearly half of the year. She happily admitted that she didn't often enjoy her working months in the US, but that was the price she was willing to pay to live that alternate life of travel, adventure and meaning. What I remember most clearly about our friend, is that she always left a 15% tip for the server when she ate in restaurants (unheard of in backpacker land), knowing that the server likely relied on such tips just as she did.

Tips for Travel Spending

There are many ways to fund your trip and the above story is an example of how a person has built her entire lifestyle around traveling and has made a clear decision on what was important to her. How you fund your travels will depend entirely on the type of traveling you want to do and the frequency of it. First, I'll share a few of the basic guidelines that I follow.

Never travel on credit

If you can't afford your trip then don't take it. Sounds simple, but judging by the negative savings rate that persists in much of the developed world, many people don't understand the concept of spending less than you earn. If you are careful with your money you will be able to reduce your overall travel cost, but no matter how cheap you do it, a trip will always cost you something and you will want to pay for it out of your savings.

Part of the fun of travel is the anticipation, planning, and build-up to the big trip, but this planning stage must also include getting your finances in order. When you return from your trip, you will have a collection of great memories and stories, but nothing will spoil this more than opening up your first credit card bill to find that you must now suffer through six months of repayments for that trip. Do you want to be forced to reflect back thinking, *I can't believe I spent $500 on that helicopter ride; it's going to take weeks to pay that off!* Or would you rather think, *that expensive helicopter ride was fun and something I'll probably never do again but I'm glad I spent the money trying it once.* The end of your trip should not be the start of saving for that trip via credit card payments.

Avoiding traveling on credit does not mean you can't use credit cards. Credit cards are an absolute necessity, just be sure you have money available to pay them off.

The time goes fast, the cash goes faster

Humans are terrible at predicting future events, but somehow we fancy ourselves to be quite good at it. We think we are much more efficient with our money and our time than we really are, henceforth the tendency to under budget time and money for our travels. This applies especially to novice travelers, but also to the more experienced ones as they too nearly always spend more than they expect to.

What is the solution for this? Simple – put a realistic budget together, making absolutely sure you've budgeted conservatively for everything you plan to do…. then add 30% as contingency and you might be close.

Maximize the use of reward programs

It seems there's a company out there to reward you for every dollar you spend these days. We do make use of these, but only selectively. The main one we use is the bank sponsored credit card that allows you to accumulate air miles for purchases you charge to the card, but this comes with a huge caveat - if you are not disciplined enough to pay your credit card balance every month then these type of cards are not for you because the interest you pay will surely exceed the value of air miles you are rewarded. I recently did a big analysis on the value of the reward card we have been using for many years. It turns out that no matter what type of rewards you take, whether it is air tickets, gift cards or merchandise, it works out to be about 1% of the expenditures you made with the card. So, for example, if you charge $10,000 to your card per year then you will be eligible for $100 of rewards. Considering you may have to pay a yearly administration fee to use them, and any missed payment will result in large interest charges, it's quite likely that it's simply not worth it for many people. On top of that, extensive use of credit cards leads many people to purchase more than they can afford since they don't actually see the cash disappearing from their wallets or bank accounts.

Ana and I use credit cards for a second reason – tracking our expenditures. I try to account for all the money we spend so that we know exactly where it is going, and having most of our expenditure done through debit and credit cards instead of cash makes this much easier to track. In this regard, my motto is "If you can't track it, it's impossible to control it." At the end of each year I do a complete analysis of where our money went during that year and we compare this spending to the previous two years' spending patterns. For example, at the end of one year, 7.5% of our total expenditures were devoted to vacations while, embarrassingly, only 0.3% was spent on charitable donations. More shamefully, we spent 1.3% on booze. By tracking our spending to this level, it allows us to take a very objective view on our finances. As a family, are we happy spending four times as much on booze as on charitable donations? No, we are not. But at least we know so that we can adjust our spending next year.

I've found that by using credit cards, on average we are able to accumulate one round trip international air ticket every year from rewards programs. Since this is money we are spending anyway, why not get something in return for it?

Work for an airline

When I make this recommendation I am absolutely serious. Ana worked for the Canadian airline WestJet for many years, which enabled us to do ten times as much traveling than we would have been otherwise able to afford. Airline employees (and usually their spouses and parents too) get terrific deals on travel. Besides getting ridiculously cheap fares on air tickets, many companies in the travel industry give discounts to employees of any airline; for example, we've received discounts on rental cars, hotels, airport parking, tours, airport transfers, and travel insurance. Most airlines partner together through Interline agreements, which enables employees to travel on partner airlines at an extremely reduced fare – sometimes as little as $25 or, in some cases, absolutely free.

During Ana's tenure with the airline, we received well over $50,000 per year in savings on travel. These benefits, at least with WestJet, were available to all employees, regardless of whether they worked full or part time. There are many people who work in the airline industry in part time jobs, from check-in staff to customer service to flight attendants so it's often possible to work for an airline in addition to your regular job. The only difficulty then may be getting the time off from both jobs to travel.

Funding a Trip

I have always been interested in talking to other travelers and asking what motivates their travels and how they manage it financially. I have met some travelers who have used very creative ways of paying for their trips, while others were just old fashioned savers. Here are a few of these ways.

Save, Save, Save

Our American friend from the opening story in this chapter was a saver – of the more extreme variety. Savers typically have good control of their spending and are focused on their goals. Some strategies that savers use are:

Pay yourself first

This concept has been done to death in practically every financial book written in the past 20 years, and here it is again. Have 10% automatically withdrawn from every pay cheque and put into a separate savings account that you never touch…until vacation time. This is a great way of saving for travel but still requires dedication and willpower.

Reduce small, frivolous daily expenses

Instead of paying four bucks for a Starbucks coffee on the way to work, brew half a pot at home before you leave and put it in a travel mug, which will cost you about a quarter. Instead of going out for a ten dollar lunch every day, pack a sandwich in the morning. You get the picture.

Write down your goals

Good savers write down their goals and review them often. By keeping your goals visible and always in your mind they will be that much easier to stick to.

Subject Yourself to Medical Experiments

When I lived in London, England, I had a great friend named Paul who hailed from Capetown, South Africa. Paul once told me of a friend of his who was desperate to go backpacking around the world, but was completely broke and didn't have the willpower to save any money. To most people, this would either mean traveling on credit, joining the circus, or forgoing the trip altogether, but not this bloke. He came across an ad in the newspaper for a local research study where they were seeking out volunteers for an experimental re-attachment surgery. Seeing a solution to his dilemma he immediately inquired and learned that he would be paid the equivalent of $10,000 US dollars if he were to allow them to sever one of his little toes then re-attach it. A quick mental calculation to value that one little piggy produced a number well below the ten grand (in fact, only slightly higher than zero) so he immediately signed up. The day for the surgery arrived and after an anaesthetic and quick slice and sew job, he was out the door with a cheque in his hand. The only lasting side effect was a moderate loss of feeling in the said digit – but to him this was actually a benefit considering the little pinkie toe is the one most likely to be stubbed.

Do I recommend undergoing experimental medical surgery to raise funds? I personally wouldn't do it but it worked out wonderfully for that guy! This story may be bordering on the realm of believability so, not wanting to spread false urban myths, I did devote ten minutes on the internet to researching this topic. I found several people who claim to have done this, although one of them was paid only $6,500. He should have held out for more.

The Life Transition

While visiting Italy, I crossed paths with another backpacker in Rome. He was a quiet, unassuming, shy Australian – yes, a rare specimen indeed. I was a very green traveler, so was therefore astounded when he told me he was into the tenth month of a two year round the world journey. To me, it was absolutely incredible that a person could undertake such a long backpacking trip. Once I got to know him a little better he told me told me more about himself and the motivations for his trip. He had been married for two years and during that time had built him and his wife their dream home near Cairns, Australia. He had done a lot of the work on his own; firstly, to save some money but also for the satisfaction of building it by himself. By the time the house was finished, it had gone up in value substantially. Unfortunately, during the same time period, their relationship had gone down in value considerably, and as part of the divorce, he was forced to sell the house. As soon as the deal was done and the split was finalized, he decided to take his portion of the net proceeds from the house and embark on a two year backpacking trip to, in his words, "rethink his life".

Again, not a typical way of paying for travel, but it certainly goes to show that sometimes one's situation, motivation and finances come together at the right time.

Ask Your Family for Money

Let's face it: lots of people have rich parents, rich grandparents and rich, childless aunts and uncles. All it takes is to swallow one's pride, tuck the proverbial tail beneath the legs, and come up with a fascinating and convincing argument why this trip is vital to your development as a human being, then approach one of these family members who have idle cash to spare. The suitability of this strategy may well depend on the order in which you were born – eldest children are the least likely to use it as they normally have an independence chip on their shoulder while middle children are usually too pissed at their family for years of neglect to consider asking. Youngest children are the most likely to adopt this strategy as they have likely been using their preferential baby status and scamming their family for years.

Join a Charity, Religious, or Social Group that Offers Travel

There are many, many groups out there that will pay for you to travel…on their terms. The prospect of finding an organization to sponsor you to travel is very high if you are willing to devote some time and energy to it and be flexible and open minded.

Three of my cousins, similar in age to me and whose parents were involved in the Rotary organization, each went on an international exchange as high school students. The eldest, Chris, went to the Philippines. The next, Kendra, went to France and the youngest, Talia, went to South Africa, and each of them spent a full year in the host country. They each had an extraordinary year and came away with many unique experiences, new friends, and no debt from the trip. I remember being very envious of them at the time and wishing my parents had spent more time in a Rotary club than driving me and my brothers around to hockey and football games!

I have met a lot of people involved with various religious groups, who are living in other countries doing volunteer work on different types of projects. These religious groups normally pay for the volunteer's trip there and back and everyday living expenses. What you provide, in trade, is your labour and skills that you bring to the project and are expected to work hard to help. This is often the most gratifying form of travel as you are contributing to the betterment of a community or individual and are making a difference.

The best way to find information on the opportunities currently available is to begin making some calls to the various organizations in your community and get involved. You can also get on the internet and start searching out more nationwide or worldwide organizations.

Find a Job Overseas

While I have a whole chapter devoted to working and living overseas, it bears mentioning here that working in your host country is a way to travel and earn money at the same time. Some occupations lend themselves to travel naturally, such as teachers or diplomats, but there are many other types of jobs that you can do in other countries, and I have met travelers from a wide spectrum of careers. For example, while living in Bahamas I met foreigners living there who were teachers, bar/restaurant servers, Mercedes mechanics, construction workers, IT consultants, marketing professionals, hotel managers & staff, fishing guides, business owners, blackjack dealers, diplomats, dive masters, tour guides, and crew on a yacht.

Many travelers originally start out traveling on their savings and then either realize that they have exceeded their budget or decide to extend their travels; in either case, there's a requirement to earn more money. In this situation it is usually not that easy to find decent paying work because you likely will not have a work visa and probably won't have any local connections to help you find a job in your field. The best bet is to find a job working in a restaurant, on a farm, or any other business where workers are transient and paid mainly in cash. Securing work in your particular field is something you will normally need to arrange before you begin your travels, although as usual, there are always exceptions to the rule.

I was lucky enough to spend some time in France during my first backpacking trip in Europe. While staying in an overpriced hostel in Paris, I had struck up a friendship with three other travelers – a Brazilian, an American, and a Dane from the Faro Islands. One of them had heard that it was possible for foreigners to get work on wine vineyards so as a group we decided to take the train out to the Champagne district and see what we could find. The Dane had been given a phone number by another backpacker of a local farmer who was looking for help, so once we arrived at the station, she gave me the number, assuming that Canadians must speak French, but was sadly mistaken. That was one of the first times, but far from the last, when I felt completely ashamed that I did not have a second language, especially when she spoke four languages, the Brazilian spoke three, and even the American knew enough German to get by. The Danish girl had enough French to tell the farmer we were at the station, and before long, an unmarked panel van pulled up and we were quickly and discretely hustled into the back of it. Feeling very much the victims of a kidnapping, we were relieved to be dropped at a farm yard after a very bumpy ride, and for the next four days we were to enjoy all the food, wine and laughter we could handle in the company of a dozen other transients, mostly French. Each time we were packed into the van and taken out to pick grapes it started to rain, which prompted us to be squeezed back into said van and returned to the farm for more wine and food. While we didn't wind up actually being paid any money, it was four extra days I was able to extend my trip and learn more about the French than I would have wandering around the tourist traps in Paris.

Beg, Busk and Barter

If you really want to travel on the cheap, and don't mind being a pain in the ass, then take a shot at the three B's – Beg, Busk and Barter. Since travel is such a great opportunity to experience things far outside your comfort zone, here's a challenge for you – try to earn ten dollars from asking strangers for money. We've all been harassed by street folks asking for money, why not try stepping in their shoes for a while? I can guarantee it will be a most humbling and possibly even enlightening experience, as nothing batters your ego and shatters your pride more than being pitied while asking for money. I hadn't planned on trying out begging, but one time I was forced to after completely running out of money on the road and needing bus fare to get to a bank machine. I felt like such a bum and will never forget how people looked at me in disgust. It gave me a small but intense glimpse into the life of street people.

If you just can't bring yourself to beg, why not put your musical skills to work and try busking? I've never tried this myself but I've sure seen a lot of buskers making pretty good money, especially in crowded tourist areas. I was once in Florence, Italy and saw a busker from Quebec playing guitar for a crowd of hundreds of people with a guitar case full of bills and coins in front of him. If you're not that talented, you still might be able to earn some pity pennies from entertained onlookers. If you don't play a musical instrument, or if it was just too much trouble carrying your tuba around, then why not try something else like putting on a puppet show? Or show off some special dance moves? Or cake yourself in mud and pretend you're a statue? Or sing foreign national anthems dressed in a ballerina tutu? The possibilities are truly endless if you use your imagination. Most people have a pretty good sense of humour and are willing to cough up a bit of money for a good laugh.

Everyone has skills of some type and being on the road may be a good chance to provide a service to somebody in exchange for the necessities of life. If you keep your eyes open you will find opportunities for barter everywhere you go. The real difficulty with bartering is getting over the fear of hearing the word "no" and building up the confidence to sell yourself. While Ana and I were traveling together in Central America and the Caribbean, Ana created websites for several businesses in exchange for all sorts of things. She built websites for El Salvador Divers in exchange for diving lessons, a Surinamese adventure travel company in exchange for a weekend trip into the jungle, a talented artist named Marcel Pinas for two pieces of original artwork, and an online bakery in exchange for local travel and some cash.

Sell Your Business

We met Robert and his wife Maureen on voyage number 350 of the Solway Lass – a magnificent tall ship in Queensland, Australia. We went on an eight day sailing trip off the coast of Airlie Beach to the famous Whitsunday Islands, a string of tropical islands characterized by crystal clear waters and stunning white sand beaches. This interesting couple had recently retired and were on an extended tour of Australia and New Zealand. Robert had been a financial planner for many years and after a massive heart attack, sold his book of clients and retired. Fortunately, this happened just shortly before the explosive popping of the internet stock bubble at the turn of the century, so this excellent timing produced a substantial amount of money and Robert and Maureen decided it was the perfect time to take the trip of a lifetime. They were in their 50's and in excellent physical shape, as both of them were marathon runners, and Robert had even run an Ironman triathlon. I have a feeling that after this extended adventure they likely went back to Canada and got involved in a new business to keep themselves busy, as they didn't seem like the type of people who could handle retirement for too long. Perhaps by now they've built and sold a second business and are off on another retirement trip.

Running your own business has a way of locking you in and locking you down, making it difficult to even take a few days off. Many business owners are true "do it yourselfers" and have a tough time trusting others to manage the businesses, which means giving up control. Selling a business can be a difficult decision, but once you have done it, and re-discovered what it is like to have free time, it will become clear why you were working so hard in the first place. If you decide that you miss the pleasures of business ownership, you can always start a new one and become a serial entrepreneur.

****

Chapter 8 – Dangers

Dangers exist everywhere and travelers must always be aware of them. There are many things you can do to avoid being a target and keep yourself safe while exploring and enjoying new places. This chapter is the end result of many perilous situations I've found myself in while traveling – some in dangerous, risky countries, but others in places where you would just not expect anything bad to happen. Traveling helps you to develop a sense of safety that is invaluable on the road, but also at home.

It was a Friday afternoon in San Jose, Costa Rica and Ana and I were walking along a very busy road, directly across from Parque La Sabana – the largest park in the city. We had been living in San Jose for several months as part of a Central America based project I was working on and were currently enjoying Christmas vacation. Ana had been doing freelance web design work, and had just finished a client meeting so had her laptop with her, which I was carrying. Normally, we would never be caught outdoors carrying valuables, as the city was known to be a dangerous and unpredictable place, but since the client was very close to our apartment, and it was the middle of the day, we decided to walk instead of drive.

As we walked down the busy street, congested with cars and thick with fuel exhaust, we were passed by two young men, one walking and one riding a bike. As they passed by, my eyes met with one of them and I gave him a slight nod, which went unreturned. I didn't think much of it, and was not surprised as our experience with Costa Rican hospitality had not always been great, so the two of them passed and we continued along our way. As we approached a small plaza a bit further down the street, we heard a noise behind us then saw the two men and realized that they had been silently following us and were now making their move. The bigger one jumped off his bike and approached us quickly, reaching into his pocket for something. Without thinking, I swung the laptop bag off my shoulder, threw it to the ground and backed into a wall. The thief pulled a knife from his pocket, grabbed my collar, pushed me against the wall and put the blade to my throat. I was absolutely paralyzed with fear and couldn't do anything. I could see that the other guy had picked up the laptop bag and was standing in front of Ana, but not touching her, so she didn't appear to be in danger. The knife wielder was grumbling something to me in Spanish, which I couldn't make out, then he ripped the gold chain from my neck, slowly backed away, joined his friend and they continued down the street. Ana and I stood there in stunned silence, watching them walk away, noticing the dozens of cars in the street driving by, the occupants unperturbed by the robbery or perhaps just unaware and minding their own business. The laptop bag contained not just our computer, but also Ana's wallet and passport, which she had needed that day for some transactions required at the bank.

In the end, we didn't get hurt, didn't lose a substantial amount of money and only suffered the inconvenience of having to deal with a lost passport and cards. That was not the first time we had been touched by crime, and would not be the last, but it was the one time a weapon was involved, which affected us much more deeply, and made us realize the severity and potential consequences of such a robbery, and the knowledge that things could have been much worse.

Crime happens everywhere and when you travel you put yourself in unfamiliar locations, unusual situations and in the company of people who may live in much different social environment than you do and act in unpredictable ways. There are many things you can do as a traveler to reduce the probability of being victimized, many of which can and should be used at home too. Beside the financial loss, the psychological losses can be dear and will probably destroy the enjoyment of your travels and your opinion of a country and its people.

Risk and Fear

Humans have a built in tendency to fear the wrong things, mainly because we are very bad at calculating risk. This is often driven by the way information is presented to us, such as the daily news articles that alarm us with grim statistics on your risk of contracting cancer, Hepatitis B, Parkinson's, MS, AIDS, Alzheimer's or being swept up by a tornado. It seems that anything we breathe, eat, drink, participate in or fail to do, is proven to cause some sort of dreadful affliction. The fact remains that the most dangerous activity you could ever do on a daily basis is getting in your car and driving somewhere, as a person is much more likely to be killed in a car crash than die of whichever rare disease is currently making headlines.

Many people are scared of flying in airplanes, but happily drive thousands of miles in their cars each and every year. It seems that the probability of dying in a plane crash is much more likely, simply because when planes crash, it is catastrophic and kills many people at once, making spectacular news in the process. While the news may report that a plane full of 100 people has crashed into the Amazon forest in Brazil, killing everybody on board, what they don't mention is that 103 other people died that same day in automobile accidents, which will happen every single day of the year in Brazil. If you live in the United States, the lifetime probability of dying in a car accident is 1 in 98. The probability for dying in an airline crash is 1 in 20,000. Which seems scarier to you?

How does all this relate to travel? Having a realistic idea of where the risks lie will guide you on the decisions you make while traveling. Are you more likely to die bungee jumping in New Zealand or taking a taxi in Egypt? Taking a jitney ride in Pakistan might well be more dangerous than going sky diving in the US. What seems dangerous is often not, while what seems perfectly safe could well be the riskiest situation you could put yourself in.

Another major factor in assessing risk is your age as people tend to become more risk averse as they get older. As a young person, you feel invincible and assume a long life lies ahead, thereby diminishing your ability to accurately calculate risks. Middle aged folks feel much more vulnerable and develop this annoying habit of clinging to life and jealously guarding what precious time and assets they have left. Real old people don't give a damn at all, if they haven't accomplished what they've set out to by that time, it's already been scratched off the bucket list and they aren't clinging to anything besides the hope of a super sized bowel movement after breakfast.

Of course, death is not the only bad thing that could ruin your day – you could also get robbed, beaten up, burned, knocked down, puked on, blinded, insulted, stranded, humiliated or even trampled by a water buffalo, though this is much more likely to happen in Zimbabwe than in Ireland. And definitely not in the Bahamas; there you are much more likely to just be insulted. I even read of a guy who was visiting Quito, Peru and had a bucket of shit dumped on him, distracting him long enough for thieves to steal his fancy camera. The point is that when you are traveling you need to be consciously aware of the real risks of what you are doing and not simply afraid of things that are not at all likely to happen. Alternatively, if you travel without a thought of the risks involved, do whatever you want to and disregard the likely consequences of actions, then you are sure to run into problems.

What is Safe and What is Not?

Living in Santo Domingo, Dominican Republic really set the bar for how dangerous driving can be in the Western Hemisphere. The term "demolition derby" accurately describes our regular commute from home to the office and some of the driving practices we saw on the weekends were mind blowing. One evening on the way home from the beach, Ana and I were driving along on one of the few divided highways when I noticed some strange lights far ahead on our side of the road. At first it was very hard to make out what they were, but as the lights became brighter I realized they were coming from vehicles traveling towards us, against the traffic and moving very fast. Within seconds, we were being met head on by a dozen motorcycles, weaving in and out of the oncoming traffic. If that wasn't bad enough, one of the riders was doing a headstand on the bike as he blasted down the highway. Fortunately, they whizzed by us without hitting anything, but I can't say what may have happened further down the road, as traffic accidents there were so frequent they didn't even make the news.

We take calculated risks every day in our regular lives but when traveling, the risks become harder to judge because of the unfamiliar environment. For example, from experience we know which streets at home are okay to jaywalk on and which ones are not, or which roads are okay for speeding. We know which areas of town to avoid when walking at night, from previous knowledge of where crimes typically occur. When we are in a new place, we are lacking all of this knowledge, which puts us in a vulnerable situation and our estimation of what is safe and what isn't will not be nearly as accurate as it is in our home environment. Using the Dominican again for an example, one soon realized that while driving the typical signals drivers make to each other were not the same as in Canada, and in some cases they meant the complete opposite. Suppose you are in a lane of traffic trying to make a left turn across the oncoming vehicles in the opposite lane. You put on your signal light, and wait for a break in the traffic. There comes a gap and the closest oncoming car sees your signal light and gives you a double flash of his headlights. In Canada or the US, that signal would probably mean, *go ahead and make your turn, I'll slow down a bit so you can make it through safely.* In the Dominican, that signal means, *don't you even think about it asshole, I'm coming through fast!* and vehicles would actually speed up to make sure they got through and didn't have to wait for you. What seems like a safe traffic manoeuvre would probably result in a smashed car and injured passengers.

When in a country for a short time, there is no way to become familiar with all such local customs so the only way to reduce the risk is to be cautious, simple as that. Don't take the calculated risks that you would at home, and always be aware that things are different and your judgement may be faulty. Try to keep out of dangerous situations, and if you find yourself in one, keep in control and find the most expedient way out of it. In the Dominican, this meant using our vehicle as sparingly as possible, but when we were in the car, I learned to drive like a Dominican – aggressive, fast, oblivious to traffic signals, discourteous, and with absolutely no concern for the safety of other drivers. If I recall correctly, we had only two minor traffic accidents while there, and we lived in Santo Domingo for nearly two years so that was quite an impressive record.

While traveling, you often have to make a decision on which is the least risky of several options. For example, let's say you are staying in a budget hotel in a new city and are going out for the day to explore. What do you do with your passport? Do you leave it hidden in your room somewhere or do you take it with you? If you leave it in your room, there's a chance somebody will go in there, find it and steal it. If you take it with you, there's a chance you will get mugged or lose it (if you are thinking you can just use one of those travel pouches that goes around your waist and is hidden beneath your clothes, good idea, but remember that thieves know all about these and expect travelers to be wearing one.) Unfortunately, there is no right answer, and I've faced this situation many times over the years. The best you can do is to evaluate how safe the accommodation is then make the call. If the room has a safe, I'll always use it. If it doesn't, and I'm going out at night, then I will usually hide my passport in the room somewhere. If I'm going out during the day I will carry it with me in a travel pouch.

We once spent a week at a cool little cabin in a rural area outside of Bariloche, Argentina. It seemed like the safest place you could ever imagine as it was owned by a lovely family, located off the main highway and hidden in the woods, and constantly under surveillance from the owners. We went into town one day and left all our important documents in the cabin in our bags, bringing along only cash and one credit card each, comforted by the fact that our belongings were safe and secure. We returned later that night to find our cabin had been ransacked and somebody had made off not just with all our passports, but also our credit cards, cash, most of our clothing and the souvenirs we had bought along the way. This was the first time in 25 years the owners had ever experienced a burglary and were shocked, angry and extremely embarrassed. It seems our calculated risk just didn't work out that time.

Contrary to logic, it is often these everyday, simple situations and decisions that can lead to problems, and not the ones that may appear risky. For example, organized bungee jumping, animal safaris, scuba diving, caving, skiing and so on do have an element of risk, but at least the risks are known and probably very unlikely to happen in a regulated, controlled environment. These are often the highlights of a trip so taking on the additional risk for these activities is likely to be very gratifying and well worth it. Going to a bar in a shady part of town with a wallet full of money is almost certainly not a risk worth taking.

Being a Target

Ana and I were on a backpacking trip in Europe and found ourselves in the central station in Amsterdam, along with hundreds of other tourists. We had some time before our train was scheduled to leave so decided to get a coffee and a snack to eat while we waited. Train stations in Europe are known to be one of the worst places for pick pocketing, and we knew that so were being careful with our bags. We decided that we'd put our bags down, Ana would stand watch over them and I would go over to the nearby kiosk to get the food.

When I returned, Ana looked a little flustered and said, "You're not going to believe what just happened." She looked fine, our bags were there and everything looked pretty much exactly as I had left it less than ten minutes before. She told me that shortly after I had left, a man came up to her and asked her what time it was. She looked down at her watch then told him the time, to which he replied, "In the few seconds it took you to tell me the time, my partner has just stolen your bag." Ana turned around to see another man had lifted one of the bags and was several metres away holding it, showing her that he could have been far away and lost in the crowd by the time she had noticed. She learned that the two men were police officers and had noticed Ana there and decided to teach her a valuable lesson about spending time in European train stations. The officer then told Ana that the best way to prevent this was to physically sit on top of your bags so that a thief couldn't easily grab them if you were momentarily distracted. This lesson has stuck with us over the years and every time we are in a public place while traveling with luggage, we are instantly returned to that train station and respectful of the lesson learned.

The time we have spent living, working and vacationing in such a wide range of countries has drastically altered our approach to safety. Growing up in Canada means not having to lock your door when you leave home, going out in public wearing expensive jewellery without a second thought, leaving expensive items clearly visible in your vehicle, opening your door to strangers without a security lock in place and being able to forget your wallet on the table of your local coffee shop and have it returned with nothing missing. We grow up to be trusting, but careless and this approach simply does not work in most countries of the world where people are much less well off and thievery more widespread.

People with this careless approach to security are an easy target, especially when traveling. There are thieves everywhere, at home and abroad, looking for easy wins. It may be a pessimistic view of the world, but it is a fact, and preventing yourself from being victimized should be a primary concern when you are on the road. The idea is not to make yourself completely impossible to steal from but, rather, less of a target than others around you, which is typically not that hard to do. The best approach is to be constantly aware of your surroundings, keep a low profile and be very careful who you trust. There are obvious places where you need to be extra vigilant, such as bus and train stations, crowded city markets, airports and fringe areas such as parking lots and walkways. In these situations you are naturally more aware of your surroundings, but when you get into a seemingly safe environment and this heightened sense of awareness dissolves into a false sense of security, you let your guard down and before you realize what's happening you have been robbed.

What specifically can you do to make yourself less of a target? Here are some tips:

Don't talk loudly

When you are in a country that speaks a different language, speaking loudly in your own tongue is the best way to identify yourself as a tourist and attract unwanted attention. Keep your voice down.

Do not dress like a tourist

Keep your camera in your bag and not around your neck, keep all maps and guidebooks in your bag and out of sight and for God's sake don't sew a bloody flag on your pack!

Watch for those who are watching you. If you notice somebody regarding you as low-hanging fruit, look directly back at them with your best stink eye, and let them know that you are not a victim. Most time they will turn away and, like a predator lion, find a weaker target.

Walk with confidence

Even if you don't know where you are going, pretend you do. If somebody approaches you to offer friendly advice, especially if they start with, "My friend, what country you from?" then get the hell away from them because they are either going to rob you or try to sell you something you don't need.

Beware of kids

Cute kids are often used as a distraction. As you are fawning over a beautiful toddler making baby noises, his uncle is stealing your wallet.

Don't look rich

Leave the brand name clothes at home and dress modestly. The only people you are likely to impress are the thieves; everyone else will think you are a careless idiot.

Sometimes, no matter how careful you are, no matter the precautions you take, there is absolutely nothing you can do to prevent being robbed. While living in the Netherlands we did a long weekend trip to Paris, France, along with my grandparents, my aunt and our friend Carmen. We arrived in Gare du Nord then proceeded to the platforms to get on the underground metro to central Paris. We were well accustomed to the dangers of trains and train stations so were being very careful. We looked for a car that had less people but unfortunately all were packed, so we boarded one of them, and instructed everybody in our group to hold their bags tight to their chest and watch for thieves. Seconds before the doors closed, a group of suspicious looking characters including a couple small kids, squeezed into the train car and we knew immediately that they were thieves as they started scanning the crowd looking for something to steal. All of us held our bags tightly and tried to manoeuvre around in the car to get away from the group of them, but as it was so packed this was difficult. We managed to make it through the ride seemingly unscathed and with all of our gear intact, and it wasn't until a couple hours later that Carmen noticed her wallet was gone. It had been zipped up in the pocket of her backpack, and even locked, but those little bastards on the train somehow found it and stole it. In this situation, it's hard to know what we could have done differently to avoid this.

Remember that not all crime is so skilfully premeditated. It is often done on the spur of the moment as a crime of convenience, and sloppily executed. If the aggressor sees an opportunity, and the moment passes due to some sort of defensive move by the potential victim, then he may simply go back to what he was doing before this potential opportunity presented itself. The key is to be aware of what is going on around you, recognizing when a bad situation is developing, and getting away.

The best way to understand how a thief finds his victims is to try it yourself. No, I don't mean actually robbing people, but rather assume the role of a mugger for a week and look for easy targets. A great place to rob people is in parking lots. Normally a person drives into a parking lot, gets out of their car, heads straight into the mall and does their shopping. When they leave the mall, they will have bags in their hands, will usually be in a hurry headed straight for their vehicle and won't be paying much attention to anything going on around them. As a mugger, you wander through the parking lot looking for people who appear particularly distracted or weak and with something worthwhile stealing. Walk up to them as they are loading their gear into the trunk of their car and ask them a harmless question. See how easy it would be for your friend to grab a handful of packages or a purse while you are having a chat with the victim.

Lesson learned: Everybody in parking lots is either going somewhere or coming back to their cars, nobody loiters around parking lots except thieves.

When you are standing in line at a retail store, coffee shop, bank or waiting to get on a bus, look at what people are carrying and how they are carrying it. Often, people carry backpacks that become unzipped, or they keep their wallet easy visible in a side pocket. Men carry wallets in their back pockets, which can be easily lifted with a quick distraction. People wear watches and jewellery worth thousands of dollars. In retail stores, women will often set their purses down just about anywhere while they are trying on clothes. As you are walking past cars parked on the street, look inside them and see the valuables people leave lying on the seats, often with the doors unlocked. Many people leave their wallets overnight in their unlocked cars that are parked in driveways or on streets. While dining in a restaurant, look how women leave their purses sitting on chairs and men leave their wallets and car keys sitting on the table.

Lesson learned: Thieves look for people who are careless with their possessions.

Let's say you are a mugger in a busy place and you want to ambush somebody. Where would you stand to be able to sneak up on somebody unnoticed? For example, when people exit an elevator to a parking garage, their attention is directed immediately to the signage indicating the level they are on, then to the direction of their car. They rarely look left or right to the hidden or dark spaces, where thieves can be watching a parade of potential victims going by, just waiting for the right one. In city parks with walking trails, there are many hidden spots for thieves to hide and wait for victims with valuables to pass by.

Lesson learned: Criminals seldom need to hide; there are spaces everywhere where they can position themselves so as not to be easily seen.

Trust Your Instincts

It was a Thursday evening in San Carlos de Bariloche, Argentina, and Ana and I were walking down a dark street after enjoying a meal at one of the many fine restaurants. The restaurant was located in a quiet area off the main street and we were heading back towards the busy downtown area to stop for a drink somewhere before returning to our accommodation. As we walked along we both noticed a group of young men walking towards us on the same side of the street. While I felt a bit uneasy, Ana was positively frightened and grabbed my hand and led me quickly across the street to the other side. The men watched us move quickly away and did not follow, instead continuing on their way. Once we were back in the well lit, busy area Ana told me that she knew we were about to get robbed. She didn't just have a hunch, or the slightly uneasy feeling that I had; she positively knew that we were in harm's way and had to get out of there immediately. I don't know if it was the way they were walking, their pace, the way they looked, the way we looked, or maybe the part of the street we were on? It was likely a combination of all those things, but when your subconscious mind picks up on things that aren't right, it will signal your conscious brain and you have to decide whether to listen to it or not. Our logical brain's natural inclination is to brush these aside as paranoia or being unnecessarily suspicious. But listening to your instincts is a very important skill to learn while traveling and you ignore them at your peril.

Many times while traveling, I have been in situations where, suddenly, things do not seem right, but I cannot pin down exactly what was wrong. Often, there isn't much you can do about the situation besides remain alert and vigilant, while other times the best response is to change your circumstance as quickly as possible. While living in Karachi, Pakistan, a few friends and I decided to do a day trip to one of the beach areas that was a couple hours drive from the city. We had a fantastic day and made sure to begin the return trip well before dark as it wasn't considered to be very safe traveling in the evening hours. On the way back, we came to a point in the road where we had to drive across a bridge. I was in the backseat while my friend Andrew was driving, and as we approached the bridge I noticed a truck heading our direction had stopped on the road just before the start of the bridge on the other side. It seemed odd that he was just sitting there, especially since there were two full lanes on the bridge where vehicles could easy pass by each other. I then looked behind us and could see that another vehicle, which wasn't there before, had pulled up behind us and was slowly following us to the bridge. At this point, my Spidey senses went wild and I relayed my worry to the other people in the car, who agreed that something didn't seem right. None of us were particularly important expatriates in Pakistan, just four regular people, so not an obvious target for kidnappers, but in Pakistan, to say things were unpredictable was a huge understatement. As we rolled toward the bridge, my panic shifted to terror and, though I tried to contain it to myself, the tension inside the car was unmistakable and my heart was racing. At that point, there really was not much we could do, as there was only a single road, and nowhere to turn. I asked Andrew if he had his cell phone, which he did, so he pulled it out and had it at the ready. As we drove onto the bridge I fully expected hooded men to jump out of the truck ahead with guns and take us hostage. But that didn't happen. We drove slowly across the bridge, met up with the stopped truck and passed by them with no difficulty. There was no explanation as to why they were just sitting there, and the vehicle behind us simply followed us along the road, and eventually turned off somewhere. I can think of few other times in my life when I have been more terrified, and it turned out that my instincts were wrong and the environmental indicators my brain was picking up turned out to be harmless, but I think it's reasonable to assume the potential was there for a very bad situation.

It's very hard to know how good your instincts are. In the case where you get a bad feeling about a situation, trust your instincts and get out of there. You will never know if you were truly in danger or not. On the other hand, if your instincts tell you to run, you decide to stay put, and nothing bad happens, then you know your instincts were wrong, which may lead you to trust your instincts even less in the future, which would probably be a mistake. I prefer to put up with the occasional false positive, act on my instincts and try to keep myself out of trouble.

****

Chapter 9 – Children

I can proudly say that we have the best traveling children of anybody I know. We have included them on our travels since they were babies and they have grown up to become adventurous, adaptable, accommodating and able to sleep pretty much anywhere, from heavily listing sailboats in rough seas, to airplanes, to benches in cantinas. But traveling with children does have its challenges and, while you can't completely eliminate these, there are many things you can do to reduce the stress of traveling with kids and make it an enjoyable trip for the whole family.

When it came to puking, our son Magnus was the world champion. His ability to vomit, both involuntarily and on demand, was matched only by the enormous volumes of frothy liquid he could produce. Sometime before his first birthday, we planned a two week holiday to the Azores, Portugal, leaving from Toronto and arriving in Ponta Delgada a mere six hours later. As the airplane started its taxi to the runway I sat with Magnus on my lap and my wife and father beside me in the same row. Without warning, the young chap unloaded a giant stream of barf directly into my chest, which ran down my shirt, arms and even part way into my favourite blue jeans I had foolishly worn that day. His skill was such that not a drop landed on him or the airplane seat – he had reserved the entire foul payload for his dear sweet dad. I was hardly happy with the situation, but it had happened to me so many times before that I was well prepared. As I gave him a few shakes to get the last drops out, Ana dug into the baby bag to retrieve the jumbo pack of wet wipes and my set of reserve clothing that was ever present. I handed the little tyke to my dad, and gently removed my dripping shirt, then my pants, and rolled them up, contents and all, into a tight ball. With my wife's ample supply of wet wipes, I gave myself a fast, yet thorough, in-flight sponge bath. I added those wipes into the pile then triple bagged the whole works in plastic Wal-Mart shopping sacs and stuffed it into the bottom of the baby bag for later intensive cleaning or, more likely, permanent disposal. By the time the plane's wheels left the ground, he was back on my lap, I was in fresh clothes, and there was only a subtle hint of vomit fragrance in the air.

Traveling with children can be aggravating, stressful, chaotic and expensive. But it is also one of the most rewarding gifts you can give your child. Children that travel from a young age develop an early appreciation for adventure, self-reliance and variety. There are few things that really rattle my chain but the one that does is when I tell somebody that we went on a vacation somewhere and they ask me, "Did you take your kids?" My snarly reply is invariably, "Of course we took our kids, why wouldn't we?" Our kids are part of our family and we do everything as a family, as doing it any other way is not fair to the kids and not fair to the parents. I do realize that we are probably in the minority here, as many people dump their kids on the grandparents when they go off to a resort for a week, but that is something that we've never been comfortable and have never done. If you have taken the decision to have kids, then why would you not include them on a holiday? I think many people like to leave the kids at home to try and relive the days as a couple without kids. But those days are gone and they are not coming back anytime soon so why not include the kids are part of the family, be adults, suck it up and accept the fact that you are now a team. Assuming that kids will hold you back on vacation is giving both yourself and your kids too little credit. When I was a kid my mom and dad took me and my brothers everywhere so I probably inherited this way of thinking from them and I'm very happy for it, as are my children.

There was one moment during our travels that illustrated perfectly the capacity for families to travel together. Ana and I were staying in a cozy hostel in Cairns, Australia and as we were getting acquainted with the place, we wandered through the communal kitchen and saw a large wall plastered with photos of the owners of the hostel. The photos were of their travels in various exotic world locations, obviously a sign of people who took the backpacking life seriously. But it was the last group of photos that shocked and amazed us. The photos were of this young couple toting around three beautiful children in what looked like one of the Middle Eastern countries. The youngest looked to be around one year old and the oldest was probably about six. We asked one of the staff about the photo and learned that they had backpacked around the Middle East for six months with their three kids. We were immediately overcome by a sense of wonder at how you could possibly do this. Were they insane? Judging by the looks on the faces of the kids and parents in the photo, they were far from insane and, rather, looked to be having the time of their lives. Back then, we didn't yet have kids, and had assumed that our traveling days would be numbered once the kiddies showed up, but after seeing what this family was capable of, we knew there was hope!

Now, two kids later, while we are yet to spend six months backpacking around the Middle East, we have together explored many exciting places and made traveling an integral part of our family culture and, as a result, have two of the best little travelers you could imagine.

Teaching kids to adapt

I would be lying if I said that our travel hasn't changed. It has, but the frequency and the things we do on those trips have actually changed very little. I think the biggest factor for us is that we started traveling with our kids from a very young age. Stella took her first airplane trip at the ripe old age of one week, while Magnus was a bit later at three weeks, and since then we've had the opportunity to travel as a family many times per year. In fact, in the first five years of his life, our son Magnus had done approximately 80 round trip journeys on airplanes! By the time Stella had reached this age, her numbers weren't quite as high, but she had still done better than average. These experiences have been a remarkable opportunity for them and one that few children will ever experience to such an extent. Traveling now comes naturally to the kids and they are experts at airport security, traveling in airplanes, being in new places, dealing with time differences, eating new foods and sleeping in new beds. For most kids that don't travel until later in life, that first trip away from their comfort zone and regular routine can be a real shock to their system.

Of course, such extensive travel at a young age isn't something everyone can afford or have the available vacation days for, but there are other inexpensive ways to adapt your kids to travel. Camping, weekend driving trips and overnight hotel stays are all usually possible for most families. Exposing them to different types of foods in your own home is also a great way to expand their palate and get them used to trying new things. I've found that music can be a great way to ignite their curiosity in other countries and cultures and our typical home play list will have songs in Spanish, Portuguese, French, Russian, and Arabic and originate from any country around the world. When the kids hear a song they like, we will often jump on the internet and look up the artist to see what country they are from, what language they are singing in and what the song is about.

Food, Milk, Diapers

The first time we left Canada with our eldest child, Ana packed enough diapers and food for the entire trip. She was a little paranoid about how they would react to the local diapers and wasn't even sure that they would have bottled baby food. In this case we were going to Portugal and didn't really have to worry as there was baby food and diapers at every corner store. This isn't the case for all destinations and the unavailability of some critical item could potentially hamper a trip. But I have found that kids are usually much more adaptable to new situations than adults are, and if left to their own devices they will do just fine. Usually, they do so fine that they make their parents look bad, so before you pack a hefty supply of baby merchandise for your precious little ones consider they probably won't need it.

When it comes to food, children can be very picky if allowed to be – just like adults. Being in another country can be an excellent learning experience for both kids and parents as it puts you out of your comfort zone and exposes you to new types of food. As I've always told my son, the first time you try a new unfamiliar food you will hate it. The second time you definitely won't like it. The third time it will be tolerable. The fourth time it won't be too bad. The fifth time it will taste okay. The sixth time you will like it and the seventh time you will love it. If you don't believe me, try toast with Marmite. I think it actually took me ten attempts to finally develop a taste for that particular British culinary delight, which is a black, gooey, sticky yeast extract derived from the beer brewing process, and a standing item on our grocery list. If you approach every new food this way, there is no way you can go wrong.

Medicine

Ana has perfected the medi-kit; which is the ultimate travel medicine pack for our family. The basic contents are as follows:

- Children's liquid Tylenol or Advil (two flavours)
- Children's and adult cold medicine
- Stool softener
- Band aids
- Cough syrup (with Codeine if you can get it)
- Antibiotics
- Cold FX (can only get in Canada and is excellent for colds)

- Imodium (stops diarrhea)
- Immunization certificates for each member of the family
- Antihistamines (for itching or swelling)
- Plenty of pain killers (Advil, Tylenol, Acetaminophen, anything stronger if you can get it)
- Afterbite
- High SPF sunscreen
- Polysporin
- An EpiPen in case of severe allergic reaction

You may need to adjust for your own specific needs as required. Fortunately none of us have allergies so if you do you may need to add allergy medicines. You may also want to consider adding a tube of "mystery cream" just in case your kid gets some sort of bite that none of your medicines seem to soothe. That way, you can always pull out the magic cream and hope for the placebo effect.

If you travel to more out of the way locations, then you will want to consult a local doctor or pharmacy if you or your kids contract anything unusual. When Ana and I traveled to Brazil she was bitten by something one night that turned into a nasty welt that didn't go away even after several days. When she went to a local pharmacy the doctor there immediately knew what it was and gave her an ointment that took care of the problem in a day or two. He explained to her that it was actually the bite of an insect that injects its eggs under your skin and if left untreated the insect babies will eventually hatch and eat their way out. We actually met a couple who had traveled to Brazil and she had been bitten by this bug and one night, several countries later, they actually watched horrified as the insects erupted from under her skin!

One area to pay particular attention to is the medicine for malaria. Depending on where you go there can be local blends of malaria medicine, which are the only effective ones against the particular variety of malaria in that country. Of course, whether you choose to take malaria medication in the first place is your decision, but if you do decide to take it you might as well ensure that the one you take is the most effective. I took malaria medication in Pakistan without doing any research and after several months of terrible nightmares and realizing my hair was falling out, someone mentioned in passing that these were typical side-effects of the medication I was taking. I immediately stopped taking it, though later in life questioned the wisdom of that decision after becoming friends with a Surinamese man who had contracted malaria and said it was the worst thing that had ever happened to him, and he had nearly died from it.

Pace Yourselves

You need to be wary of your pace when you are traveling with children. While you may want to hit three Smithsonian museums in Washington, D.C. in the span of one day, chances are your kids won't have the patience for this. Kids have plenty of energy, but you need to make sure you don't over plan the days, especially with activities that appeal more to adults. Kids will be happy to spend an hour or two in a museum, but after that all they will want to do is go to a park, run around outside for a while or just find some other kids to play with. We have made this mistake many times as we like to pack as much into a day as we can while traveling, but if you overdo it the kids will just get impatient and cranky, which will make it hard for you to enjoy yourself. As our kids are a bit older now, we include them in the planning process and decision making when on a trip so they have a say in what we do, though not the final word. If there is a potential trip to the playground after the art museum visit then you can keep the threat of a cancelled trip in your back pocket to counter any animalistic behavior their boredom may lead them to. But since we've been dragging the kids to non-kid venues since they were infants, they know the routine and are usually well behaved and actually enjoy adult activities more than many other kids we see.

The Kids Bag

The kids have a role in preparing for a trip — each of them have one small, roller bag that they are responsible for packing with the non-clothes items they will need for the trip such as toys, books and games. Giving the kids this job gets them involved in the planning process and lets them work on their decision making skills. We always have a final check on what they have packed, first to ensure that they have left some space for the new items they will inevitably pick up along the way, such as shells, rocks, fancy hats and small toys, but also to make sure they haven't packed anything that airport security will confiscate. A couple years ago we were at the security checkpoint at Toronto's Pearson airport when Magnus's bag was pulled out and searched after going through the scanner. I asked the security guy what he was looking for and he said it looked like there was a toolkit in his bag. Knowing we were obviously not carrying a toolkit, I let him search until he found a small box Magnus had recently received as a present. The security guard dumped the contents of the box to expose a dozen small metal pieces, an assortment of tiny screws and a mini wrench to put it together. He picked up the wrench, which was about one inch in length, displayed it to me and said, "No tools allowed on board the aircraft." Ana, knowing my fondness for scrapping with idiotic airport security guards (and history of failure), quickly stepped in, relinquished the deadly weapon to the triumphant guard, and shuffled us out of there before I had a chance to blow a fuse. Incidentally, the tent I was carrying on as hand luggage had been searched after going through the scanner and found to contain two dozen 12 inch, sharpened steel spikes, used to secure the tent to the ground. But as they weren't on the banned item list, the security guy put them back in the tent bag and let me pass.

The Surprise Pack

To get the kids excited about a vacation, we always put together a surprise pack, which they are allowed to open after the airplane tires have left the tarmac or, if a driving trip, once we're on the highway and settled in for the ride. Ana usually goes to the local thrift store and picks up a pre-assembled bag of small toys, which only costs a few bucks, but provides a whole lot of entertainment during the trip. As the kids get older, we're now including items such as cards, games and books, but we've found that they generally like whatever we put in there and keeps them from getting bored, at least for the first couple hours of the journey.

Disney World, MarineLand, Chuck E. Cheese and Other Houses of Horror

If you have kids you can assume they will start pestering you about a trip to Walt Disney World shortly after they begin to talk. We managed to tack on a single day to Disney World while passing through Orlando, Florida on the way to the east coast where we were vacationing. It is fortunate I had not visited this vast, obnoxious money pit before having children, otherwise I likely would have decided on a life of perpetual bachelorhood. Walt Disney wrote the book on child marketing and his company has been holding parents ransom for decades – from the moment you arrive to the moment you leave, you will be assaulted from all sides by people, products and systems designed to relieve you of your funds. But don't take it personally as there will be thousands of others queued up ahead of and behind you, waiting for their turn to be financially assaulted. This is the corporate money machine at work and they are experts. Here's a typical family conversation we heard over and over that day:

Kid 1: Dad, I'm tired!

Kid 2: Daddy, I'm hungry and I have to go to the bathroom

Kid 3: Mommy, that big walking dog is scaring me!

Wife: Honey, we need to find somewhere to eat and take a break.

Dad: There is nowhere to sit! Can't you see all the goddamn people here taking up the few benches! And I'm not paying fifty bucks for another round of shitty hot dogs.

Wife: Don't swear in front of the kids.

Kid 2: Daddy, I have to go – it's an emergency!

Kid 1: Mommy, can you carry me, my legs hurt?

Dad: Everybody just shut up! Shut up! You kids better start having fun, and I mean right now otherwise we're leaving. This trip is costing me a fortune.

Kid 3: But Daddy, this is only the first day; we have a whole week here.

Kid 2: I think I had an accident.

You may think I am exaggerating but I am not – I've never experienced so many stressed out parents pretending their hardest to have fun. After a day of stress, lineups, overpriced food and merchandise and complaining kids, I vowed that we would never return. Of course we did see some neat things there, and I don't regret going, but anything longer than a day would have driven me mental.

I will warn you that this is just my experience and there were actually a lot of young couples we saw there without kids, which truly left me flabbergasted. I learned later that many couples travel to Disney World year after year, which makes me wonder if they simply have no imagination or perhaps are just clinging to childhood, but in any case, the American marketing machine is a wonder to behold and nearly irresistible.

I have always found theme parks, carnivals and kid-centric venues such as Chuck E Cheese to be the worst rip offs for your travel and entertainment budget. Their business model relies on using your kids are marketing pawns and having them guilt you into taking them there, at which point the company steps in and juices you for money. It's not likely you will be able to permanently avoid these places, but certainly don't limit your family outings to these; it's a big world out there and you can find much more gratifying destinations that will leave you with your own, real memories and not corporate sponsored ones.

****

Kris Olson

Chapter 10 – Expatriate

Living in thirteen different countries has given me special insight into the lifestyles of people who leave their own country to live and work elsewhere. These people, called "expatriates" truly live in a different and exciting world, and the opportunity to do this is available to anybody who is willing to work hard and pursue that goal. This chapter is a brief guide on finding overseas work, preparing to leave your country, what you do when you get there, and how you eventually come home.

Barbara is my dad's oldest sister and she and her husband Gerry were the first international travellers I knew. Gerry was born and raised in Northern Ireland then educated there as a petroleum reservoir engineer. After graduation he moved to Canada where he met my aunt and they settled in Calgary, Alberta, which is the business centre of the Canadian oil patch. There they lived for a decade, and while Gerry was climbing the corporate ladder with Esso, Barb stayed at home to raise their two daughters Nicole and Erica. They were a typical middle class Canadian family living cheque to cheque, struggling like everybody else to make ends meet, much like my own family. Gerry did very well in his field and in 1983 was presented with an opportunity to do a two year overseas posting to Kuala Lumpur, Malaysia. When I heard about this as a youngster, you might as well have told me they were moving to the moon, for all I knew about world geography. In those days international travel was certainly not as cheap and accessible as it is today, nor was information readily available about exotic sounding countries such as Malaysia. After what I can only assume was a difficult decision making process for their family, they decided to go for it and were soon living, working and schooling in Kuala Lumpur. From then on, our contact with them was limited to the annual, highly expensive Christmas phone call and their summer visits where Barb and the girls would return to Saskatchewan, though Gerry was usually only able to visit for a week or so.

It was during these summers that we heard all about what living in Malaysia was like, and I'm certain this is when the travel bug first started nibbling at me. We heard tales of cobras in the garden, geckos in the bedrooms, strange foods in the streets, international schools with classmates from all over the world and school trips to Thailand. We were very envious of our cousins as they were living this exotic life as opposed to us living on the frozen, boring prairies, but were always very happy that we could still spend the summers with them. These stories really opened up my eyes to the world, to what was possible and what incredible things were out there to discover.

This original two year contract would be extended several times and the Davidsons would end up living in Malaysia for ten years, after which they were transferred to Stavanger, Norway and would remain for four years. Their final international posting was a short stint in the Netherlands, after which they finally returned to Canada to live in Calgary, Alberta.

The Davidsons' time in Norway coincided with my own time in London, England, and this is where I learned intimately about the world of expatriate overseas living. Since it was short plane ride away, I was invited to spend Christmas with them in 1995 and again a year later. The memories of these visits are some of my best as the Davidsons are the most gracious hosts you could imagine, and really made me feel at home. Most days Gerry and I would go out to do manly exercise activities such as back country hiking, mountaineering, jogging and these were always followed up with Norwegian beer on uncle Gerry's tab. The time I spent with Barb was irreplaceable; we got to know each other very well, had some amazing conversations and became best of friends.

They had a very busy social life and I was introduced to what I assumed to be the typical expatriate lifestyle. Gerry explained it to me like this - whichever spouse is the working spouse, usually the man but sometimes the woman, gets posted to a company that really needs the help and does not have any staff that can handle a particular job. Their compensation package includes not just an excellent wage, but also premium housing, living allowances, yearly or more frequent trips back home, and so forth, but in return the company grinds their ass and expects them to deliver results. This often requires long working hours, major stress, frequent travel and weekend work, but this is just what is expected of the role, and since expatriates are so expensive to employ, they have to be top performers, and if they are not they get sent home.

So if the working spouse spends all their time working, what does the non-working spouse do? Well, this is where Buddhism plays a role. You see, Buddhists believe in reincarnation, and if you lead a good, selfless life, then your next reincarnation will be into a better social position. For example, if you live your life as a scoundrel and spend your days lying, cheating and stealing, then in your next life you won't come back as a lawyer again. No, you will surely be reincarnated as an accountant, and it will just continue to get worse for you after that.

On the other hand, if you lead a good and noble life, then get reincarnated into a better position, then lead a good and noble life again and repeat this about a thousand times, then one day you will be rewarded with the ultimate reincarnation; namely, you will be reborn as an expatriate wife. This is the reward for millenniums of selfless acts, charity and good will. Your days as an expat wife will be gloriously lived out playing bridge, organizing dinner parties, collecting ceramic elephants, wiring money to your kids in boarding school, attending aerobics class, drinking fancy tea, buying gifts and directing household staff. The only downside to this ultimate reincarnation is enduring the bitching from the working spouse, but any good Buddhist learns to simply smile and nod, then get back to the Suduko, Chardonnay and Nirvana as soon as possible.

I would discover later in life that this whole expatriate wife thing that uncle Gerry educated me on did have elements of the truth (auntie Barb truly does have a world class ceramic elephant collection), but once Ana and I were in the position ourselves, we learned what it was like living day to day as a foreigner in another country. Yes, the lifestyle was good, but there certainly were plenty of challenges for the non-working spouse. Having the opportunity to become an expatriate, just like my aunt and uncle had, is something I am very proud of, and having that experience made me know and understand them even better.

Luck and Opportunity

When discussion expatriates, one can't help but wonder why some people seem to get more "lucky breaks" than others. One of my favourite quotes is from Seneca, a Roman philosopher from the 1st century. He said,

"Luck is what happens when preparation meets opportunity"

I have held this close as a motto for many years and believe in it with all my heart. Over the years I have had many lucky breaks and opportunities, but so has everybody else, it's just a question of whether they were ready and willing to act on them. This is often the difference between those who end up traveling the world and those that do not.

During my third year of university I made a difficult decision that would prepare me for all my future travels. After a difficult and stressful year I was considering taking a break from school and going to visit my Danish friend Marten Olsen, one of my best friends I had met in high school. For me, the urge to get the hell out of school and travel was agonizing and it was feeling to me like the right thing to do. I called Marten, told him of my plans and to my surprise he told me in no uncertain terms that it was a terrible idea. "You only have one year left," he said. "Get your school over with then come to visit, that way you can stay as long as you like and not have to worry about going back." This was probably the best piece of advice anybody has ever given me and fortunately I took it. I stuck it out, graduated from the College of Commerce with Distinction and that degree made a world of difference in my career opportunities. Without that, there is no way I would have been able to take the path I have, so for me that preparation has been the cornerstone of many things I have done. Many of the opportunities that have come my way would not have been possible without that credential.

Shortly after Ana and I met I asked her why she didn't have her Portuguese citizenship and passport. Since both of her parents were born in the Azores she was definitely entitled to this. She said that she had never really thought about it before, but after talking about it she got the process in motion and after a laborious, complicated and frustrating experience, finally got her citizenship and passport. Several years later, Ana would be contacted by a friend of ours with a lucrative offer to work in The Netherlands. Because she had her Portuguese citizenship she was eligible to work in the EU and because we were married, I was also eligible to work there and managed to get a contract position on the same project. In this case, once again, without adequate preparation, this "lucky break" would not have happened. We were able to bank more money during this short contract than we would have been able to living and working at normal jobs in Canada for years.

If you are sitting there reading this book, and have parents or grandparents who were born in another country, immediately drop what you're doing, get on the internet, and find out if you are eligible to gain citizenship. For many countries, eligibility can depend on whether your grandparents or parents are still alive, so time can be of the essence.

Although you might not see the value of it now, you might have need of it in the future. In our case, because Ana has her citizenship, it automatically makes our children eligible so we will soon be applying for them to become Portuguese citizens. If they end up becoming world travelers themselves, this will provide them with many future opportunities, and we'll be expecting lots of invitations to come and visit them in exotic locations, all expenses paid!

Having opportunities come your way may be of no use if you are not prepared for them. Few expatriates will tell you the opportunity to work abroad came without a great deal of previous hard work and preparation.

How to Find Overseas Work

There are many excellent books and guides that have been written specifically on how to find overseas work. In fact, just this week at the library I picked up a 700 page book on finding work overseas – it was in the discard bin and available for 25 cents. I believe I have found the secret to finding overseas work and I'm sad to report, it's not that earth shattering. Here are the two things you need to do to find overseas work:

- Work your ass off at whatever you do to build a reputation as a hard worker and an expert in your field
- Cultivate a wide network of friends and contacts and treat them like gold

You must question yourself, why would a company or organization in another country want to hire a foreigner? An out of country worker is likely to be more expensive, will be subject to working visa requirements, which can be an administrative nightmare, may not be familiar with local working culture, be subject to health afflictions more readily than a local, and can always decide to leave and go back home if the going gets tough. With all those reasons not to hire a foreigner, what reason could there possibly be to do it? Well, I've found it's one of two things; either there is nobody available in the local labour market with the required skills and experience for the job or the hiring manager knows somebody capable of doing the job that they trust in and are assured that if hired, that person will do whatever it takes to get the job done. It's no coincidence that these two reasons dovetail with what I believe it takes to find overseas work.

While working in London, England back in 1995, I received a call one afternoon from the temping agency I worked through to advise me that they received a work order from Shell International for a person who was an expert with the software Microsoft PowerPoint. It was to be a two week contract with the possibility of an extension and paid more than I was currently making. Beyond that, I was growing tired of the daily hangovers from being out drinking every night with my boss Johnny Eyre-Walker, so decided it was time for a change.

Upon arrival at the Shell International headquarters I quickly realized this would be a very good place to work so I spent those first two weeks busting my ass hammering out PowerPoint slides that were, admittedly, desperately mediocre, as I have no visual design talents, but my bosses must have appreciated the effort because I got my extension and ended up working there for nearly a year. This single job would lay the foundation for nearly all my future travels. You see, I worked for a team that was responsible for the strategy and performance of all the Shell companies in the Far East and Pacific. The people I worked with day to day were professional expatriates who had worked in senior roles for Shell companies worldwide, which meant I got to work with some of Shell's smartest and most experienced people. Beyond the obvious advantage of being able to learn from such high calibre individuals, I became friends with many of them, which would be very helpful in finding overseas contracts later on. The one gentleman I worked most closely with is now the CFO of Shell International worldwide and the others are either retired or in very senior positions in Shell, working in countries all over the world. During my tenure at head office, there were many times when I worked into the night, supporting the team, or was in the office at the crack of dawn helping out. I wasn't doing this to impress anybody, I was just dedicated to the team and trying to do a great job and learn as much as possible. I knew I wouldn't always be in a position to be working with this calibre of people and, in truth, after returning to Canada I am still yet to work with any senior managers who even come close.

Finding overseas work begins well before you actually start looking for particular opportunities. Building a solid track record in your field or getting specialized education or experience in an uncommon field will be critical. You must have something that makes you stand out from other candidates and be able to show that you are a safe bet. It doesn't hurt to have some recreational travel under your belt, as this at least demonstrates that you have done some personal traveling along the way and are familiar with the general aspects of overseas travel.

Most, if not all industries have trade shows, conferences, user group forums, seminars and symposiums. All conferences feature speakers who are experts in their field so pursuing the opportunity to speak at these is an excellent way to not just build your reputation, but also to meet people in your field from other countries, or even fellow countrymen who know about overseas projects that may be scheduled or underway. And in many cases, taking on a presenter role will get you a free admission to the conference, which makes it an easier sell to your boss.

There are some fields that are much more conducive to overseas travel than others. For example, many professions such as engineering, medicine, information technology, and accounting are quite portable, meaning jobs in these fields do not change much from country to country so the skills you acquire in one country can be easily applied to similar jobs in another country. My educational background is in Finance but early on in my career I got involved with installing Enterprise Resource Planning software systems, in particular, one called J. D. Edwards, which is similar to other packages such as SAP, PeopleSoft and Oracle. This software is generally used to replace a lot of smaller systems, so that all of your main business processing is tightly integrated and the various parts of the organization such as Human Resources, Payroll, Accounts Payable, Budgeting, Accounts Receivable and Asset Management are able to use the same system, see the same information and process transactions quickly and efficiently. I soon realized through meeting people in this field that these software packages were being rapidly installed in companies worldwide and the supply of experienced consultants was much less than the demand. Despite taking years to become an experienced consultant, after I had one project under my belt it was quite easy finding new projects, and as I gained experience, it became easier every time.

Finding a very small niche market is an excellent way of preparing for overseas work. I remember years ago talking to a friend of mine, Marc Haugen, who told me of a mutual friend Alex who had been working with specialized piece of software that was used in designing airports – it simulated traffic patterns in a typical airport and identified design problems that created bottlenecks. Talk about a specialized skill set! I can imagine that if he became a recognized expert in this software, he would have no trouble finding overseas contracts as airports worldwide are very similar so his experience would be directly relevant to airport design in any country. I don't know if Alex ever did do any overseas work but that always struck me as a very intriguing career.

There are other fields that you wouldn't expect to be portable to any country but certainly are. I met an Australian couple in the Dominican Republic who ran a huge dairy farm for a national dairy products company. In a typical scenario, when living overseas, you go out to dinner with a group of expatriates and do the "round table", where people explain what brings them overseas, and typically goes something like this:

"I'm a reservoir engineer for a big oil company, here on a three year project."

"I'm doing consulting work on a corporate merger."

"I'm a tax accountant, we've got a shell company here that we run a lot of our business through and I'm here on a year long project."

"My wife and I are here doing consulting work for a branch of the government working on improvements to their health system."

In this case, the answer was,

"I'm a farmer."

When I think of farmers the image that comes to mind is not exactly a high flying expatriate but apparently I didn't know much about the dairy industry. Their operation was an extremely high tech modern farm where everything was automated and monitored using complex control systems. My assumption of a wrinkly necked old man wearing rubber boots sitting on a wooden stool milking a cow was somewhat incorrect. This served as a good lesson to me; there are many avenues that can lead you to overseas work – the key is to be an expert at what you do.

Latch Onto a Guru

Early on in my career I met an English consultant named Heinrich and discovered very quickly that he was one of the few gurus in the field – knowledgeable, experienced, connected, reliable, meticulously thorough, and an extremely hard worker. He was doing the sort of work that I aspired to and there is no better way to learn the ropes then to latch onto somebody who knows what they are doing. His fondness for quality steaks and good beer made it that much easier to strike up a friendship, and we soon became personal friends and would cross paths many times over the years. Heinrich could see that I was willing to learn and ready to work hard so he mentored me and opened up opportunities for me that I wouldn't have otherwise had. I met several other important mentors along the way, each of whom passed on their tricks and secrets and I soaked it all up like a sponge. When starting out in your career you must actively seek out the experts and influencers in your field, get to know them, show them you are willing to learn, then watch them and do exactly what they do.

The Internet

The explosive growth of the internet, particularly with respect to communication tools, has truly changed the world. When I first left Canada in 1995, email was not widely used, the web was in its infancy and online communications were limited to message boards. International telephone calls were prohibitively expensive and internet connections were done using dial-up. Communication with overseas friends and contacts was handled via paper letters and the occasional telephone call. Today I can send and receive messages, pictures, files and videos instantly with friends and contacts all over the world for free every single day. The question is, has this change in technology made it easier to find overseas work? In many ways, I think it has made it more difficult. The real benefits have gone to the organizations looking for people as it is now simple and practically free to advertise your requirements to candidates all over the world. For potential candidates the competition is fierce and the field of suitable candidates is now larger than ever so the basic principle of building a good reputation and having a network of known and trusted contacts is even more important than in the past.

Neither Ana nor I have ever found an international contract using the internet – we have always found our opportunities through personal and business contacts. What we have discovered in recent years, though, is we get a lot of agencies and head hunters contacting us about international work. This is one way that the internet becomes extremely valuable – it enables jobs to find you instead of the other way around. The key is to build a solid online presence and advertise your skills and experience, which is not difficult as the tools available for this now, such as social media networks, are absolutely incredible. Using these tools to build an international network of professionals in your field has now become simple and free, while in the not too distant past, it was very hard to keep in contact with past colleagues, especially if you did a lot of overseas work and worked with many people on various projects. When it came time to start looking for your next project, you would basically pick up the phone and start trying to track people down to see if anybody knew of current opportunities. Today, using LinkedIn for example, you can see exactly where all your business contacts are currently working, when they change jobs, mutual people that you know and what projects they have recently worked on.

Recruiters for jobs are increasingly using these tools to not just locate candidates, but once they have identified candidates, to verify their information. Making oneself easy to find on the internet can be helpful in this regard, which means building up a substantial internet presence. In my business, I come across the same people again and again on software support sites, chat rooms, connections of connections on LinkedIn, professional sites and so on. It is safe to say that if you've seen a particular consultant popping up on well regarded industry chat boards, with published articles in the various journals and connections to good consultants you have worked, chances are they are a solid bet.

Working Holiday Visas

If you are between the ages of 18 and 35 then your best bet for an international work opportunity is applying for a Working Holiday visa. My initial foray away from Canada to the United Kingdom was on such a visa, and it gave me the opportunity to spend two years in the UK working and traveling. This was a one time only visa and as soon as I entered the UK, the clock started ticking. It was an excellent program that allowed me to use the UK as a base for two years, and use the money I earned from well paying, short term contract jobs to fund my travels in the UK and beyond.

This program has now changed and is now available for a one year period and for many other countries besides the UK. For details, look to the Canadian Foreign Affairs website at www.international.gc.ca and look for information on the International Experience Canada (IEC) programs. They are now split into three categories, Working Holiday, Young Professional, and International Co-Op. The IEC negotiates bilateral youth mobility agreements with other countries, providing young citizens of each to work in each others' countries. The list of countries is long and includes such diverse places Australia, France, Germany, Hong Kong, Mexico, Costa Rica and Poland.

There is an application process you will have to go through, and will also have to prove that you have enough funds, generally around three thousand dollars, to at least get you started and settled in your new location. As an introduction to living and working in another country, this is about as good as it gets so if you are between these ages and looking for an international opportunity, have a close look at this program. You can either travel independently or enlist the help of any of a number of government recognized organizations that can help you locate work, make the required visa application and generally help you along.

Deciding to Leave

You have found an international project or job assignment, been offered the position and now need to make the decision on whether to take it. You will consider the financial aspects of it, do extensive research on the country you will be going to, get as much information as you can on the exact job and working conditions, ask the opinion of your friends and family, but in the end, you will have to make that final decision, which will be based as much on emotions as on the hard facts of the opportunity. This decision may be tougher than you think, as it is difficult to imagine a situation so substantially different than the one you are in, and you will naturally be scared of making a bad decision. But remember this one fact – if you decide to take it, you leave, and find that it's the worst decision you ever made and hate the job, then you can always go home. Even if you have to quit your current job and break a few ties, it is likely that you will be able to re-establish yourself at home without too much trouble. The last thing you want is to decide not to go, then spend the rest of your life wondering what it would have been like and regretting that missed opportunity. Throughout my travels, with all the people I have met, I cannot remember a single person telling me that taking up a new opportunity in a different country, province or state was a bad decision, or didn't somehow work out in the end, or lead to a better future. In the end, you can leave your home for a year or two and come back to find that nothing much has changed – your friends will still be doing the same things, your family will still be there, and your favourite watering hole will likely still be in business. What will have changed is you, and upon returning you may find things don't really feel the same, or you may see your old situation in a different light. Nothing saddens me more than hearing somebody tell me of a past experience where they were presented with an interesting work opportunity away from home and turned it down, for whatever reason. I can assure you, the decision is only tough the first time, after that it gets easier and easier.

Preparing to Go

You have made your decision to leave and now need to prepare for your departure. There have been hundreds of books written on this subject so I'm not going to cover all the details, but rather point out some of the most important things you need to look at.

Your Stuff

Chances are that you have a lot of stuff and by stuff I mean your car, house, furniture, dog, cabin, boat, photo albums and seven hundred pounds of camping gear you use once every three years. When I first left Canada I was very lucky in that I really didn't have much of anything. My possessions consisted of a 1968 Dodge Dart, a giant stack of textbooks and class notes and a couple boxes of junk ranging from old ball gloves to photo albums. I moved the boxes into my dad's basement and sold the car to a friend of my brother, who soon learned that taking sharp corners at high speeds in the Dart causes its passenger door to fly open, spilling any unfortunate occupant onto the road. I was told my beloved car was shipped to the junkyard shortly after such an episode, which resulted in hospitalization of the co-pilot and some embarrassment to the new owner.

It is good to have a short term and long term plan for your possessions. In the short term, try to arrange to keep most of your things somewhere temporarily and perhaps find a renter for your home and a trusted friend or family member who can manage things for you while you are away. That way, if things don't work out, you can always come back and pick up where you left off. In the event that your time away turns out to last longer that you initially expected, and it probably will, then you can decide on a longer term plan at that point, which may include selling your home and possessions, or at least the ones you don't care about. You will find that the longer you are away, the less concerned you will be with these old possessions. When my aunt and uncle went on their first overseas posting, they put all their things into one of those big self-storage rooms, expecting that they would be moving back to Calgary in two years. Well, twenty years later when they finally moved home, walking into that storage unit was like stepping into a time capsule, and they were then faced with the decision of what to do with that pristine Barbie Malibu Beach House.

Your Residency and Tax Situation

Yes, it's boring and nobody wants to think about taxes and residency but this is something you must thoroughly investigate before leaving, as the rules are complex and depend on your citizenship, residence and many other aspects of your particular situation. A few years back I wrote an article on the tax rules that cover this area, which will serve as an excellent starting point. It was written based on the rules in Canada, but many of the same concepts are used by other countries. The article may be accessed for free at my website www.lifeisgrand.org.

It is critical that you know exactly how you will handle your residency and tax situation as many of the things you can do to reduce your tax obligations need to be done before you leave your country, and trying to make this right after you have left is much more difficult. The same applies if and when you decide to move back to your home country – you must investigate the process well in advance and make all the necessary arrangements to allow a smooth and predictable return.

Ongoing Commitments

By this I mean who will take over your duties as the Soccer Club treasurer, how will you file your tax return, what happens to your mail, will you be able to renew your vehicle and home insurance online or do some steps need to be done in person, can you put your gym membership on hold and so on. There is no way to generate a comprehensive list here, so sit down think about all the administrative things you typically need to do and list them out. Have a look at a year's worth of credit card and bank statements, some of the transactions in there will jog your memory. The goal is to take care of as many of these things as possible before leaving so you don't need to worry about them when you are away. Your new life will bring about its own hectic schedule and trying to manage two lives at once will become overwhelming.

The Ones You Leave Behind

You will move on – don't expect anybody else to. Having moved to a new country, you will now be experiencing dozens of new things everyday, going on weekend trips to new and exciting places, meeting interesting people with diverse backgrounds, trying new foods and possibly learning a new language. It's easy to forget that people back home are still doing the same things they were before and they will probably not share the same enthusiasm as you do for your new life. And let's face it – you have consciously chosen to leave your friends behind in search of something new and different, which can be awkward. But your real friends will always be there, no matter how long you are away.

Thanks to social media technology, we are no longer limited to boring one's friends and family with our fabulous travel photos during occasional trips home. Now, we can do it each and every single day with the help of the internet. Let me put this bluntly – nobody really cares to see your photos of the Taj Mahal, they can see much better ones with a click or two on the internet or on the Discovery Channel. Most people who have moved away from their home country find that the majority of their friends and family aren't that interested in the intricate details of their adventures. And yes, the irony of me saying this while writing a travel book of my adventures is not lost on me; I guess I'm just holding out hope that at least my mom will buy a copy! Since returning to Canada, I don't often bring up stories of my travels unless it comes up naturally in a conversation. I suppose it's because I don't want to chance appearing as a braggart, but also because I prefer to discuss travel with people who are as similarly interested in it as me.

Getting Settled...Fast

In your new country, things will be different than what you are used to, in some cases radically different. But don't let this stop you from immersing yourself in the culture and society as quickly as possible. When Ana and I were working on projects where we moved frequently, she became the master of high speed acclimatization. In one case we arrived in a new country one evening, checked in at a hotel, and by the time I finished my first day of work, she had already found us an apartment, arranged for internet service, rented us a vehicle and made dinner plans for us that evening! It is best to dive in fast and not loiter around waiting for things to get done for you. If your company is responsible for arranging a lot of this for you, there's a good chance it will take three times as long as doing it yourself; taking care of the spoiled expatriate's tender needs is not always at the top of the HR department's list. So if possible, get involved yourself and speed the process along. If there are other expatriates with your organization, get to know them and ask their advice as they will usually be very happy to help and will have some experience under their belts.

The best tip I can pass on for getting settled in a new place is to learn how to use your ears and keep your mouth shut. People on vacation don't need to do this as they are surrounded by other obnoxious tourists and have the right to complain endlessly about the lack of fresh towels and poorly stocked fruit plate at the buffet. Your goal is to learn as much as possible about your new location, so your mouth should be used primarily for asking questions and not telling people about how much better things work at home or how more efficient the processes are.

Coming Home

You have lived as an expatriate, possibly in several countries, worked your arse off, explored new places, met many new people but, for some reason, decide that it is time to go home. Quite often it may be for family reasons, but could also be a change in your health, a job opportunity, a bad experience, or perhaps you have just had enough and begin to crave the comforts and predictability of your own country. For me, it was purely a family decision. Before meeting Ana, the thought of returning to Canada to live permanently did not cross my mind, as I was very happy living as a vagabond, moving from place to place, earning great money, meeting new people and expanding my job experiences. Even while both working and traveling together internationally, our plans were never to return to Canada to live. But after we got married and decided that we wanted a family, the decision to return to Canada was obvious and painless. By that time, we were quite satisfied with the amount of traveling we had done and looked to Canada as the perfect place to spend this next, important phase of our lives. While many expatriates successfully raise happy children in foreign lands, it was important to us that our children would be able to know and grow up with their grandparents, cousins, aunts and uncles, and to have a place they could look back on later in life and know that it was their home. Some expatriate kids have a tough time with this, as they may have lived in three or four childhood homes in countries they may never return to, and can feel like they never really had a permanent base. But for most, the incredible experiences they have as children more than compensates for this.

The concept of "reverse culture shock" is very real. Returning to you own country to live after an extended time away can make you feel like a foreigner in a foreign land. Things might not work as efficiently as you remember, the bureaucracy and paperwork can be crushing and, worst of all, your countrymen may not place the same value on all your experiences as you do, particularly your work experience.

When Ana and I returned to Canada, I assumed it would be fairly easy to find employment. But I was wrong. I quickly developed an empathetic appreciation for the Pakistani and Indian lawyers and accountants working as taxi drivers in Toronto. People in hiring positions, who may not have traveled much, will often assume that experience gained in other countries is simply not as good as the same experience gained at home. It is understandable for people to assume that experience and credentials claimed by candidates who have worked out-of-country are not relevant, not comparable or perhaps even not believable or verifiable. Look at it from their perspective – why would they take a chance on a candidate with wild claims of international experience, when they have a perfectly good candidate, perhaps with less experience, but who has spent their whole working lives in their home country working for recognizable companies?

The good news is that once you finally land that first job, and get recent home country experience on your resume, then you will be fine. And your employers will immediately realize that all that international experience is relevant and useful.

Once you get established with a home and a job, everything else will click into place. You will connect with old friends and family, make new friends, and start getting involved in your community. Integrating yourself back into your home country and culture is really the same as integrating yourself into a new country and culture – all the same rules apply!

You will be a different person than when you left. You will likely find much greater joy in local travel. You will have a better appreciation for security. You will be more tolerant, patient and very interested in meeting people from other countries and hearing their stories. Above all, you will be overjoyed to meet travelers visiting your country, as you will look into their faces and see yourself.

****

Conclusion

Every person has limited resources and must decide on how to best use these resources to maximize the benefits they experience. We are all looking for something to provide a release from the everyday grind, to keep ourselves occupied in our spare time and to give meaning and purpose to our lives. For my family and I, this has always been travel. If the budget gets tight, we will usually find a way to reduce our normal everyday living expenses to be able to afford a trip. Fortunately, over the years we have made decisions with our careers and finances that have allowed us to travel, but also to have the resources to raise children, live in a decent house and have enough material possessions to provide for a comfortable lifestyle.

I feel privileged to have traveled to so many remarkable places, yet I still feel like there is so much more to see, and I've really only scratched the surface. When Ana and I first met in 1998, she bought me a small, beautiful leather-bound traveler's atlas, and in the back we made up a list of all the countries we wanted to visit together. So far, we have visited 21 out of 40 of these, so we are slightly over the halfway mark, but still have plenty left to go.

Traveling changes you in ways that you cannot predict. A day spent in a new, unfamiliar place exploring, watching, and understanding can be a life changing experience. Traveling helps you to approach the world as an inquisitive child does – always asking questions, wondering what's out there and knowing always that anything is possible.

****

Part Two– Ten Travel Adventures

How to Miss Your Own Bachelor Party

Ana and I were married in Canada, but at the time were living in the Caribbean. More than two thirds of our guests were to be flying in from some other location, many international, so planning and scheduling everything was a big job. The terrorist attack on Sept 11 happened 11 days before our wedding so all of our plans where thrown into chaos. It was a time of great international worry and hatred, and that attack would shape world events for years to come. But that did not stop our party – in the end everybody arrived safely, we all pushed that terrible event from our minds for an evening and celebrated together.

With only four days and a short plane ride standing between me and my fishing trip weekend bachelor party, I was a happy fellow. I had finished my last day of work after being on a project in San Juan, Puerto Rico and I was ready to get home. Ana had returned to Canada a few days before as she was taking care of the final preparations for our wedding, scheduled for the following weekend.

My flight was leaving San Juan, Puerto Rico at 11:00 am on Tuesday, September 11, 2001. Yes, that's right, September 11. I left my apartment at 8:00 in the morning, drove to Budget, dropped off my rental car then jumped in the courtesy van for the airport. On the way we were listening to a Spanish radio station and they were talking about an airplane which had crashed into a tower in New York. Moments later they reported that a second plane had crashed into another tower, which obviously sounded a bit suspicious. I arrived at the airport, checked in as normal then went through to the American Airlines Admiral's Club to check out what was happening on CNN. Just as I sat down to watch, I saw the first of the World Trade Center towers collapsing in a mushroom of black smoke, then shortly thereafter watched the second one collapse. By this time all the flights to the US had been cancelled, but fortunately my flight was going to Dominican Republic, where I was planning to spend the night before leaving for Toronto via Miami on Wednesday morning. The lady at the airline reception counter assured me that the international flights were still flying and only the US ones had been affected, but before long the voice over the loudspeaker announced that all flights were cancelled, the airport was closing immediately and all remaining passengers had to collect their bags and leave.

Oh oh, I thought, *that's not good*. I went down to get my checked bags and watched them drop down the luggage carousel, one by one, all except the bag containing my clothes. I searched the airport for about two hours trying to find the missing bag but it never materialized, which would later turn out to be a blessing in disguise.

I picked up my three large, overstuffed bags, one of which contained about 40 pounds worth of Ana's shoes, left the airport and took a taxi to a hotel so I could make some calls and try to figure out what to do. I first called Ana to let her know I was okay then we both started checking into every possible airline and cruise ship option but there was absolutely nothing leaving from Puerto Rico except the ferry that runs to Dominican Republic. At the time there were still flights arriving to Canada via Cuba, which planted the seed for Plan B. Ana called a colleague from our project and had her buy me an air ticket from Santo Domingo to Havana, Cuba, then one from Havana to Toronto. The plan was simple and foolproof - I would stay overnight in San Juan, take a ferry the next day to Santo Domingo, then catch my flights and make it home for my bachelor party!

With Plan B solidly in place, I was feeling pretty good. I checked into a hotel, watched CNN late into the night then was up early the next morning and on a bus headed for the ferry terminal located on the western end of the island. I bought a ticket, hung around the terminal for a few hours, then boarded the ferry and settled in for a nice overnight run to the Dominican. The ferry experience was delightful as I had my own little cabin and bed and was able to enjoy some cold Presidente beers in the huge onboard bar. I was actually fooled into believing the rest of the trip would be as enjoyable, but I was soon to discover otherwise.

I woke up Thursday morning feeling confident, well rested and ready for action after the smooth overnight sail. I stepped off the ferry at exactly 8 am, collected my mass of luggage, and then grabbed a taxi to the Shell office. I ran in, grabbed my air tickets, thanked the receptionist, and then had the taxi take me to a friend's apartment to pick up another heavy bag that we had left there before going to Puerto Rico. The taxi driver then raced me out to the airport and got me there in time to get checked in for the flight to Cuba, which was scheduled to depart shortly. The airport in Santo Domingo was practically deserted as there were almost no flights coming or going, though I failed to recognize this for the omen it was.

The Cubana flight arrived in Havana on time and everything was looking good until they took all the transfer passengers to a special area to wait for further instructions. *Oh oh*, I thought, *that doesn't sound good.* I was soon told that my connecting flight to Toronto had been cancelled and there were no more flights that day. Shit. So I went to the accommodation counter and made a reservation at a government hotel in Havana. The airline people told me to be at the airport the next day before noon to try and get on another flight. About then I figured it was time to play the "wedding card" so I told them my wedding was Saturday and they somehow had to get me home. Sure, it was a little lie, but times like that call for drastic measures. After relaying my sob story I left the counter, found a bank of telephones, stacked up my luggage, then bought a telephone card so I could call Ana and give her an update on the situation. After several failed attempts I finally figured out the correct series of international codes to use and managed to get through to Ana, whose nerves were shattered and was desperate for a reassuring update on the status of the flight, which I was unable to provide. As I was explaining the situation to her, the bag that I had picked up in Santo Domingo, strategically placed on top of the others, shifted, slid down the luggage pile, hit the floor and made a crashing sound. *Oh oh*, I thought, *that really didn't sound good.* I then noticed an ample volume of brown liquid leaking out and was overcome with the smell of alcohol. I had forgotten that we had put a 60 ounce bottle of rum in there, which had just broken and soaked all my stuff. At that point, frustration began to set in. My conversation with Ana was cut short as the time on the card abruptly ran out, so the last words she heard were probably "fuck" and "rum". I spent the next hour in the bathroom emptying out the bag, throwing out the ruined items, picking shards of glass out of the remaining objects then trying to wash up whatever was salvageable. The whole time this little Cuban washroom attendant was listening to me and was clearly intrigued to be learning so many new English obscenities. When that mess was finally cleaned and I was stinking of alcohol I took a taxi into Havana, found the hotel and immediately sought beer and cigars to try and soothe my frazzled nerves. The hotel was a total dump and it seemed that at any moment the building could quite easily collapse and put me out of my misery. Unfortunately, it remained standing.

I left the hotel as soon as possible on my hunt for tobacco and cerveza. I bought a cigar from a nearby shop, lit it up, found a nice patch of pavement, then started puffing away and thinking of where I could go to consume some beer. Just then a Cuban guy walked over and started talking to me. After a few minutes he still hadn't tried to con any money off me so I took him for a decent dude and asked him to go for a beer. He led me to a local bar that I never would have found on my own, and then I started buying us ridiculously cheap rounds of Cristal, which is the most common brand of Cuban beer. But after four bottles he said he had to quit because he had a problem with one of his organs. We were talking in Spanish and because my Spanish medical vocabulary leaves much to be desired, I didn't know exactly what organ he was talking about, but it may have been spleen or liver perhaps. Once we left the place and got to an empty part of the street he pulled up his shirt to show me. What came next seemed like a hallucination, and I watched as he displayed the previously concealed plastic bag protruding from the side of his body, which protected a pink pulsing organ. He told me he had been hit by a car and for some reason they had to remove the organ from inside his body, requiring him to wear these medical plastic bags to protect it. Before the situation slipped any further into the macabre, I bid him adieu, returned to the seedy hotel and fell asleep in about half a second.

It was now Friday, the kick-off day for my bachelor party. I got up early and ate a disgusting government sponsored breakfast of dry bread and super sugary juice-free juice. As I choked down the bread I looked across the breakfast area and saw a prostitute and her fat German boyfriend who I reckon had a scorching case of AIDS judging from the open sores all over his body. I didn't stay for a second cup of rank coffee.

I packed my things and took a taxi to the airport, all the while thinking there was a good chance I would be back home in Canada in mere hours and on my way to a wild weekend with the boys. What a fool! When I arrived at the airport I found out that the 15:00 flight to Toronto had been cancelled but there was still a chance the 18:00 flight to Montreal would go. I begged one of the airline employees to help get me on that flight and she did help me after I told her that my wedding was the next day. There was that little lie again, but I was getting dangerously close to missing my bachelor party! How could I miss my bachelor party, especially since it involved such a motley crew of hard boozing family and friends doing all sorts of damage to their livers and digestive systems in my honour?

Well, the 18:00 flight didn't fly, which made me wonder if I would ever get out of there. I couldn't bear spending another night in the government hotel so I managed to contact the owners of this lovely bed and breakfast Ana and I had stayed at once before. I took a taxi to their place and was overjoyed to be in a familiar environment with kind, normal people. The lady of the house even washed my filthy clothes for me, which I was desperate for since the only clothes I had were my emergency stock, which I always include in my carry-on bag. But they were not just dirty; they were still reeking of the rum they had been marinated in when the bottle broke at the airport. Once all my clothes were in the wash I realized this was the first night of my bachelor party weekend so, trying to make the best of a difficult situation, I put on a pair of swimming trunks and one of Ana's shirts and went out for dinner by myself to celebrate, looking extra gay in the process with my banana hammock and skin tight glitter blouse. Fortunately, my favourite restaurant in Havana, called El Ajibe, was within walking distance, so I hustled over there, being careful to avoid eye contact with any potentially gay men, and laced into a an extra large platter of rice, beans and chicken then followed it up with a couple beers and a cigar. Although it was a delicious meal and my surroundings were cozy, I still felt sad and lonely, and tried not to think what the Olson boys were getting up to that night. And I missed Ana badly.

Well, next crappy day, same routine. I got up, rounded up my freshly washed, though not quite fully dried clothes, and took a taxi to the airport at 6:00 in the morning. With a soggy crotch I realized it was Saturday and there was still a chance that I could make it back for one day of the fishing trip. Of course when I arrived at the airport I found out that my flight was cancelled yet again and there was no hope at all of anything leaving that day. Aaaarrrgggggg!!! Desperation set in and I found myself running around the airport, frantically trying to find a flight going anywhere. I just couldn't take being stranded in Cuba any longer. I found a flight going to Nassau, Bahamas that afternoon so I bought a ticket, deciding that I would have a better chance of getting home from anywhere besides Cuba. Besides, even if I couldn't get to Canada or the States from there, at least I could go to my favourite bar Hammerheads and get completely shitfaced on Kalik beer, which would be a decent bachelor party consolation prize!

Surprisingly, the flight left on time and arrived in Nassau airport, which was a total mess and full of angry, nasty people trying to get back to the States. Once I got there I explained my pathetic situation to a guy at the first class counter and the great man gave me a standby ticket on a flight to Miami that afternoon! It helped that he remembered me from all the flights I used to take from Bahamas the year before when I used to live there. After that I called my good Bahamian friend Ruthie and she picked me up and we went for a delicious meal of grouper fingers and conch salad at Traveler's Rest restaurant. I also succeeded in downing about four Kalik beers in the space of thirty minutes, which was not a bad effort, though well off my peak. The only reason I didn't drink more was that I could not risk getting kicked off the plane for being drunk. Ruth and I had an excellent visit and my spirit and mood was dramatically improved. On the way back to the airport we stopped and picked up a crate of Kalik cans, which we somehow managed to cram one by one into the remaining space in the bags. Ana would later mention that she was missing a couple pairs of shoes but I didn't know anything about that.

I checked in and proceeded to US immigration where they made me completely empty my spring loaded bags after not liking my answer to "Where are you coming from?" which went something like this:

"Cuba, but I didn't mean to go there, I'm really coming from Puerto Rico but I had to pass through Dominican Republic to pick up a bag. I'm missing my bachelor party and getting married next weekend. Please have mercy."

Well, turns out they had no mercy, but at that point I didn't care; I had a ticket to the USA in my hand, a nice Kalik buzz and the prospect of getting home in time for my wedding, which was all that mattered. The flight left Nassau late and when it arrived in Miami I found out that there was actually a flight leaving to Montreal in thirty minutes that I may be able to catch if I ran. My God, I could still make it for one day of the bachelor party! So I got my bags, somehow roped them all around myself and ran like hell, wildly optimistic, to the American Airlines counter where I was faced with a crowd of about fifteen thousand people and complete and utter filthy chaos. I pushed my way through the first class line and begged the lady to take me first. I was informed that I was a couple minutes too late, the flight was closed and there were no more flights to Canada that night. Aaaarrrggggg!!!

Beaten, humiliated, and exhausted, I made my way up to the Admiral's Club to see if they could help me, but also to take a nice big dump in a clean toilet. I waited in line for about forty minutes then finally got to the front and explained my situation to the nice lady at the counter. I was left in stunned disbelief when she told me she reserved me the last seat on a flight to New York, with a connection to Toronto the following morning. I should have been thrilled, but at that point I didn't have the energy to get excited, plus I just assumed something would go wrong and it would end in disappointment. I wasn't even that happy when she gave me a $30 food voucher for dinner that night at the hotel, all I wanted to do was to be with my fiancée whom I was missing terribly, especially now that the prospect of making the bachelor party was impossible.

I sat down in the lounge for a while, caught my breath, ate some peanuts then called Ana to give her the good news. After talking with her I was feeling much better with things so I celebrated by joyously polluting the nice lavatory, which was a real treat after those third world cans. I limped away from that effort weighing twelve pounds lighter and feeling one hundred percent better. I grabbed a coffee and doughnut then gathered my bags and pushed my way back out through the airport to find a taxi to a hotel. The airport was total chaos, unlike anything I have ever seen before and, hopefully, will never see again.

I arrived at the hotel, got my room, and ordered the best steak on the room service menu, which cost forty bucks and looked and tasted like Goodyear rubber. I tried paying with my food voucher but they told me the voucher was only good for food purchased in the airport. Damn those insensitive bastards, kicking me when I was down! This was the biggest night of the bachelor party weekend and here I was all alone gnawing on a foul piece of overpriced meat without a beer; definitely one of the lowest points of my otherwise charmed life.

I awoke Sunday morning at 5:00 am, had a delicious breakfast of bottled water, and went to the airport. If it was bad the night before, it was worse now. The line-up to American Airlines check-in was about 300 meters long and snaked its way from one end of the airport to the other. As I walked sherpa-like, overcome with luggage, I kept asking people in line, "Am I almost at the end?" and they laughed at me. So I kept walking and walking. When I finally got to the end of the line (and the airport), I was relieved to find that the American Airlines staff were walking through the whole line and calling flights are they were ready to check in. After a while mine was called and I proceeded, not triumphantly, but rather suspiciously to the check-in, fully expecting a last minute cancellation of the flight. I checked in my bags then continued to security where they looked through everything except my bowels. I then continued to the boarding gate and was shocked to find the boarding areas of the airport completely tranquil and quiet, totally unlike what was going on in the check-in side. It was as if I had passed from the Twilight Zone back into reality. I assumed it was a trap.

The flight boarded and pushed off from the gate right on time. During the taxi out to the runway the plane passed about 80 ground workers who were all standing in a line waving American flags and saluting the plane, as it was one of the first planes headed for the recently re-opened La Guardia airport in New York. As we passed them the captain came on and said, "America loves you, we love you, God bless New York and God bless America!" People on the plane started shouting, "God bless America" and laughing and even crying. Christ, I didn't know what to think! I was just glad I was on the way home.

The plane flew without incident into New York right over top of the smouldering ruins of the crumbled towers and not a single person said a word. They were all just quietly staring at the wreckage, as was I. I thought of all those people who had died because to this senseless violence, what their families must be going through and how insignificant my problems were compared to theirs. But yet, I was happy to be this close to home and only hours away from seeing my fiancée.

The plane landed safely and, as expected, I found out that the connection to Toronto had been cancelled, which is why Ana had already booked a rental car for me at the airport. Throughout all the connections, transfers, shuttles and taxis, my bags had miraculously accompanied me the whole way, and yet again they rolled off the luggage carousel undamaged and just as heavy as before. I loaded them up, jumped on a shuttle to the car rental company and before long I was blasting down the interstate headed for upstate New York where Ana and my Australian friend Todd, who had arrived in Canada a few days before, were going to pick me up.

After seven hours of exceeding the speed limit, making only a single stop for gas, a squirt and to grab a big bag of dill pickle chips, I finally arrived in Rochester, New York at the rendezvous point, which was a Budget Rent-A-Car drop off in a gritty parking garage. The moment I stepped out of the car, I saw my beautiful fiancée, and man did she look good! She gave me the biggest hug of my life and I just held her for what seemed like a very long time, though I did take a moment to high-five Toddy partway through the embrace.

The ride back to Brantford, where our wedding was to be held, passed by quickly as we talked and visited. We were even able to start laughing about the whole arduous journey, even though the pain was still fresh in my mind. I was so happy to finally be reunited with Ana that the six torturous and stressful days of airports, hotels, taxis and bad food had already begun to fade from my memory, and thoughts began to focus on the upcoming wedding and all the joy and excitement that would bring.

We arrived in Brantford around 11:00 pm that night and I was tired, weary and overjoyed to be back on Canadian soil. I have probably missed out a lot of things that happened to me during my journey, but if I try to recount you every piece of bad luck I had, I will never finish writing this little story.

Mr. Osama Bin Laden, thank you for teaching me the value of persistence.

****

All Hail the Power Weekend

The American Style Power Weekend is when you make an ordinary weekend extraordinary by packing in an impossible amount of activity. I have had many, many such weekends over the years, but one in particular stands out. It was accomplished right in our backyard and should serve as inspiration for anybody who has ever slogged through a boring weekend and felt let down and demoralized on back to work Monday.

Taken from my blog on July 27, 2009

June 23

Over drinks with friends Andrew and Jess (People of the Cul-De-Sac) we decide a summer weekend trip is in order. The only July weekend free for both of us is July 25/26. Date is set, promises made, and the destination brainstorming begins.

July 6

Destination decided – Boston and other nearby salty, fishy sites of interest.

July 9

Watch the movie *The Perfect Storm* for the 10th time to brush up on local dialect and customs.

July 10th

After checking map and talking to cousin, Ana finds out it's at least a nine hour drive to Boston. Shortly thereafter, plug is pulled on Boston, new destination planning begins. Emails circulate in earnest.

July 21st, Tuesday

Cul-de-sac meeting called. Charges of procrastination are exchanged since destination has yet to be decided. Team congregates around internet explorer browser and begin googling. After Chicago (too windy), Kingston (too much traffic), family cabins (already full), Niagara Falls (too close), New York (too far), Cleveland (already went there), are considered and dismissed, we finally decide on Rochester, New York with a day trip to Ithica. It is a good compromise. Meeting dismissed, people of the cul-de-sac disperse.

July 24, Friday

Disaster strikes. Andrew has to work Saturday night as his food and beverage manager has gone AWOL. Rapid brainstorming ensues. Within moments a new plan emerges like a summer mayfly. Hotel in Toronto Friday night, followed up with a trip to the Woodbine horse racing track on Saturday. Disaster averted. Weekend trip back on.

Friday, 6 pm

Cram bags into car. Take a week's worth of luggage along for the night just in case. Kids narrowly miss being run over by Andrew's 4x4 as he rallies into the cul-de-sac. Everyone in van, depart.

Friday, 7 pm

Arrive at the Keg in Hamilton, eat big juicy steaks. Andrew manages to get them to comp us the meal, what a star. Pile back into van, crack a beer, head to Toronto and battle traffic all the way.

Friday, 11pm

Arrive at downtown Marriot. By some miracle kids are both sleeping. Haul kids and bags to adjoining rooms, dump kids in bed, proceed to drink heavily, say lots of bad words, and enjoy the spectacular view over downtown Toronto.

Friday, 2am or thereabouts

Lights out.

Saturday, 7:40 am

Awoken by two very alert looking children ready for action. A flurry of plastic animals ensues and the room is soon alive with the roar of a high horsepower hair dryer, which ignites the morning headache.

Saturday, 10 am

Breakfast at Eggspectations, delicious as expected. Talk of life, children, choices, dreams and bowel movements.

Saturday, 11 am

Walk to Andrew's single brother Kyle's super cool downtown condo. Find multiple specimens of women's underwear scattered on bedroom floor. Fondly reminisce of the "good old bachelor days". Get slapped by my wife.

Saturday, 11:30 am

Leave Kyle's place with his entire Playstation 3 set of Rock Band gear, a well received donation to spark my children's future musical career. It's really not for me at all.

Saturday, 12 pm

Drinks at a scummy downtown Toronto bar. Beer for me, Rum and Coke for Andrew, Margarita for Jess, Diet Coke for Ana, juices for the kiddies. Jess complains of strange and offensive odours in ladies toilet. Leave shortly thereafter.

Saturday, 1 pm

Arrive at AGO – Art Gallery of Ontario. Elongated heads, little ships, squirrel mannequins, furry cubes and ivory carvings intrigue, inspire and amaze us.

Saturday, 3:00 pm

Leave Toronto in a blinding rain storm, fight traffic, drop Andrew off at hotel in Hamilton for the evening shift. Along the way, we decide to go to Cleveland after he's done work to look at boats. No sense stopping now, the weekend is not even half over.

Saturday, 5:00 pm

Arrive home, have a nice dip in the hot tub, eat dinner, put jammies on kids. Jess spends quality time with Andrew's dog Belle.

Saturday, 9:30 pm

Pick up Andrew in Hamilton, proceed to drive to Cleveland. Along the way Andrew suggests trying to find a ferry to take across Lake Erie Sunday afternoon. Idea well received.

Sunday, 1:30 am

Arrive in Cleveland, only one 15 minute stop required for entire trip, must be a new record. Get checked into hotel. Too late to embark on drinking session, feel the ravages of old age.

Sunday, 7 am

Wake up. Get kids and women moving. Jess does Stella's hair and she looks like a beauty queen. Mental note that "ragamuffin" is not the only look Stella can pull off. Investigate ferry options. Quick brekkie in hotel lobby. Leave hotel. Note that it's a gorgeous day.

Sunday, 10 am

Arrive at National Liquidators boat yard after driving through the inner city slums of Cleveland. Feel good about our situation in life.

Sunday, 10:13 am

Find our ultimate dream boat. 1996 Catalina 40 foot, pristine condition. Call broker to make offer. Find out boat already sold that week. Feel bad about our situation in life. Andrew continues shuffling through Sun Rays and Rinkers, looking for the ultimate deal.

Sunday, 12 pm

Arrive at WWII submarine, right between boat yard and Rock and Roll Hall of Fame. Women stay outside and sun themselves while kids join the men inside and cause trouble the whole way through. Amazed and astounded that 97 men could live on such a vessel. Imagined smells are overpowering. That exact moment Magnus farts and Stella craps her diaper. They both laugh.

Sunday, 1 pm

Depart for Sandusky, 40 miles west of Cleveland. Arrive, buy tickets, eat lunch and drink beer in shabby but cool downtown pub.

Sunday, 3 pm

Ferry departs for Pelee Island. Lovely ride on a beautiful day. Girls mix us deadly strong rum and cokes.

Sunday, 4:45 pm

Ferry arrives. Clear Canada customs. Drive around island to public beach. Remove shoes, play in water, skip stones. Magnus picks up dead fish and brings it over. Later, inspects flattened garter snake on roadway. Nature trip over, back in van.

Sunday, 5:15 pm

Arrive in the southern-most tavern in Canada. Listen to country music, drink Old Vienna beer, eat greasy stuff, watch the strange people.

Sunday, 8 pm

Ferry departs for Kingsville, Ontario. Much larger ferry this time, retire to canteen to drink, eat popsicles and talk about life. Conversation gets very serious. Andrew is talked out of a career as a low paid pilot.

Sunday, 9:30 pm

Arrive Kingsville. Grab a Timmy's coffee. Girls take over driving duties while boys make obnoxious comments from back seat. Kids watch movies. Along the way, try to figure out why on earth we weren't able to fit a blimp ride into the weekend.

Monday, 12:15 am

Arrive Paris, Ontario. All hail the Power Weekend.

****

Don't Piss on my People

Ana and I spent six weeks in South Africa as part of a round the world backpacking trip back in 2002. We rented a tiny Volkswagen sub-compact car called a Golf Chico and put thousands of kilometres on it, driving from one end of the country to the other, discovering so many amazing places and people along the way. This is a story about one of those people we met who made us feel welcome and gave us a brief insight into his life.

Finally, a genuine African village tour, I thought to myself as Ana and I hurriedly finished eating our backpacker style tuna fish sandwiches (no butter, no mayo, dry tuna flakes dropping all over the floor) and rushed out to the bar area of the hostel where we were supposed to be meeting up with the guided three o'clock village tour. We were situated in Coffee Bay, located in the Transkei region of South Africa. This region was only incorporated into the country of South Africa in the early 1990's and as a result is much, much less developed than other parts of the country.

In true punctual Canadian nature, we arrived at the bar at exactly 3:00, expecting to find the rest of the people waiting for the last few to turn up. Naturally, the bar was empty, save a small yellowish green parrot named Joey who was chewing on a South Africa guide book hastily forgotten on top of one of the picnic tables in the bar.

"I wonder if they've left already," I asked Ana.

"I doubt it, they're probably just late," she replied. I agreed effortlessly, realizing that backpacker staff and their residents rarely lived by the clock; rather, they preferred living by their stomachs and a shoestring.

We had a quick look around the hostel, found nobody, then sat ourselves down at the picnic table and were confronted by the parrot Joey. Not being much of a bird expert, the only thing I could think of doing was offering Joey my upturned hand, much like I would do to a dog. Joey walked over, looked me in the eyes, then sunk his beak into the palm of my hand and gave me a hard nip. Trying to play it cool, I only slightly jerked my hand, then turned it around, palm down and offered it to the little green troublemaker. This time, finding much less loose skin to bite, he hopped on my hand and started working his way up to my shoulder. As he walked up and I was able to have a closer look, I realized he was a very nice looking little bird. He was coloured yellow and green like any budgie, but the intelligence in his eyes suggested he was much better travelled than the standard issue pet store variety. He reached my shoulder then stopped and looked me right in the eyes and said, "Pretty boy, waaaaakk". As I hadn't shaved for at least a week, nor changed my clothes for several days I knew he definitely didn't know what the hell he was talking about. So I answered back, "Pretty boy, pretty boy, pretty boy," but received no reply and concluded that he was likely here for a handout, not intelligent conversation.

We played with the bird for a very long time, in fact long enough to drink a coffee and even start discussing world problems, when Silas the tour guide arrived, out of breath and sweating, then asked us if were ready for the tour. By this time, a young and very tall German fellow who introduced himself as Kristof had arrived and was also waiting for the tour. So off we went, following Silas into the bush and onto our day's adventure.

Silas was an employee of the hostel but was also a local resident and part of the Xhosa tribe. He was short, young looking, dark skinned, and constantly beaming an infectious smile. He spoke excellent English and told us that he was currently taking a tourism course and one day hoped to open up his own backpackers hostel. After first introducing himself he told us the walking trip would include a stop at a typical Xhosa home, some sacred pools, then finally the "shabeen", which was the local village bar. With that brief introduction we left the confines of the hostel and began our walk, following Silas up the hill directly across from the hostel entrance. Upon reaching the top of he hill we were startled with a magnificent view! To the north and west we could see miles of rolling hills and patches of bush populated with many small circular huts painted mostly blue. To the east we could see the village of Coffee Bay with its stretching beach and foamy surf crashing up onto the shores. To the south, it was the blue Indian Ocean stretching off into the horizon. We continued walking westward through the hills until we came to a collection of buildings.

"This is my family's house," said Silas proudly. There were two circular huts with thatched roofs separated by a rectangular, partially finished building. The structures appeared to be made from mud bricks. "What are the houses made from?" I asked.

Silas answered succinctly, "The bricks are made from a mixture of soil, grass, and cow shit." Fair enough. Silas then showed us into the first of the huts and explained that this is where his parents slept. The inside of the hut was quite dark but you could see there was a gas cooking stove, two beds, and an assortment of clothes, tools, and other bits and pieces scattered about what looked like a hard packed dirt floor.

"What's the floor made from," asked Ana, "dirt?"

"Nope, it's made from pure cow shit," Silas replied, "As you can see, cow shit is very important to the Xhosa people." Seemed very true, and it was interesting to learn just how versatile cow shit was. Silas then showed us the chicken cage, which was made from twigs bound together with some sort of grassy rope. Next, came the rectangular building, which we learned was in construction and would eventually be used as a kitchen and entertaining space. The second round hut was Silas room, and was built exactly as the first. I was happy to have such a close up look at a typical Xhosa home, as during our drive to Coffee Bay we had seen thousands of these buildings, but didn't expect we'd have a chance to actually visit one.

We continued on our way with Silas in the lead followed by Ana and I then our German friend at the rear. We marched this way for a good thirty minutes with Silas stopping now and then to point out an interesting tree ("This one's used to make good bass drums.") or plant ("We make our sleeping mats with these.") or animal ("Don't get bitten by that spider, it will kill you!") We eventually came across a small stream and followed it for a few hundred metres until we came to a large pool. Silas explained that this was a pool of the ancestors and used for religious ceremonies where everybody in the village would attend. It was also common for people to throw chickens into the pool, to keep their ancestors well fed. He recommended against swimming in it.

We were then led back up the stream, passed our original entry point, and walked up to a second pool that, Silas explained, was used solely for baptisms and for swimming. I had no inclination whatsoever to go for a dip as the water looked a little brown and there was the occasional gob of shiny blue stuff, which appeared to be either motor oil or perhaps soap floating across the top. There was also another one of those nasty spiders spinning a web in the branches of a tree right behind us, which I stayed well clear of.

And that was it for the pools. So far our tour, though interesting, was far from extraordinary. A great walk to be sure, but nothing that was likely to permanently stamp its impression on the squishy grey matter. Things took a comical turn when Silas suddenly disappeared into a hut. I asked Kristof where he went and he told me that Silas was occupied.

"What do you mean occupied?" I asked.

"He's making a piss on the side of the hut," he plainly replied.

When Silas returned, he asked me "Do Canadians have another way of saying go to the toilet?"

"Sure," I replied, "Sometimes men say 'I've gotta hang a rat.'"

"Hang a rat? What does that mean?" he asked. I made the appropriate or perhaps inappropriate, zipping, flopping, and shaking motions with my hand, then it all become very clear to Silas.

"Ahhhhh, hang a rat! Yeah, I like that!" he exclaimed. And as we trotted up and down the hills Silas practiced his new expression, bursting with laughter after each repetition. The German guy was also thrilled to learn some Canadian slang and joined Silas in his profanity session.

We soon reached the shabeen, which is the African version of the village pub. As expected, it was made of a mixture of dirt, grass, and cow shit and was being patrolled by half a dozen little wild pigs. We stepped inside the shabeen and found a number of Xhosa people, both men and women, inside including an old lady sitting in the corner smoking a foot-long homemade pipe that gave off a most unusual odour, perhaps a mixture of dirt, grass and...well, everything else seemed to me made of that! There was a wooden plank for a counter and behind it a Xhosa woman waiting to serve us.

"You're going to try some of the local Xhosa corn beer," Silas proudly exclaimed. The lady behind the counter passed over a large, rusted tomato juice can with a thick layer of froth on top. Silas sat us down then spilled a small amount of beer on the ground between us. "That is for the ancestors. They must be offered some before we drink," he said as he then took a sip. He motioned for the German to try some so he picked up the bucket and had a big swig.

"Not bad," he said passing the can to Ana. Ana brought the can to her lips, had a sip and nodded in agreement then passed it to me for my turn. It was very grainy, reminiscent of corn and didn't taste exactly like beer, but more like a mixture of beer and wine. We repeated this circle tasting until the bucket was finished, then Silas ordered up a round of more traditional brew – Castle Milk Stout, made in South Africa in wonderfully large 750 ml bottles. So we sat in the small hut drinking our beer, smiling at the locals and feeling fine.

Once we were finished that round our young guide put another cold one in our hands immediately, checked our eyes to ensure we were slightly inebriated, then announced, "Now it's time to dance!" The lady behind the bar fired up the battery powered boom box and the sound of Xhosa rock filled the smoky hut. Silas got us up into a circle, along with several of the ladies in the shabeen, and told us to dance however we liked. So we started stomping our feet and shuffled around in a circle. That circus went on for several revolutions when Silas announced, "Okay, now we're going to dance Xhosa style, do like me!" He switched to this groovy dance where he was pumping his right foot up three times and shuffling his left foot forward once per set, all the while nodding his head first to the right side then to the left. After a few circuits, we joined in and did our best to imitate. I glanced over at Ana, who has much better rhythm than I, and her attempts to do the dance were a perfect impression of a wounded pigeon. Kristof the German looked even more ridiculous, as was well over six feet tall, scrawny and presented a blur of knees and elbows. Fortunately there was no mirror inside the shabeen so I could not see how absurd I must have appeared. Silas must have decided to leave us with at least a shred of dignity so we were instructed to go back to doing our "own thing" to the music. So I reverted to the standard Canadian prairie shuffle, right foot left then left foot right, suitable to any beat, style or speed of music and definitely recommended for rhythmically challenged persons such as myself. After the song finished the dancing faltered and we all were there standing around in the smoky den. I noticed Silas had disappeared so I asked Kristof what happened to him.

"He's hanging out a rat somewhere," he informed me. Although not the grammatically correct usage of the slang, I certainly applauded his efforts. Silas soon returned, called for another round of beers then started up the music again. The ladies resumed dancing including one who had this huge hump on her back and a blanket wrapped around her. I knew it was either a serious deformity or perhaps a baby. Only seconds after I noticed this, the lady sat down, untied the blanket and out dropped a beautiful and very fresh young baby. Ana asked her if she could hold it and the lady gladly obliged. It was surprising that a baby could actually breathe under all that material, but it seemed to work quite exceptionally well judging by the baby's relaxed state. Ana cuddled the gorgeous little girl and looked over at me as if to say, "Don't I look wonderful with a little baby?" I agreed.

Our trusty guide Silas now appeared behind the counter switching cassettes in the boom box. From the speakers came a very steady, low, infectious drumming noise whose volume was slowly increasing. Silas hopped back to centre stage and announced, "Okay, listen – here's the beginning!" The drumming grew louder. "Oh yeah baby, here it comes!" he exclaimed. The drumming was joined by African chanting, which was getting steadily louder and clearly coming to a crescendo. Then there was a huge crash of cymbals, the instruments screamed to life and the frenzied beat took over the little mud hut.

"SUMMMMMMBODY, HANG ME A RAT!" Silas spurted as he leaped up and lost himself in the spastic pigeon dance, except at twice the speed of the first demonstration. I was proud of the lad's efforts to use this new bit of vulgarity, but realized that we needed another lesson to fine tune the usage. He will be sounding like a native speaker in no time.

Soon, it was time to go. A traditional Xhosa meal was being cooked for us back at the hostel and we didn't want to miss it. So we bid adieu to our new friends, paid for the drinks and followed Silas out into the darkness of the South African night. And it was pure darkness with not a single light to guide us apart from the pale quarter moon. We followed behind Silas in formation and tried our best not to trip on anything. Up and down the hills we went again, but this time three quarters pissed in complete darkness. At the crest of a hill Silas turned back and informed us, "Make sure you don't step into the really dark spots on the ground because those are holes."

"That works for the holes, but how do we see the cow shit?" questioned Ana.

"If your foot sticks to the path, that's cow shit," answered Kristof. That won a laugh from the group as we continued our late night stumble down the last hill and toward the bridge at the bottom, which we would have to cross to reach the hostel. With Silas in lead, Ana and I actually managed to make onto the bridge and nearly to the end without tripping.

Suddenly a high pitched scream erupted from the bridge behind us, followed by a flurry of Xhosa clicks, yips, and squeals. We all quickly turned around to see the German, rat in hand, spraying a stream over the side of the bridge, but doing a sideways shuffle, obviously trying to divert the stream. Silas yelled, "Hey, what are you doing? There's a lady down there shitting in the river and you just pissed on her head!" This was obviously what Silas translated from the Xhosa screams piercing the night. "Why didn't you tell me you had to hang a rat??" he asked Kristof, who was still shuffling, trying his best to finish up, "I would have told you not to piss over the bridge!" By this time both Ana and I were doubled over with laughter, nearly sprouting tears.

"I didn't know there was a lady down there, it's totally dark!" the German said.

"I can't believe you pissed on my people!" burst Silas. It was quite obvious that Silas, far from angry, was instead having a great laugh at the German's (not to mention the poor Xhosa girl's) expense. The German finally zipped up and we hustled out of there as fast as possible before the girl could scramble up the bank and find out who these horrible foreigners were.

Within minutes we had reached the safety of the hostel so we moved inside to find some food, and a few more beers!

And thus ends the tale of the Xhosa village tour.

****

Peaceful day in La Paz

At the time I really did not care for Bolivia. Compared to surrounding countries, the people were less friendly, the Spanish accent was much harder to understand, it was dirtier, and simply had a less positive vibe. But I recently realized that several of the most breathtaking photographs we have were taken there and when I think back, the memories I have of Bolivia are some of my most vivid. At the time, you really don't know which memories will stick and which will not. The following story is an example of some of the things that can happen in South America and a look at a less glamorous day on the road.

Ten days of early mornings, busy days, late nights, and an altitude of over 4000 metres can take its toll. Besides the stomach upset and the mild altitude sickness both Ana and I had both been experiencing, we were also having a lot of trouble sleeping at nights. But last night, in a superb hotel in La Paz, Bolivia, we had the best sleep we've enjoyed in weeks. And the best part was that we had absolutely nothing planned for today except to relax and prepare for our departure tomorrow on a big five day tour of the south west of Bolivia.

At around 8:35 I start to approach consciousness. I'm in the denouement of my dream where I had fought off a dozen terrorists with a Swiss army knife and saved my woman.

At around 8:40 I am conscious but have not yet opened my eyes. I'm listening to the sound of La Paz and to the sound of my wife's breathing. I can hear a large truck honking its horn repeatedly, almost in time to the man shouting, "Uvas! Uvas! Bananas! Bananas!" There is no hurry to get out of bed so I lay there and listen to the melody of the city.

At around 8:45 Ana stirs, says good morning, and gets up to check the time while I lay in bed absorbing sounds and expelling bad breath. We decide to go for breakfast, hoping to avoid the stale bread and cold coffee, which are inevitably fed to the late risers. After a breakfast of stale bread and cold coffee we return to the room to jump back into bed, listen to some music and read for a while, perfect activities for a lazy morning. After a volley of Sade and Mario Vargas Llosa, I head for the shower - left arm, left pit, left shoulder, upper back, right arm, right pit, right shoulder, rinse, left leg just reaching the foot when I hear Ana shouting something.

"What?" I holler.

Ana appears in the bathroom and says, "It's the tourist agency on the phone. Apparently some of the countryside people are planning a big protest tonight and might be barricading the road, so she thinks that we better get the bus to Oruro as soon as we can today in case the road gets blocked tomorrow and we miss our train connection. What should we do?"

"I guess we better go, we don't want to take any chances."

That was the end of our peaceful day. We quickly packed our bags, checked out, and stored our things with the hotel while we went out to finish up a couple things. Our first stop was the tourist agency to pick up train tickets. Next stop was the music shop to pick up a couple packages of strings for the brand new charango, a small ten stringed Bolivian guitar I had purchased the day before. On the way back to the hotel, we stopped at one of the witch vendors in the market to take a photo of the llama fetuses she was selling. She wanted me to buy one in exchange for the picture but I wasn't really hungry at the time; instead I gave her two Bolivianos and her large toothless grin indicated her satisfaction with the deal.

We called a taxi from the hotel and he pulled up in front of the doors in about twenty seconds. En route to the bus station we passed through a chaotic market where there were vendors selling mangoes, charangos, soap, rope, glasses of strange yellow liquid, huge bags of popped corn, fluorescent lamps, cocoa leaves, charms, yarns, and alpaca sweaters.

"Seis bolivianos," requested the taxi driver. I gave him the coins, which was the equivalent of about one American dollar, then gathered the bags and we proceeded into the station. It was remarkably peaceful, except for the sales representatives standing in front of each of the bus company kiosks, one humorously named Jumbo Aroma Bus Company, screaming destination names. "Oruro! Oruro! Santa Cruz! Arequipa!" We laid the bags down on the cleanest part of the floor we could find and Ana walked over to one of the kiosks (not Jumbo Aroma, that one looked a little risky) and bought tickets for the Oruro bus at 1:30. We then went through the exit door and waited beside the bus for someone to load our bags. A young snotty punk finally appeared and begrudgingly fired our backpacks into the bowels of the autobus. We asked him about the problem with the road blockades but he wasn't inclined to answer. We then asked the bus driver on board what was happening only to be told that the bus was not going anywhere since there was already a blockade just outside La Paz and nobody knew how long it would take for the police to sort it out.

"Well, that was nice of them to sell us tickets," I said to Ana, "do you want to sit on the bus for a few minutes until we get some more news?"

"Okay, we might as well," she replied.

We found our seats and sat down. After a few minutes, some snotty punk climbed aboard the bus and informed us that all services to Oruro were cancelled due to the road block, but that we should come back tomorrow and try again. Strangely enough, we could still hear the shouts of "Oruro! Oruro!" coming from within the station. We got off the bus, collected the bags, returned to the station, found some clean floor and bench, then sat down to consider our options. Once again, I guarded the bags while Ana put on her boxing gloves and went to get a refund on the tickets, which was surprisingly easy. Once she returned, she became the watcher of the bags while I went to several of the other kiosks to see if they had busses to Oruro. They all said no except one chubby lady who said they may have a bus at 1:30 and to check back at 12:00 to confirm. That gave us time to sit and stew over our options.

"How long can they possibly block a road for? Wouldn't the police just go and break it up?" Ana wondered aloud.

"Who knows? I talked to one guy over there who said this sort of thing happens quite frequently and it can take some time. Why don't we phone the tour agency and see what they recommend?" I said. Ana volunteered for the job and left to make the call but was back shortly to get some coins. The call would cost only two bolivianos but, as usual, the vendor did not have change, even for a ten boliviano note. This is certainly a common thread through Latin American countries, they never have change. The most important tip for traveling around Latin America is to have at least two kilograms of coins in your pocket at all times.

Ana returned shortly thereafter to report that the tour company was not answering the phone, which was hardly surprising. We had the distinct feeling that they had sold us the tour knowing full well that there was trouble in the countryside. What was our next move? Go back to the agency and demand a refund? Return to the hotel and wait until tomorrow? Sit in the bus station all afternoon waiting for news? Find a bar and get loaded? It is situations like this that are the best and the worst part of traveling. You cannot have a real adventure without surprises, unpredictability and hassles, where you have to make decisions in a foreign, unusual environment surrounded by locals who look a lot less stunned than you do. But hey, if you don't get your kicks that way, then take a nice Caribbean cruise where the biggest challenge of the day is waking up in time for bacon and eggs with the rest of the fatties.

As we sat pondering, a man wearing dark glasses approached us holding a ticket in his hand. We recognized him as one of the passengers on the original bus. He told us that he had found a company that was indeed sending a bus to Oruro and it was leaving in five minutes. We asked how it was possible that this company was going when all the rest had cancelled their services. He explained that this bus would be taking a back road shortcut to avoid the blockade. Ana and I looked at each other, telepathically weighed the pros and cons of embarking on this dodgy sounding journey, then Ana was off running to the kiosk to buy tickets. Ana elbowed through the little Bolivian mob and got us the last two tickets on the bus. *That's my girl*, I thought.

We rushed out to the bus, had our bags loaded, and found our seats. Although this was not the Jumbo Aroma Company it might as well have been. The dank air was thick with hot, sticky Bolivian body odour. The bus took off before many people had sat down but after several blocks, all bums had found seats except for two old Bolivian women standing at the back of the bus next to us. And they smelled horrible. I recognized the odour from the stands in the La Paz markets selling the llama fetuses and charms.

"They're witches," I whispered to Ana, "don't piss them off."

"I wasn't planning on pissing them off," she replied in a hushed voice.

I moved as far to the right as the seat would permit and nuzzled my face into the safety of Ana's perfumed neck. Every once in a while I looked over to make sure they weren't casting any spells on me for my insolence. The first witch lady was chewing something and had a small stream of black paste leaking out of the sides of her mouth. Neither of them was paying attention to me but the smell was almost making me retch. After a little while the bus conductor walked to the back and asked the ladies where their seats were. They said they didn't have seats or a ticket. He asked them where they were going. They didn't answer. He asked again, but got no response. Instead of risking a horrible afternoon hexing, he charged them five bolivianos each and left them alone.

We passed through the slums of La Paz with all its stray dogs, stray people, stray litter, and stray colours and were soon out of the city and into the countryside. The countryside was desolate and bleak, the barren altoplano periodically decorated by muddy villages where the only non-brown colours came from the signs advertising Pacena beer and Coca Cola. Everything was constructed from mud bricks and rebar, though most buildings were unfinished and there were very few people walking around the villages, making them appear eerily deserted. The only bit of action we did see was at village number seven, where an old Bolivian man was emptying his bowels on the side of the road, timing his release perfectly with the passing of our bus. In fact, this was a common occurrence in Bolivia – from the windows of busses, trains, and taxis we had witnessed dozens of Bolivians of all ages and sex relieving themselves on walls, streets and signposts. But once you have experienced the quality of Bolivian toilets, you too would probably shake free your inhibitions and let loose in the relative sterility of the open land.

When we got tired of looking at the brown out the window, we watched the Mexican movie that was playing on the televisions in the bus. I couldn't quite figure out the plot. The main character was a short, chubby Mexican man with a huge moustache and unbelievably white teeth, and the scenes alternated between him laying in bed singing ballads and a never-ending poker game where, between raking in chips, he was telling the rest of the bandito gamblers of his love for this woman who was married to his sworn enemy. Boredom overcame me and I fell asleep but was soon awoken by the sound of gunshots. The chubby Mexican was now wearing a sombrero and had just shot his enemy in the chest, multiple times. The dead man's wife looked sad for a moment, and then ran into the hero's arms, eyes wet with glee. Next scene, they were in bed together and he was singing her a love ballad. I felt sorry for her.

At that moment the bus slowed, stopped, and turned off the engine. Ana opened her window, stuck her head out, and reported that we were stuck in a huge queue of traffic. *Splendid*, I thought, *so much for the shortcut around the roadblock*. There was no room to turn around and the cars and busses continued to arrive behind us. I noticed that the witches were gone; their supernatural senses must have prompted them to get off sometime before. The other passengers started to look a little nervous and some were doing inventory on the amount of food and water they had brought with them.

"This looks like it may take a while," I sighed to Ana, "what do we have to eat?"

"Half a bottle of water and a bag of Peruvian corn nuts," she replied.

"Can I have a corn nut?" I asked.

Just then we saw a bus pull out of the queue ahead of us and drive down a rough dirt path to the left of the highway. The bus descended down a hill slowly and we notice there were five or six people chasing after the bus. They caught up to it, passed it, and ran ahead to a part of the road that looked as if it was piled high with dirt. They stood in the middle of the road and blocked the bus from progressing. The bus sat there for quite some time but it was quite far away so we couldn't see exactly what was happening, but there did seem to be some movement of people, perhaps the bus driver negotiating with the protesters. Then the people moved away and the bus lurched forward over the dirt pile, but it must have been larger than he estimated because the nose of the bus lifted into the air and the ass of the bus ground itself into the dirt. The brake lights flashed and the bus remained there, poised for launch, for several minutes. It then slowly reversed and resumed its horizontal position. There was again some movement of bodies, a few more minutes passed, and then the bus again lurched forward, this time faster, and plowed itself over the embankment leaving a large crowd of people behind it, evidently the passengers. The bus, having gained momentum, continued along the road and up the incline with all its passengers running wildly behind trying to catch up.

"Yeah!" somebody on our bus shouted. I hope that was not the go-ahead for us to attempt a similar maneuver as the bus had appeared to come very close to tipping over as it went over the embankment. We were happy when our bus remained in its place; obviously our driver was not a psycho.

About an hour passed. During that time many of the passengers' bladders had reached the bursting point so they had left the bus and watered the side of the road, some of them even having the courtesy of pointing their weenies away from the bus. Ana refused to drink any water, in case we became stuck here for the night. I was starting to have horrible thoughts. It would be very easy for bandits to come onto the bus and rob us of everything. Or the protesters could take some shots at the bus for trying to cross the blockade. Perhaps we should have cancelled our tour and played it safe in La Paz. I was then overjoyed when I felt the engine of the bus fire up and the bus begin to slowly move forward. I reached over Ana and stuck my head out the window. There were quite a number of Bolivians walking on the side of the road in both directions. I could see nothing except the line of vehicles ahead of us slowly creeping forward together in unison. We continued at this slow but steady pace for twenty minutes when we finally reached the source of the problems. There was a huge mob of perhaps two thousand people, all wearing blue rain ponchos shouting angry words at the bus. The roadblock, hundreds of medium sized rocks, had been pushed away and were scattered all along the side of the road. Nobody knew why they had removed the roadblock, but I was just glad to get out of there before the mob got the urge to push our bus over. A Bolivian man who had been sitting behind us returned to his seat after talking to the driver. He told us that there had actually been ten thousand people at the rally, which had eventually fizzled out. We never did find out what the rally was all about, we were just happy to be on our way to Oruro.

We passed more brown villages and more bleak countryside, then a few more brown villages. I pulled out our guide book to read about Oruro. It said that Oruro was one of the main cities in the region and quite a pleasant place to spend some time. "Maybe we can have a nice peaceful day in Oruro tomorrow, it sounds nice," I said to Ana. We were soon to reconfirm our belief that most guide books are crap.

The bus motored along the highway and at around 7:30 pm, we approached what appeared to be a huge mud flat, except that there were half built houses floating in it. The rain was coming down hard and the mud level seemed to be rising before our eyes. If there was an uglier suburb in the world, this one must have been a close second - it had the same mud brick buildings, same lack of colour, but a whole lot more mud. *Must be because of the rain*, I thought, *but can you imagine the dust storms around here when it's dry?*

The suburb turned into Oruro proper, and it was a true dump. Muddy, unpaved streets, mud brick buildings, beer signs, and shady looking characters hanging around shops selling car parts. I looked over at Ana and she was not impressed. "I can't believe we left our beautiful twenty dollar per night hotel room in La Paz for this filthy pueblo," she complained. I couldn't agree more. But, at the very least, we were here and we beat the roadblocks. At least we wouldn't miss our trip tomorrow.

We continued through the town and things actually began to improve a little. Not much, but a little. The dirt streets ended and the paved ones begun. There were a few more lights around and a lot more people. Soon, the bus just stopped in the middle of the road in front of a decrepit hotel and the driver told everyone to get off, which we did, then immediately grabbed our bags from the luggage hold and found a taxi. Ana had gotten the name of a decent local hotel from the lady who worked at the hotel reception in La Paz so we gave it to the driver and he drove us to the hotel. I paid him six bolivianos and we walked into the hotel, which was actually a very large building, rising into the sky at least ten stories. Inside the hotel we found two shocked looking girls working behind the desk and a family of Bolivians, from granny right down to kiddie, glued to the television in the reception watching The Simpsons in Spanish. "Dos cervezas Moe," I heard Homer say. Can this really be the global cultural connection that binds all countries, great and small, together? I hoped not.

"Buenas noches," we said in unison. Then we asked if they had a double room available. The first girl looked doubtfully through the register then said they did, and it was forty-one dollars. "No! Fifty-three!" blurted the second girl as she shot the first one a very dirty look.

"Fifty-three dollars American?" I asked astounded. How could that be? I told her that we had been sent by an agency in La Paz and that we should get their discount. She asked which agency it was and Ana showed her the business card.

"No," she said, "we don't work with that agency. I can give you a discounted rate of forty-one dollars but that's it." We were not going to back out into the rain looking for a better deal so we took it. We asked her if we could at least have a late check-out since our train didn't leave until 7:30 the next evening. "Sure," she replied, "but you have to pay another twenty-one dollars." We told her to forget it.

A young man appeared out of nowhere and motioned for us to follow him. He summoned the elevator with a concentrated push of the yellowed button and when it did finally arrive Ana tripped getting in as the elevator floor was about six inches higher than the ground. Fortunately, the elevator was so small there was no room to fall. The third floor is where the elevator stopped and as the doors opened we were struck with an indescribable, horrible smell, which was likely the result of disuse, cheap or perhaps no cleansers, and rotting building materials. We reached the room and were not immediately pissed off. It was very old and not particularly attractive, but it was good enough, and there was a television with lots of channels. The rumbling of our stomachs reminded us that we should dump our bags in the room and hunt for some food so we returned to the ground level, minding the tricky elevator floor, and asked the reception girls if there was a restaurant nearby. They told us there were two pizza joints, one around the corner and a block down and the other on the far side of the plaza the hotel faced. We stepped out into the rain and jog-walked around the corner, down a block and found ourselves standing in front of a Juan's Pizza sign and large aluminum door covering the restaurant front.

"Shit!" I blurted, "How the hell can those girls not know which places are open or closed?" We hustled through the rain back to the hotel when Ana pointed up and said, "Look!" The entire building was black except the light coming from our room.

"We're the only people in the hotel?" asked Ana in disgusted amazement. "I can see why it was such a problem giving us a late check-out," she said sarcastically. We had that familiar feeling of a royal tourist-screwing.

We continued across the plaza and found the second pizza joint, thankfully open for business. We found ourselves a table and were soon attended to by the waiter who took our order of a large pizza, a diet Coke for Ana and a nice beer for me. The drinks arrived and we finally had a chance to relax and collect our thoughts. Soon, four teenage girls burst onto the scene, took seats at the table next to us and all lit up smokes. The waiter arrived and took their order of one large coke and one large beer. Several filthy grey clouds of smoke later, the waiter returned with the bottles and four glasses. He placed one glass in front of each of the girls then half filled each with coke. To my horror, he then filled each of the glasses with the foamy beer. The girls put straws into their glasses, gave a stir, and started sucking away. This incredible disrespect for lager and the plumes of smoke convinced us to change tables so we went to the other side of the restaurant.

The pizza turned out to be very good and we enjoyed our meal then returned to the hotel, only to find that there was no hot water for a shower. After three trips down to reception and some shocking Spanish profanity, we finally got enough hot water for a quick shower.

I climbed into bed after scanning for bedbugs, briefly wondered what tomorrow had in store for us, and then dropped into sweet unconsciousness.

****

Dance lessons from a six year old

Suriname is a spectacular, special and truly undiscovered country. We lived there for a short time and had the rare opportunity to make a trip deep into the jungle and stay with a Maroon tribe in their village. This was probably as far off the beaten track as I have ever been in my travels and it was an extraordinary experience.

The images and thoughts from the evening danced and swayed and pulsed in my brain, refusing my body's demand for sleep. As I lay in my hammock in the middle of the Suriname jungle, trying to make sense of things, I feel exhausted from the fury of the dancing and the strength of the jungle moonshine I had consumed. The gentle sway of the hammock seems to keep the room from spinning. As this is my last weekend in Suriname, I want to relish this moment.

My wife and I had been stationed in the capital city Paramaribo for about two months working on a business improvement project for a big oil company and during that time had ventured into the jungle on several occasions, learning a bit more about this fascinating country each time we traveled. The country was a myriad of cultures, religions and quite unlike any place I had ever experienced. Each day brought intriguing new discoveries and incredible sights. But tonight's experience gave me a single image which seemed to embody all that I had learned.

It was a six year old boy and he was dancing like nothing else in the world mattered. He kept me entranced as he worked his jiggy across the wooden floor boards of the jungle dance floor. He appeared to be the youngest of a small group of dancing boys and was dressed in what looked like blue pyjamas, which immediately conjured images of Hugh Hefner. That limber little boy was throwing down moves like I'd never seen – feet moving together in small jumps, body pulsing in unison to the beat of the drums, head swaying, frantically trying to keep up with the torso. He vibrated around the floor to the music, like a bean dancing atop a powered subwoofer turned up much, much too loud. He didn't actually move his feet, yet somehow seemed to hover and float as his body throbbed to the sounds. The other boys were amazingly rhythmic but it was this one boy who captured my gaze and wouldn't let go. Before long, I had joined in the dancing and did my best to emulate the smooth moves of the jungle boy. I felt in my heart that I had somehow been possessed by the beats, controlled by the jungle rhythms, overcome by the spirit of Suriname and completely conquered by the magic of the Amazon.

In reality, I'm pretty sure I looked like a spastic fool. My white, Scandinavian heritage did not bless me with much natural rhythm, though I am quite proficient at drinking large quantities of Danish schnapps.

The rustic, rampant rhythms were produced by a band of five young boys, each playing a different sort of drum. The music began with one drum, one hard pounding drum. It was then joined by another, then another joined in and soon all five drummers were furiously hammering their instruments. The beat infected all who were there, but the first to respond to the call of the drums were the five little boys, lead in style by the energetic young swinger.

As I too danced, I remembered an experience at home in Canada many years before. It was a jungle party of sorts; at least that was the theme of the bar for the evening as the organizers had draped green plastic vines throughout and adorned the table tops and bar with life-sized plastic monkeys and bunches of yellow wax bananas. The patrons were of course dressed in their best "Tarzan and Jane" garb including leopard print mini-skirts (or maxi-belts, depending on how you looked at it), fur underwear and bare, hairy chests. I too fell into a trance that night as I danced to the techno beats exploding out of the giant sound system. It seemed wonderful and deep at the time, but looking back now, from here, it was simply comedy.

Now I lay here in my hammock. The room is spinning one way and my mind is spinning the other. I could have never predicted the effect a mere nine weeks in Suriname would have on me. But is it not always that way with travel? Quite often when our expectations of a place are high, we leave unusually disappointed and wondering if perhaps we should have gone somewhere else. It's when our expectations of a place are low that the potential for amazement is the greatest.

I think back to three days before. Our canoe slid gracefully into the muddy groove worn into the bank from a thousand other launches and dockings. Despite being narrow and overburdened with gear, the vessel had easily and solidly navigated my wife and me through twenty miles of the Upper Suriname River. There were several others in the boat, including our Surinamese friend Nesta who had arranged the trip to this Maroon village called Jaw Jaw to transport some supplies to her friend, the chief. The Maroons are the descendents of the runaway African slaves who were originally brought from Africa to work on the plantations owned by the Dutch colonists in Suriname.

We were met at the shoreline by a hundred white eyes and a thousand white teeth. The naked village children gathered anxiously on the muddy banks to greet their friend and see what gifts she had brought. There were not disappointed with the payload, which included picture books, candy and toys, but they were somewhat surprise to see two foreigners staring back at them from the canoe with interest.

We clumsily lurched our way out of the skinny dugout canoe, nearly falling into the water, which I would later discover was full of piranha. Nesta led us up to the village and showed us to a small cabin that had been constructed for guests of the chief. After dropping off our bags, Nesta took us for a walk through the village, which consisted of 500 people and almost as many huts. During our walk, we visited some of the older ladies making cassava bread and were offered samples, which were lacking in flavour but sported a most pleasurable texture. The villagers communicate together in their native language but many also speak Dutch, a leftover from colonial times. We also learned that men are allowed to have several wives, but with this privilege came the responsibility of building each new wife her own hut and giving her a full set of dishes. The wives would sleep in their own huts but cook for their communal husband in a communal kitchen. I giggled silently to myself as I wondered how well this system would work in North America.

After our walk, we spent the afternoon swimming with the village kids in the river as well as fishing for piranha in the same water, which seemed rather risky to me. Unlike the children, at least I was wearing swim trunks to protect the dangly bits from attack, which offered some comfort. And as a lifetime fishing enthusiast, I was thrilled to actually catch a piranha.

After dinner that night, which Nesta and her friends prepared, we gathered in the main village hut for a special treat. The local band from a few villages away would be there to play traditional African drum music. It seemed that the whole village turned out for the event. As one would imagine, there is not normally a great deal to do after dark in the middle of the jungle. The village did have a diesel generator used to generate light until 8pm but for the show the village chief authorized the generator's use until 10pm to keep the lights going for the party.

And what a party it was! The drummers, the dancers, the smiles and the frenzied release of jungle energy, were all pulsing in time to the chirps of ten thousand tiny faceless Amazon creatures. But most importantly, that little boy whose moves I will never forget.

Many skills can be studied and learned. I believe that dancing cannot. But every time I find myself dancing, I think of that boy and wonder where he is and what he could be doing at that moment.

And I hope in my heart that he is dancing.

****

The Plural of Platypus

I struggled with whether I should include this story in the collection as I feared it was one of those "had to be there" experiences, but in the end I included it, mainly in the hopes that my experimentation with sarcastic, funny dialogue would entertain. Plus, I love the title of this story!

"The Tablelands Tour?" I asked aloud, reading a brochure, as Ana and I sat in a Cairns, Australia guesthouse one morning wondering what to do with ourselves for the next couple of days. "It says there's a good chance of spotting platypus since one of the days involves a canoe trip around a dammed lake," I said.

"Don't start swearing so early in the morning," she replied.

Decision taken, we signed up with the lady at reception, an American woman named Michelin who seemed to have an endless reserve of physical energy, especially when used for talking. She told us to be ready at 7:30 the following morning for pickup.

Fast forward to 7:28 the next morning to find me preparing my first cup of the hot black stuff consciousness is made of.

"Are you sure you have time for that?" my dear wife asked me.

"For sure, these tour companies are never on time," I replied confidently. Exactly two minutes later a bus screeches to a halt in front of the guesthouse with "Tablelands Tour" painted across it. With a slight tear in my eye and the beginnings of a nice caffeine withdrawal headache that only a true coffee addict can appreciate, I poured the morning magic down the drain and we walked out to the bus.

"Hellllloo!! You must be Kris and Ana!" the enthusiastic or perhaps slightly overeager tour guide hollered.

"That's us," Ana replied. I stuck my index finger up to confirm that I was indeed one of us and mostly awake.

"Great, my name is Emma and I'm the guide. Jump aboard and find yourselves some seats, we have to be at the next hostel in three minutes!" Emma said. Our bums hit the vinyl, Emma's foot hit the accelerator, the rubber hit the road, and the pedestrian ahead of the bus hit the dirt. Three minutes and several two wheeled corners later we were in front of the Pirate's Cove backpacker hostel. I felt pity in my empathetic heart as I looked through the hostel kitchen window to see some poor sod pour his coffee down the drain then head out to the bus.

This was the start of the first day of the two day tour. By the end of the first day I was convinced that we had made a big mistake. Our guide, while extremely friendly, knowledgeable and likable, had the remarkable ability to talk non-stop, not even taking the time to breathe. I can normally overcome a chatterbox by simply switching off mentally and enjoying the scenery. But she was also able to remember every person's name and ensured that we were all included in the conversation. "So, Kris, what did you and Ana do last night?" she asked. "Bill, what do you think of Australia?" was another one, as well as "Eva, what other countries have you been to?" By the end of the day I knew more about these people than I know about some members of my family. This system of indiscriminate inclusion also applied to the short forest walks we undertook.

"Ooohhh, there's a rare bush lizard!" Emma hissed with maximum effect and minimum volume so as not to disturb the little beast. This was the second of the bush walks and, despite trying my best to enjoy the trip, was not really into it. We had all been huddled into a group and instructed to direct our gaze down Emma's arm, over her fingers, through twenty feet of rain forest shrubberies, and onto this beautiful reptilian specimen. I summoned all my optical strength to see the creature but I just couldn't.

"What colour is it?" I asked Ana.

"Green and brown," she replied.

"The whole bush is green and brown, how can you see it?" I asked, annoyed.

"It just moved, did you see that?" she said.

"No"

"Well, don't worry, it's not that exciting."

"Can everybody see the lizard?" Emma asked. A few bored responses. "Well, can you all see it? Mark, can you see it?" she asked.

"Yah, I see it," said Mark.

"How about you John, can you see it?" she probed.

"Yep, there it is," he said confidently.

I knew somebody was lying. These two guys were looking in completely different directions. Emma went down the line asking each individual if they could see the lizard, all nodding enthusiastically, until she got to me, hiding behind Ross the American trying not to be seen, obviously not as successful as the invisible lizard.

"Kris, can you see the lizard?" she asked, ensuring I didn't feel left out.

"No, not really," I replied, shamefacedly. Everybody looked at me, the only kid in class busted for not doing his homework. I was the kid that couldn't throw the medicine ball, or climb the rope ladder, or conjugate the bloody French verb "ser". The poor bugger the other kids look at and make that "tch, tch" sound when he displays yet again his inability to keep up with the rest of the class.

"It's just over there, about twenty feet, sort of brownish and green," she encouraged.

"That's all right, I trust you," I said, desperately trying to get her off my case.

"Aw, c'mon, it's just over there. Look harder," she persisted.

"Yeah, c'mon Kris it's just over there, can't you see it?" somebody asked. All of a sudden, they were all on me, encouraging me and my poor vision, pointing their fingers (in slightly different directions) trying their best to help the poor little blind kid. "Kris! Kris! Kris! Kris!" I imagined them chanting as I squinted my lids closer and closer together until I felt my contact lens dangerously close to launching out of my eye and sticking on someone's cheek. I was Superman with X-ray vision. I was wearing super spy glasses. I was a great bald eagle spotting a field mouse three miles away.

Kris Olson

"There it is!" I lied, "I see it now!" Everybody cheered and congratulated me. Emma smiled and looked skyward, as if to say "Another happy customer." I wanted out of there.

The remainder of the day included ogling a few waterfalls, a swim in a freshwater pond, and a drive by a sugar factory, where we were entertained with the story of the disastrous introduction of the South African cane toad to Australia. I made sure to nod my head enthusiastically whenever anybody asked me anything, and I was able to make it to the end of the day more or less anonymously.

That evening turned out quite nice, as Emma left us alone to mingle with each other at our outpost home for the night, a comfy wood-built lodge called On the Wallaby. I had a nice chat with Ross the American, who I initially mistook for a shell shocked Vietnam vet judging by his camouflage clothing, wiry frame and inky black tattoo on his arm, which was a perfect replication of an inky black splotch. But after hearing his outrageously loud giggly laugh and noticing his effeminate mannerisms I decided I was probably wrong – he was likely a university professor. I also met Shayne the Welshman who had stringy red hair and buggy marijuana eyes that seemed to move independently at times. He also reeked of fried bacon, constantly. Additionally, there were a few Germans, a few English, and a Scottish fellow who sold insurance for a living and reckoned Australia was the best country in the world. At one point in the evening I was sitting at the long wooden table beside a young Canadian guy named Mark and across from a Swedish couple.

"What's your last name?" I asked Mark, striking up a conversation.

"Gustafson," he replied.

"You're kidding! My mom's maiden name is Gustafson too!" I replied, amazed.

"Yes, that's our last name," said the Swede across the table.

"Sorry?" I said to him.

"You just said Gustafson, that's our name," he explained.

"You've got to be kidding me! Mark just told me his name is Gustafson, and that's my mom's maiden name as well," I answered.

So there we were. Four Gustafsons at one table, and the first non-family Gustafsons I had ever met in my entire life. We celebrated this ancestral bond by drinking a few beers, after which I excused myself and left for bed, determined to avoid a hangover that would make the next day's task of defending myself against the tour guide's friendly onslaught much more difficult.

The morning began with a hearty feed of fresh fruit, eggs and bacon, which I saw Shayne the Welshman eyeing ravenously. Once finished, Emma announced that the morning activity would be a mountain bike ride to a nearby lake where we could either go swimming or do a short hike. Thank *Good*, I thought, *a nice solitary bike ride with no guided commentary*. We each selected a bike outside then off we went. The day began a little rainy but that soon cleared up and we were able to enjoy a lovely ride on a paved road through thick green forest. We soon arrived at the lake, jumped off the bikes, and Ana and I set out for a hike around the lake. Along the way, we joined up with Mark, the Canadian fellow from Vancouver and we got onto the topic of Anglo-French relations in Canada.

"I've been to Montreal," he began, "and I met a lot of nice Quebeccers. But I also met a few jerks. One night I was in the city centre looking for a particular restaurant I heard was good. I was having trouble finding it so I asked a fellow on the street if he knew where it was. 'It where it ahs always bin, dey aven't moved it,' he replied, annoyed, in his thick Quebeccer accent. So I asked a lady who was walking nearby and she said, 'Why should I tell, eef you do not already know?' she answered. Such lovely people. I eventually just gave up and went to Burger King."

We moved on to discussing some of our traveling stories as we walked together around the lake. "I've learned some new slang words for Canadians," he said, "I was in a bar one night talking to some English people and when they asked where I was from I said, 'Canada'. One of them said, 'Oh, so you're a frozen Yank!' Another night, same scene, but this time I was talking with a group of Americans. When they asked what part of the States I was from I said, 'Canada'. One of them said, 'Oh, so you're an American Pom!' After that I decided to stop talking to people in bars."

At the end of our walk we went for a quick swim in the crystal clear freshwater lake then hopped back on our bikes and returned to the lodge. We had lunch together then were back in the bus with Emma barrelling down the highway towards a different lake where we would be partaking in a canoeing adventure and searching for the mysterious and shy platypus. The lake was created for the purpose of an irrigation reservoir, as the area was very prone to drought, as it was in currently and as a result the water level was quite low. There were a few cabins around the shoreline and a large number of standing deadwood growing out of the lake, creating a rather eerie sight.

"Has everyone here canoed before?" Emma asked. As usual, there was a flurry of enthusiastic nodding and Emma issued paddles to each of us then directed us to pair up, grab a canoe, and get onto the water. Ana and I picked up one of the canoes and launched it and ourselves without too much trouble. We paddled out fifty metres and turned to watch the rest of the people launching their canoes. Among the several reluctant pairings were the tall German girl and Shayne the Welshman. They somehow managed to launch the canoe without capsizing and were soon afloat and paddling madly.

"Paddle on the left! No, no, paddle on the right, we're going the wrong way!" he shouted from the back of the canoe. I looked on to enjoy the frenzy underway and knew that this guy had never been in a canoe in his life. The laws of physics dictate that the motions of the paddler in the back of the canoe, the Welshman in this case, will determine in which direction the canoe travels. His experiences in motor vehicles obviously led him to believe that he provided the power while the front paddler chose direction.

"You goddamn idiot, you don't know what the hell you're doing!" she screamed back at him, "Look at how the other people are paddling you dummy!"

"Left! Left!" he screamed at her hysterically, "Paddle harder on the left!"

"Shut up! Shut up!" she grunted as she paddled wildly on the right.

Left to right, right to left, splashing and shouting, they progressed across the lake slowly, erratically and loudly. Eventually they caught up to our congregation of canoes and the German girl said something in German to one of the other Germans in a different canoe. Then she said in English, "Get me away from this guy!" She transferred canoes with the German fellow and he was left to struggle with the Welshman.

We paddled ahead across the lake and into a channel then slalomed around the standing deadwood. We saw and heard many colourful birds but unfortunately no platypus. The channel eventually ended in a bank of muddy flats. Emma instructed the group to paddle to shore, get out and pull the canoes up onto the mud so they wouldn't float away when we went for our short hike. As Ana was at the front of our canoe she was the first to get out – and sank up to her knees in smelly mud. "Can you pull the canoe up a bit?" I asked. I was then able to get out of the canoe and sink merely up to my ankles, what a lovely wife I have.

Most of the people decided to go barefoot so we all lined up behind Emma and she led the way. We walked across the muddy flats, over a mostly dried up creek, and up a hill into a thin forest. Emma stooped and picked something off the ground then laid it on a large flat rock and instructed us all to gather around. "This," she began, "is a dried up cane toad." It was certainly toad shaped and definitely dried. She went on to tell us a story about this ninety year old couple she had seen on television whose favourite hobby was to sit on the balcony and watch the toads mating. Perverts. We then continued along the forest path.

After a few minutes of marching along the path like kiddies on a potty parade, we heard a voice scream, "Emmmmaaaaaaaa!! Heeelp!!" We thought somebody had been attacked by a snake or wild boar or, judging by the horrific scream, perhaps a rhinoceros. It turned out it was the American Ross, who had wandered about ten feet off the path and thought he was lost. Somebody said, "Jesus Ross, we're right over here, take it easy!" Ross stepped back on the path, emitted a huge sigh of relief, and continued on the trail walking directly in the footsteps of the person in front of him.

A short while later, we reached a small stream where Emma showed us that the creek bed was littered with special oxidized rocks the Aborigines used for painting their faces. She said, "It's not just kiddies that get their faces painted, give it a go!" The assembly of gentle folk once again paired off and started mixing paints on the flat rocks. It was quite simple, just dip the rock in water and rub it in circles on a larger rock, adding more water as required until a nice pasty paint was produced. And different rocks produced different colours of paint, from a deep Indian red to magnificent gold to sea blue. I mixed up a colourful palette as Ana was desperately trying to remove the caked mud from her toes and feet, creek-manicure style, as she has a severe allergy to dirt and grime. The symptoms usually include restlessness, a foul temper and extreme agitation, so I just stayed out of her way. When she had finished scraping the last fleck of mud out of her toes I sat her down on a rock then started plastering the paints on her face. I did the traditional furious red war stripes down her cheeks, and then filled it in with other ferocious, menacing colors and patterns until she resembled a war chieftain ready to wage war on some unworthy tribe. It was then my turn. I sat facing toward Ana as she dipped her fingers into the colours and dragged them across my face. I was an Aboriginal warrior and my Indian wife, coveted by all but consort of solely me, was readying me for the big battle. The rainbow scars across my face would strike fear and paralysis into the hearts of my enemies and I would surely lead our tribe to victory. "Aaaagghhhhhhhhh!" I roared in my inner mind, a roar like an enraged lion, like a silverback pouncing on an unworthy rival, like thunder. As she finished I stood up, took the small mirror she had and held it up to my face to see the fearful war mask, ready to emit an unholy death cry. Looking back at me was a red, smiling happy face on my forehead, a triangle on my nose, and sperm-like squiggles swimming down my cheeks. This instantly hauled me back to reality and I looked around the assembled group to see a multitude of ridiculous looking paint jobs. I guess it takes some practice to get the war look just right.

Emma soon gathered us and we set back on the forest trail to return to the canoes. Ross the American, terrified of getting lost, walked in her footsteps the whole way while the rest of us simply enjoyed the stroll through the forest. We reached the swampy mess of a shore and started launching the canoes. A couple of the other men and I were helping people push off their canoes, and in the process sinking knee deep in the thick mud. As we were pushing away I noticed Shayne the Welshman standing on the only dry bank skipping rocks across the water, oblivious to the tasks underway. "Hey Shayne," one of the other guys yelled, "Are you having fun?" He smiled back and waved. He didn't get it.

There were only two canoes left, ours and Emma's. I asked Emma if she wanted help launching hers. "No, that's okay," she replied, "I'll get Shayne to push us out." I pushed our canoes out as far as it would go then climbed in and crawled down to the stern. Ana then jumped in the front of the canoe, freshly manicured feet again covered in mud and a disgusted look on her face, and we pushed ourselves off the bank. Once in the open water we turned to see how Emma and Shayne were making out. Emma, planted in the thick mud, was shoving with all her strength on the canoe, which appeared to be quite lodged in the mucky bank. Simultaneously, gentleman Shayne was desperately trying to pull a dead tree out of the ground. The rotten roots gave way and he heaved it out of the mud, dragged it over to the canoe, and toppled it onto the bank, creating a nice little tree bridge he could tip toe across to reach the canoe without getting his feet dirty. As Emma was pushing the canoe into the water, sneaky Shayne walked past her on top of the tree and made himself comfortable in the stern of the canoe, just as Emma had finally wrenched it free of the mud. Looking extremely perturbed, our brave tour guide bit her lip, jumped into the front of the canoe and pushed off.

We watched transfixed from our own canoe as the predictable happened. Wild flailing of paddle from the back of the canoe as Emma shouted at Shayne from the front trying to direct his random paddling as she did her best to steer from the bow. I couldn't help laughing. They meandered from side to side but seemed to be making progress so we turned and began paddling our way back through the narrow lake.

"Look!" cried Ana from the front of the canoe. I looked ahead and saw something swimming toward us on top of the water leaving a perfect v-shaped wake.

"What is it?" I asked Ana.

"It looks like an otter with a duck's head," she answered excitedly, "and the ass looks like a duck's head too!"

"It must be a platypus" I said, "Cool!" The platypus swam by our canoe, only metres away, giving us a close-up look at him. It is a very strange, no, frightening creature indeed when one cannot tell the arse from the head. As it past by us we heard a splash and it was gone, submerged into the muddy depths.

Ten minutes later we were passing some scarcely submerged deadfall when I saw a small splash and dark fur. "Look Ana, there's another one!" I shouted. And mere seconds later yet another platypus broke the surface, much to our delight. I informed Ana, "Now we've seen three, uh, uh, what's the plural for platypus? Platypie? Platypusen? Platypice? Or maybe it's Platypussies?"

"Okay, that's enough!" she said, disgusted. I laughed and kept paddling. The sun was now beating down upon us and I could feel my beak starting to smoke. Luckily a strong wind had blown up, which kept the heat manageable but made the paddling more difficult as it was pointed directly against us. After some hard paddling we made it across the lake and back to the shore where we had begun the trip. Almost all of the other paddlers had arrived and put their canoes away. We reached the shore, jumped out of the boat onto the grassy shore and hauled it out of the water. Ana immediately found a rock to sit on and began furiously cleaning her toes. Then we all waited together for Shayne the Welshman and Emma the Patient to arrive, which they eventually did.

After locking up the canoes, Emma led us up the hill and back to the bus for the trip home. I had my last laugh of the day when I turned to my dear wife who was sporting clean, white, mud-free feet, and saw her looking with horror at the German guy walking ahead of us who had thick clumps of gooey mud caked all the way from his toes up to his knees, obviously oblivious to the filth and certainly not interested in cleaning up before getting into the bus. I could see her bite her tongue as he jumped into the bus, now with bits of grass stuck to the mud, and left a trail of muck and weeds on the floor all the way to the back of the bus where he plopped down and fell asleep.

After a short stop at the lodge to pick up our luggage we were on the road and soon arrived back in Cairns. Emma pulled up in front of our guesthouse where she got out, helped us with our bags, and said good-bye. We gave her a big hug and expressed our gratitude for such an unforgettable trip. She drove away and we walked into the guesthouse, where I immediately went to the kitchen, made a big cup of coffee, and sat down for a relaxing mug.

****

South Africa Shark Scare

Great white sharks are enormous animals. You can watch "Shark Week" all you want on Discovery Channel but you just cannot get an appreciation for the size of these creatures until you see them in real life. Ana and I went on a cage diving expedition to get in the water with these beasts but Mother Nature had different plans for us.

Knock, knock.

"Hey, you guys, you have to get going now if you want to make the shark dive," summoned Joe as she knocked on our hostel room door. Joe was one of the girls who worked in Hermanus Backpackers hostel where Ana and I were staying in Hermanus, South Africa, the whale watching capital of the country, and great white shark territory!

We quickly gathered our gear, locked the room, jumped in our rental car (actually "car" is generous – it was more like a tomato can with wheels, branded a "Chico") and we began our short journey to a neighbouring town called Gansbaai. After forty minutes of splendid coastline driving we arrived. The instructions from Joe were, "Drive to Gansbaai, take the exit to Kleinbaai Harbour, then look for a lady named Christine who should be wandering around waving her arms". Sure enough, just as we had parked our little Chico in the harbour parking lot, this lady walked over to us waving her arms.

"Are you Christine?" asked Ana.

"That's me. You're here for the shark diving?" countered Christine

"Yup," I replied.

"Great! Go over to the Carcharias shack and get your waiver forms filled out."

"Hmmm, waiver forms?" I said to myself. As soon as we reached the shack and joined the rest of the people who had arrived before us, a white form on a clipboard was passed around for our careful review, which was met by most with the standard backpackers blank hangover stare and a "Look, just where do I sign?" That task completed, we were given the safety briefing by Christine.

"Morning folks! Glad to see you all here and welcome to the Great White Shark Cage Diving Adventure! You will be going with Captain Brian McFarlane and his divemaster Ughhh."

"Sorry, what's his name," somebody asked.

"Ughhh," she repeated.

To the uninitiated, this would have either sounded like nonsense or perhaps some sort of Neanderthal greeting. But, knowing that the local language Afrikaans is very similar to Dutch, and having spent a considerable amount of time in the Netherlands surrounded by Cloggies making bizarre guttural barking noises to each other, I reckoned the guy had an Afrikaans name that the English language just couldn't handle.

Christine continued, "The most dangerous part of your day is going to be leaving and returning to the harbour as the weather and winds in this area are very unpredictable. Captain Brian is a professional shark handler and you have absolutely nothing to fear from the sharks. If any of you do happen to get seasick while on the boat, just remember that if you are able to heave it over the side into the water, that will help with the chumming effort and Captain Brian will offer you a 5% discount on the trip. Okay, you're all set."

Thus began our adventure. Ana, me and the other eight people walked down to the dock and climbed aboard "Predator", the shark diving boat. It was not difficult to find as there was a huge steel mesh cage hanging from a large beam and pulley mechanism on the back of the boat. Captain Brian was waiting for us and helped each of us on board. He was a tall, solidly built, sea-worthy looking fellow whose smile lines surely held a thousand tales.

"Welcome aboard the Predator! My name is Brian McFarlane and this is my divemaster Ughhh. Everybody find a seat and we'll be off shortly." Divemaster Ughhh was somewhat shorter than the captain with a slightly darker complexion. He didn't speak much, but when he did it was with a very thick Afrikaans accent. He looked like he knew a lot of jokes.

Once everybody was seated Captain Brian hit the switch, the engines roared to life and we were off to sea. And what a beautiful day it was! The sun was bright and there were only a few clouds to the west, with hardly a breath of wind. "This is the most beautiful day you can hope for." said the captain, "We're going to see a lot of sharks today." After about twenty minutes we arrived at an underwater reef where several other shark dive boats were anchored. The captain continued past these boats with the expectation that the sharks would be off the reef in the morning, so he found the spot he wanted, anchored the boat, dropped the cage, and started preparing the bait. As he reeled out several long strips of strange brown gut chunks, he explained to us that shark livers were the key to attracting the great whites. He packed these livers into a burlap-like bag, sealed it then threw it into the floating cage. He repeated this process but instead stuffed the bag with various chunks of mako sharks then threw it into the cage. He then told us that it would take up to half an hour for the scents to work their way out into the ocean and begin attracting the sharks so instead of waiting, he would release the cage, attach it to the anchor rope, and we would make a quick side trip to Dyer Island, home to a colony of 60,000 Cape seals.

Captain Brian cranked up the engine again and off we sped towards the islands in the distance. As we approached the island a horrible smell came over the boat. I thought perhaps it was the pail of chum at the back of the boat boiling in the sun but the intensity of the odour increased the closer we came to the island. "What do you guys think of the smell of seal shit, eh?" laughed Captain Brian, which explained the mystery. It was easy to see how the shit could accumulate, considering the small rocky island we were approaching was blanketed with barking, coughing, howling and obviously shitting, brown Cape seals. The noise of the creatures was incredible! Besides the seals on the island were hundreds, no, thousands of them swimming and diving through the waters on all sides of the boat. Some were small babies, others were large cows, but all appeared to be enjoying themselves immensely as they leaped out of the water then dove deep only to return again to the surface, rear their heads out of the water and bark "Hello!" to these idiotic tourists hanging off the edge of the boat gawking at the show before them. Captain Brian piloted the boat slowly down the length of the islands so we could see the immense number of seals on this little island. He explained that during the winter months you would not see a single seal in the water since during that season the great whites would cruise up and down the island looking for seals to eat. During the current season all the sharks had moved to the reef area to breed and therefore the seals were safe and they knew it. But even when the sharks are around the island the seals still need to visit the sea to find fish to eat, and that is when the great whites got lucky. "One day," he said, "I was here with a boatload of tourists and we saw twelve seals taken by great whites." I hoped to myself that there had been a few Greenpeace loonies on that trip.

We could have quite easily stayed there for hours watching the playful seals but we had sharks to find, so Captain Brian turned the boat around and we cruised back towards the anchored cage. Approximately half way back, first mate Ughhh jumped to the bow of the boat pointing to the starboard side hollering, "Whales! Whales!" A couple hundred metres from the boat were two Southern Right Whales with their backs protruding out of the water. South Africa law does not allow powerboats to come within 300 metres but since we were already well within that range Captain Brian cut the motors and we drifted forwards until we came to a halt. The whales must have decided to investigate us because they turned toward the boat, dropped just below the surface and moved directly towards us. Seeing a whale from shore can give you an idea of how huge they are, especially if you are fortunate enough to see them breaching, but when two fully grown whales swim directly beneath your boat you get a new appreciation for their size. They were probably twice the length of the boat and even their tail width was half the length of the boat. A chorus of "Ooohs", "Ahhhs", and camera shutter clicks came from all the thrilled passengers aboard. As they passed beneath us Captain Brian said, "If they decide to surface now, we could be in a bit of trouble." Luckily, once they were well clear of the boat the whales surfaced and played on top of the water. At that point we could have gone straight back to shore and I would have been very happy with the tour. But our host said that it was time to go see the sharks so off we raced to the main course.

We reached the cage and Ughhh tied the anchor rope back onto the boat then repositioned the cage directly beside the boat. Captain Brian pulled out a rubbery seal imitation named Gladys, tied it to a rope then threw it out into the water. "The great whites will see Gladys all the way from the bottom and think it's a seal," he explained, "and when they surface we'll lure them towards the boat with a piece of shark meat tied to the end of another rope." He also threw another pail of chum into the water...and we waited. Fifteen minutes past. Thirty minutes past. Captain Brian pulled out a mobile phone and called one of the other shark boats anchored near the reef. They had seen no sharks yet. An hour passed. Two hours passed. Captain Brian would call the other boats every fifteen minutes for an update. One of them had seen a couple sharks, but they had disappeared after seeing the boat. Luckily, it was a warm day so most of the others on our boat were just sitting back enjoying the sunshine. "Don't worry guys, they will come. We just have to wait," said the Captain reassuringly.

Ughhh finally piped up, "If anybody wants to do a few laps around the boat, feel free as the sharks really like that. And if the girls do it naked, they get the trip for free!" Strangely, there were no takers.

Captain Brian decided that we would have lunch and give the sharks thirty minutes more before we tried a different location. So the sandwiches were handed out and eaten promptly by the hungry and increasingly anxious guests. As the thirty minutes passed, our trusty Captain made another couple calls and found out that two of the other boats by the reef had some "players", which is the word they use to describe great whites that aggressively go for the bait and stay around the boat for a long time, giving the cage diving tourists the show they were waiting for. "I can't believe it!" he said in an irritated manner, "I'm always the first guy to get sharks around here! I don't know what's going on." Ughhh pulled up the anchor and the dive cage and Captain Brian moved the boat over to the reef where the other boats were. With anchor and cage back into the water, they laced the water with a couple more pails of chum and we waited. And waited. Another thirty minutes passed. I noticed the wind starting to pick up. A few more phone calls, only to find that one of the other boats had three sharks circling it! "Jesus, I can't believe this!" said Captain Brian, exasperated, "I'm always the one who's inviting the other boats to join me after I've found the sharks! If we don't see anything soon we'll go and anchor beside that other boat and share their sharks. That guy owes me. I must have called him over to share my sharks a dozen times this season!"

After a few more minutes with no action our devoted Captain threw in the great white towel, pulled up the anchor and cage and powered us over next to the other shark boat interestingly called "The Shark Lady". By now the wind had not just picked up, it was really starting to howl and the sea was getting choppy. Anchor down, cage down, more chum, and we waited hard. I was standing on the viewing platform, which was a small second level over the cabin when I saw a very dark shadow approaching the boat. "Here comes one!" announced Captain Brian gleefully as he launched the piece of shark meat over the side. The shark approached from the port side with the dorsal fin slicing through the waves. And in all his infamous grey splendour surfaced the first great white shark I had ever seen in my life. The shark went for the bait but Captain Brian pulled it away just as the shark's eyes were rolling back and his huge mouth opening. "Oh yeah!" somebody from the boat shouted.

"Can we get the wetsuits on now to go in the cage?" asked a skinny Englishman.

"Yep, you two get those suits on," he directed towards the Englishman and a Dane who was standing next to him, "and make it quick as this is a nasty wind blowing up." The wind had gone from a howl to a near gale and the sea was starting to foam. The "Predator" was rocking wildly with the cage bashing up against it. I was still on the viewing platform holding tightly to the railing with one hand and my hat with the other when I saw another dark shadow approaching, except that this one was surely a small whale or...something, as it was much too big to be a great white. The shadow came up from the depths and towards the surface and I realised that it was no whale. It was a great white shark. And the beast was bloody enormous.

"Holy shit!" bellowed Ughhh, which grabbed everyone's attention as he radiated all characteristics of a seaman salty with experience and not easily impressed. Captain Brian saw the beast and threw the bait in its direction. As it hit the water the shark's huge jaws broke the surface and his eyes rolled back, expecting to consume this little morsel. The Captain pulled the bait away, but not fast enough. The shark clamped down on the meat and began a tugging match with our fearless captain. Somehow, Captain Brian managed to yank the bait, or at least most of it, from the jaws of the monster and it dove back down into the ocean then resurfaced and circled around at the back of the boat trying to figure out what happened to the rest of its meal. Several other sharks appeared and the captain continued throwing the bait out and tempting the sharks to bite. Sometimes they would surface and go for the bait while other times they followed the bait for a few seconds then shied away. I was quite surprised at how slow the sharks were moving. They appeared more to be pushing water like a barge rather than gliding through it. But I was to soon found out just how fast they could move it they wanted to.

A medium sized shark was lured into the bait and went for it. The Captain pulled the bait away but the shark carried on toward the boat until it was directly beside us. A huge gust of wind pushed the boat right into the shark, which obviously scared the hell out of it. It gave a powerful thrust of its tail and soaked everybody on the lower deck, but principally Ana who was the closest to it, then shot off into the ocean.

By now the wind was screaming in my ears, the temperature had plummeted and huge waves were rocking the boat. All the other boats had reeled in their cages and anchors and were heading back to shore before things got worse. In a space of thirty minutes the day had gone from dead calm to 80 kilometres per hour winds, something I had never experienced before. Captain Brian was still bravely firing the bait out and luring sharks in, but the water was so foamy from the smashing waves that the sharks could hardly be seen. Just then the two jokers in wetsuits came out from the cabin and were motioning for Ughhh to open the cage so they could jump in. They must have either been blind or completely suicidal as the wind was causing the cage to swing around wildly and bash into the boat.

"I don't think you guys want to try getting into that cage," suggested Ughhh, "You'll end up falling in the sea and I don't know how long you'll last with these players circling the boat. I'm definitely not coming in after you."

At this point the captain said, "Well guys, I hate to say it, but I think we better pack up and get out of here before things get any worse. I don't want to jeopardize your safety. And since none of you were able to get into the cage, we'll give you a discount on the trip. Is that okay with everybody?"

"YES!" was the group's unanimous reply. I have spent enough time on the ocean to see that conditions were getting worse by the minute and I was starting to get a little nervous. Unfortunately for Ughhh and Captain Brian, they had to reel up the cage and get the anchor clear. Captain Brian started cranking the handle to pull up the cage while Ughhh attempted to steady it. When they finally wrestled that in Captain Brian started retrieving Gladys, the plastic seal. As he started his retrieve a big shark bolted through the water with jaws wide open and narrowly missed the seal, although did manage to bite the rope clean off. "Goodbye Gladys!" said the Captain merrily. I don't think it was the first time it had happened.

Captain Brian fired up the engines while Ughhh hauled himself to the front of the boat. Most of us were cowering inside the cabin to keep out of the way and from there I could not even see Ughhh through the front window for the foamy sea spraying over the front deck. He eventually somehow managed to pull the anchor in as the captain was attempting to stabilise the boat. The two lads in wetsuits were attempting to remove them when the captain said, "You guys may as well leave those on because we're going to have a wet ride back! Plus, great whites don't much like the taste of rubber." They couldn't make up their minds whether to look relieved or scared witless so they just laughed nervously.

Ughhh appeared out of the foam and organised us inside the boat. He shoved almost all of us into the small cabin and left the two frogmen in the exposed area in back of the boat. The captain hit the throttle and we charged up our first wave, then down with a huge crash! It was actually quite fun, but not after a dozen. I could barely see out the window for the sea spray, but at one point I could make out a huge swell approaching. As Captain Brian gunned the engine to make it up the wave he roared, "Hey, this is just like *The Perfect Storm* all over again. Haarrrrr!!" Up the wave we surfed then down we crashed, this time extremely hard.

"I just want to let you guys know," voiced the Captain as he furiously grappled with the wheel, "that if this boat sinks into these shark infested waters...I GET THE CAGE!"

Good God. Was this a man or a beast? Then, to keep my eyes off the threatening waves and my mind off our impending doom, I started reading his operator's license, which was pasted on the wall of the cabin. The line that begged my attention was, "...licensed to operate this shark cage vessel in strictly calm and flat waters only". *My God*, I thought, *we're never going to make it back to shore.* Not wanting to spark a mutiny, I kept keep this discovery to myself and decided to just close my eyes and hope for the best.

Captain Brian's mobile phone rang. It was a distress call from a dive boat in a nearby bay, which had lost both engines and was being forced towards the rocks in the bay. The captain of the boat could not get the engines started and was calling desperately for somebody to help save his vessel. Looking back towards the bay, Captain Brian told the man that there was no way he could make it back there with a boat his size, especially with a load of guests. Although we felt sorry for the guy, I think that if he had tried to turn the boat around to go back into the storm there really would have been a mutiny. Instead, Captain Brian called a couple of the other larger boats he knew were on the way back into shore. The decided amongst themselves that they would all first return to the harbour, drop off the guests, then head back out to try and help the distressed vessel. He then tried to call the distressed vessel back but there was no answer. That brought a wave of silence from all of us sitting on that boat.

"Don't worry too much about it guys," the captain said, "it was a dive boat so if they were getting too close to the rocks, they would have just put their tanks back on and bailed out and swam to shore. They will be fine. If anything, just the boat has been lost. Or maybe he just dropped the phone overboard. Don't worry."

By this time we were through the worst of it. We soon reached the harbour and amidst the crashing waves and wind, Captain Brian and Ughhh got the boat to the dock easily and quickly. Before allowing us off the boat the captain said, "Well, sorry about the disastrous day folks." I was thinking, "Disastrous? We saw thousands of seals playing in the sea, floated next to giant beautiful whales, saw lots of great white sharks, and survived a flash storm. You call that disastrous?"

The captain continued, "How about I give you all half your money back since none of you were able to cage dive with the sharks?" There were no objections, though I'm sure most of the people would have been happy to pay the full price for a day full of such adventure!

Once the guests were off the boat, Ughhh threw off the dock lines and Captain Brian manoeuvred his boat toward the angry sea. And as the boat sped away they both turned back to wave good-bye.

****

Mount Botox

While on a trip through South America Ana and I met a pair of fellow backpackers whom we connected with instantly and traveled together for a month across four countries, experiencing dozens of unforgettable moments along the way. It was one of those times on the road when you let your guard down, let others in and truly enjoy each other, explore together and share everything. We haven't seen them since that trip but I know that we will meet again someday.

Fraser was a New Zealander and his girlfriend, Bec, was Australian. They were both crazy. We met them on an overnight train in Bolivia and, after the briefest of conversations, immediately clicked. They had both been living large in London, England for years and were now doing a backpacking trip around South America on their round-a-bout way home to Australia to live permanently, or at least permanently for now. Frase was a tall, stocky bloke with an outstanding sense of humour and an unusually narrow range of facial expressions; he either looked happy or worried. Bec was a tall, thin, striking, red headed vegetarian who ate meat. We got to know each other over a few beers in the dining car and were dazzled by their knowledge of card games, which would end up providing us with hours of entertainment throughout the following weeks. We eventually laboured our way back to our seats on the packed train, stepping on at least half a dozen Bolivian kids sleeping unnoticed in the dark walking aisle. They merely coughed a sharp yelp then fell straight back asleep; apparently well accustomed to being trod upon by stupid foreigners. Once settled in our seats we shared a bottle of cheap red wine while watching the onboard movie about an American who gets kidnapped by rebel drug dealers and held for ransom in a dodgy country in South America. Impeccable choice of films considering the country we were currently in. But at least it was in English.

The train arrived at its destination, a town called Uyuni, with a grinding steel squeal at three in the morning. Half awake and half hung over, we gathered our packs and found a taxi to the hotel we had booked then checked in with relative ease and crashed out for the remainder of the night.

Our little black alarm clock rang us to consciousness a few hours later. We grudgingly arose, had showers, breakfast, and packed our bags. Frase and Bec met us at breakfast then we walked together over to the agency with whom Ana and I had booked our three day trip into the Uyuni region of Bolivia. Luckily, they had space left for our new friends and we were directed up the block to where the vehicle we would be traveling in was parked. Two others were standing there, Patricia and Mark, both from a French speaking part of Switzerland, and we introduced ourselves. Mark spoke very good English while Patricia spoke only a little. As we were chit chatting a Bolivian fellow walked up to the truck, pulled himself on to the roof then impatiently motioned for us to pass up the luggage. Assuming he was our guide we passed up the bags while he strapped them to the top of the vehicle then covered all the gear with a blue tarpaulin. He hopped down then motioned for us to get in the vehicle and once the last door had shut we took off, leaving only a dust cloud and a parking space.

After half an hour on the road I finally plucked enough courage to ask the guy driving the truck who he was and what his name was. In Spanish, he replied, "Guide. Emilio." He was obviously the strong and silent type. Since conversation seemed not to be an option, most of us just looked out the window at the passing terrain, which slowly transforming from a dusty brown colour to snowy white and before long we found ourselves at the edge of a giant, stretching plain of pure white salt as far as the eye could see. My first impression was that of a frozen lake, but with a temperature of over 30 degrees centigrade that was unlikely. Our vehicle came to a stop in the midst of a series of small, run down buildings and Emilio directed us to get out. In Spanish, he explained to us that the residents of this tiny village operated a co-operative venture producing table salt. He led us over to one of the building where one of the workers took us on a short tour. The raw salt was collected in truckloads from the huge salt flats then it was dumped onto a large belt and dried by a fire that roared beneath it. Once the salt was dried it was shovelled into bags by the children of the village then sold in the local markets.

We piled back into the vehicle and Emilio sped off into the whiteness. The intensity of the glare from the white landscape was blinding. Luckily, I was wearing a pair of polarized sunglasses, which cut down the glare, but most of the others in the vehicle were not so fortunate and I could foresee some large headaches. Emilio soon stopped the vehicle again and we got out to explore. Everywhere around us were piles of salt drying in the hot sun and people loading it into trucks. There was one area of the ground that was brown and bubbling and Emilio explained that it was some sort of underground gas being released. Yet again we were stuffed back into the vehicle and sped away. The next stop we made was to look at a salt hotel being dismantled. Apparently, the hotel had been constructed entirely of salt bricks and was a luxury destination for tourists but studies done by the Bolivian government had shown that the sewage from the hotel was contaminating the salt fields so the hotel had to be destroyed and reconstructed elsewhere.

The next ninety minutes were a snowy blur. Emilio sped across the perfectly flat surface at well over 100 kilometres per hour. His single comment along the way was that this basin used to be a huge salt lake but had dried up thousands of years ago leaving this salty speedway.

Around mid-day, we approached an island in the middle of this ancient sea and realized that it was covered with giant cacti! Emilio sent us off to explore the island while he prepared lunch and we were very happy to stretch our legs after the long ride. Standing at the top of this cactus dominated island looking down across the blinding white sea of salt was an experience I will never forget. This bizarre landscape was something I think even the mind of the maddest madman could not conjure. The green, spiny arms of the giant cacti reached up for the hot rays of the sun while the roots below somehow feasted on the salty soil below. I could imagine a giant icebreaker ship crashing towards us through the salt, with the sailors wearing board shorts and shades instead of parkas and woollen hats. I could imagine bikini-clad Inuit sawing holes in the salt looking to spear seals or catch fish. But instead of these things I saw my wife and new friends sweating from the heat and huffing from the high altitude as they hiked all over the island marvelling in the beauty of this natural wonder.

We returned to the few small buildings to find Emilio had prepared lunch, which consisted of canned meat (which smelled suspiciously like dog food), hard bread and, luckily, plenty of fresh fruit. We had a nice chat with our companions over lunch and I felt quite lucky that we had been placed with such a great group of people.

After lunch we took off in the vehicle across the salt and after several more hours of snow blindness, finally arrived at our final destination for the day, which was a pleasant surprise. It was a newly constructed building with clean rooms, a large dining area, electricity, and running water. Frase, Mark and I suspected the presence of beer so we went in search of suds while the ladies freshened up. Our supernatural beer senses proved correct and to our delight the cervezas were cold and cheap, so we settled ourselves into some chairs outside and enjoyed the sunset while discussing the standard topics for international travelers: English accents, tax avoidance, memorable hangovers and food poisoning. I also pulled out the charango I had purchased in Bolivia and proudly picked out the initial banjo riff from "Deliverance". A charango is a ten stringed instrument that resembles a small guitar and is often used in South American music, in particular, music from Bolivia and

Peru. Judging by the tortured expressions of my compadres as I strummed away, my skills were sadly lacking.

After our arrival, several truckloads of travelers from the same tour company had shown up so there was now quite a gang of people, and we all got to know each other over a delicious dinner that night, prepared and served by our guides. After the meal we all sat together, played cards and drank beers for a few hours. Our core group eventually returned to the large dorm room, which we were all sharing, but once there Frase and I decided that we should fire up my laptop and watch one of the DVDs I had purchased in the market for a few pesos. Like a couple of kids we pushed the single beds together, doubled up the pillows and settled in for the movie, but before it began there was some commotion coming from Marc and Patricia's corner of the room so Frase yelled out, "What the fuck's going on back there?" There was a double click, two blinding lights then a chorus of laughter when they turned to us with identical head lamps strapped to their noggins. They looked like two hopelessly lost coal miners. After the laughter subsided we got back to our movie and everyone else went to bed.

Dawn arrived right on schedule and Emilio was banging on our door telling us to wake up and get ready. We gathered our things, had a bread and cheese breakfast in the kitchen then helped Emilio load the gear onto the truck. By this time I had figured out that Emilio was an egomaniac; he liked to be first. We jammed ourselves into the vehicle, Ana and Bec being kind enough to sit in the cramped back row, and Emilio patched out leaving a cloud of dust for the other groups to chew on. The scenery was completely different this day; we passed by the edge of the salt lake then snaked through a hilly, dry area along the makeshift roads until we finally reached a small village called San Juan where we stepped out to take a break. Emilio parked in front of the town's general store and we picked up some important supplies; wine, chips and a few eight ball key chains, which were a great bargain that could not be passed up. As we loitered in front of the shop someone pointed out the two kids wandering up an alley toward us. One of the kids had a white furry thing stuck to his leg, making it difficult for him to walk. Upon closer inspection this white furry object turned out to be the horniest dog on the planet. It was completely in lust with the little boy and humped his leg ferociously and constantly. The kid would shake the dog off but the five legged beast would be right back on him grinding away. His little friend even gave the dog a mighty kick, which gave the kid's leg only temporary relief as the perverted little puppy barely missed a stroke.

Frase and I judged this as quality entertainment and took a dozen photos.

The other three groups soon arrived and Emilio timed our exit perfectly, leaving another cloud of dust on them as they were getting out of their vehicles. We left the town and continued along the sketchy road until it disappeared and we found ourselves on a large flat plain racing toward what looked like a giant lake, and Emilio showed no signs of slowing. Incidentally, he still hadn't said a word all day, but after seeing him humiliate our fellow tour groups so fully completely, I had total confidence in him. Besides that, he had also dipped into his pocket and offered us each a mouthful of cocoa leaves to chew on, which was the local equivalent of Pakistani pan or American chewing tobacco. It gave a slight narcotic buzz and, as any backpacker will tell you, any free buzz is a good buzz.

As we approached the lake, Emilio did not slow down, in fact he seemed to be speeding up, and soon the truck tires hit the water and we went slicing through it like a speedboat. The water was only a few inches deep but that was sufficient for us to leave a beautiful wake behind us – all I could think about was having someone take a picture of me waterskiing behind a vehicle in Bolivia.

Imagine our surprise when we reached the halfway point of the lake to be only to be confronted by a railway crossing sign sticking out of the ground! The train tracks originated from god knows where, split the lake in two then disappeared in the distance, obviously on their way to god knows where. Emilio let us out of the truck for a quick stretch that actually turned into a long stretch, since the other groups were still nothing more than a slight moving splash in the distance. As expected, we were ushered into the vehicles as the others approached and Emilio left two beautiful rooster tails of mud that landed on each of their windshields. He didn't even crack a smile, but I could tell he was laughing inside, likely a very demented, maniacal chortle.

For the third time in the day, the scenery changed entirely and we found ourselves speeding by giant orange rock formations. These formations stood grandly on a scrubby plain, which was otherwise dotted with tufts of toupee grass, and the entire scene was bordered by enormous snow capped mountains. Once or twice Emilio slowed down to point out the rock rabbits that lived on and around the rocks, though they were so large they looked more to me like woodchucks to me. We continued through this area until we reached one of the largest rock formations we had seen and Emilio announced it was time for lunch so he pulled over into the shadow of this mini mountain. He told us it would take a little while for him to get everything ready so we were free to entertain ourselves. One activity he heartily recommended was to collect some nice round stones and try to knock the rock bunnies off the formation. Frase and I immediately began scouting for ammo and were rewarded with slaps in the head from our respective kind hearted, though thoroughly unadventurous, better halves. So instead we climbed the rocks and took photos of the bizarre countryside, leaving the bunnies unscathed. I'm such a crappy shot I probably couldn't have hit one anyway.

We were soon back on the dusty trail and of course the scenery changed almost immediately. We arrived at a high altitude lake that was full of handsome pink flamingos. Bec almost flipped at the sight of these magnificent birds and she was snapping pictures as fast as her finger could hit the button.

"BiiiKK!" Frase shouted in his Kiwi accent, "Enough pictures of the goddamn seagulls!"

"But they're so beautiful," she answered, "I want to make sure I get a good shot."

"You can see those anytime you want in the bloody Sydney Zoo!"

This short interruption slowed Bec's pace of rapid photography, but only just. Emilio soon rounded everybody up and packed us back into the truck. Twenty minutes after leaving the once in a lifetime flamingo flock, we came to the second in a lifetime flamingo flock and I could hear the machine gunning of Bec's camera shutter even before the truck came to a stop. Frase didn't say much this time; he knew it was of no use. Bec could hardly believe her luck; two flamingo flocks in the same day, and she squeezed off half a roll of shots before Emilio pushed on.

The next stretch of the journey was a large, flat orange and pink coloured plain that was obviously well hardened and almost bump free, giving everyone in the truck a chance to doze off, even Emilio a couple times, evidenced by the periodic frantic jerk and fishtailing of the vehicle. When I awoke from my shallow slumber I saw that we had reached a large lake with a background of ominous fluorescent mountains and a blanket of, you guessed it, flamingos stepping in unison through the waters.

"Quick Bec, get your camera!" shouted Frase as he shook Bec to consciousness, "You won't believe it, there's a flock of wild flamingos down on the lake!"

Ignoring the obvious sarcasm, Bec did exactly that and cranked off another half dozen photos. I don't think that particular half role contained any nice close ups since as soon as the truck stopped Marc the Swissman had leaped out and ran psychotically down the gravel embankment screaming, "Yeaaaaahoogahooga!!" and waving his arms, which scared the droppings out of the pinkish fowls, causing them to furiously splash-dash across the lake to the tourist-free side. By the time the other two trucks arrived, the only things they could possibly have seen were splatterings of bird shit on the lake, feather clouds, and dust plumes in the air where our vehicle had been. Emilio was always in the lead.

We finally arrived at what we thought would be the last spectacle of the day; a tree-shaped rock in the middle of a dusty brown flatland. Snap, snap of the camera shutters and we were gone. We were all getting tired and were looking forward to a good sleep. I faintly recalled the lady who sold us the tour saying that the second night's accommodation wasn't quite as nice as the first; it was more "rustic", so I was a little fearful of what awaited us. We approached what looked like an abandoned military camp, littered with rubbish and populated by decrepit buildings and shells of vehicles. To my horror, Emilio cranked the wheel and two-tired it into the mud pit, which sufficed as a parking lot for Hitler's Hotel. I looked over to my horrified wife who was shaking her head and mouthing the eff word. I looked over to Bec whose blank look confirmed a state of pure shock. I looked at Frase who said, "I wonder if they sell booze here?" For the first time of the trip, Emilio was smiling, and I realized immediately that it was our fear that was entertaining him.

If I were a rat surveying the scene I would have said to my rodent buddies, "This place is a real shithole, let's get out of here." The floor was a mess of broken, cold concrete and offered up limitless tripping opportunities. The only running water was the rain spilling in through the holes in the roof. Ana sent me to check out the bathroom and the first thing I noticed after the terrible smell, was that the ceiling panels had been partially pulled off and people had stuffed their used toilet paper into the openings. The toilets were slightly more than holes in the ground, but you would much rather take your chances of holding it and rupturing a bowel than get anywhere close to those forbidden stinkholes. I reported back to Ana that she might want to explore other restroom options.

The common bedroom consisted of three bunk beds held together by rusty wire and topped with rotten mattresses and thin pillows that looked frighteningly similar to feminine sanitary napkins – used, of course. After seeing this I looked at Frase, he looked at me, and without words, we agreed that the best course of action would be to get blind drunk as soon as possible to numb our senses to this catastrophically unclean situation. The gods must have been smiling down upon us – after a quick inquiry we discovered they sold wine! Yes it was wine, but after our first sip we realized it was a horrific, blood curdling, foul tasting variety made from Bolivian grapes, which we could only assume grew exclusively in landfills.

Frase grabbed the cards and we started drinking and playing. Ah, the sweet buzz of cheap and nasty alcohol. The horrible common room in which we were playing was not getting any warmer, but that Bolivian wine was jacking up my own body temperature rather quickly. We reluctantly broke away from the card game at the urging of some of the others who had been for a walk and told us there was some interesting things to see we wouldn't want to miss. So we filled our cups, grabbed a reserve bottle and went for a look. We initially headed off in the wrong direction and found ourselves in the middle of a sewage field without rubber boots. "That way!" said Mark, pointing in the direction of some white hills in the distance. We changed course, began walking and continued for a good while until we came to the white hills, which looked like giant piles of cocaine. A person from one of the other groups was on her way back and told us that it was some sort of naturally occurring mineral called Botox.

"Botox?" somebody asked.

"Yeah, Botox…or something like that," she replied.

Good enough, Mount Botox it was! We wandered around on the huge drifts of powder and took a few pictures and, although my memory of this is dim, I seem to remember peeing my full name into the nice white palette. It must have been the artist in me.

We headed back and along the way Fraser and I decided we needed more wine to solve our walking problem; namely, that we could still walk. On the way we were stunned by an unbelievable sunset over Mount Botox. We all took photos but, like most photos of sunsets, they did not come close to capturing the beauty of the sight.

We returned to the shoddy common area and the card game resumed. Three hours later I was completely plastered and starting to feel blackout stage creeping up on me, though I had likely been on blackout autopilot for some time by then. After I had trumped Bec's seventeen of hearts with my fourteen of spades I knew loss of consciousness would soon be following my loss of vision. I staggered back to the bunk bedded chamber of filth and happily plopped my weightless body onto one of the rotting beds. I hope to hell my tongue wasn't hanging out onto the Tampax pillow as I slept that deep, yogic slumber common to drunken backpackers.

Emilio had promised us an early start and at 4:45 he was banging on the wall telling us we were leaving in ten. My autopilot drunk switch was still activated so the body attached to my head jumped up, packed my things and marched to the vehicle while my mind enjoyed a few more minutes of creepy sleep. I remember noting that my companions, otherwise known as the forgotten cast of *The Dawn of the Dead*, were all on autopilot as well and none looked back when we peeled away from that ranch of rot.

A most beautiful thing happened two hours later. We wound our way around a mountain and came to a river that had an unusual amount of steam hovering above it. Emilio told us it was time for a bath and brekkie so with aching head in hand I dug out my swim gear, changed behind a rock, and slid into the beautifully hot, clear spring water. It was heaven! I could feel the hangover being slowly cleansed away by the delicious hot spring. Several more vehicles soon arrived and before long there was quite a group of people wallowing in the wonderful waters. There was only one thing that could have ever convinced me to leave that luxurious spa...the smell of frying bacon! I followed my nose back to the vehicle where Emilio was cooking up the grease feed, and after changing into dry clothes, I tucked into several bacon and egger sandwiches. The rest of the crew was looking much, much better now.

If I had been a chemistry scholar, my goal would have been to understand the mysterious healing properties of bacon and eggs and use this knowledge for the betterment of mankind.

Although we didn't know it at the time, this was to be our last memory of Bolivia, as shortly after leaving the hot springs, the vehicle pulled up to a border station, where we would soon be met by a bus that would take us across the border to Chile. Here we had the pleasure of paying ten Bolivian pesos to use a real (filthy) toilet that actually had a supply of toilet paper. After holding it for two days, I'd say we got our money's worth.

We helped Emilio unload the gear from the truck then said our tearful goodbyes to our faithful guide. Well, maybe not quite tearful, but we were a little sad; even though he didn't talk much he did get through everything and provided a few unintentional laughs along the way.

Our next stop was to be Atacama de San Pedro and we had been told it was a beautiful, charming Chilean town, perfect for spending a few days enjoying first world comforts and cheap beer. What we found was something completely different. But that's another story....

****

15 Days on Lake Erie

Since purchasing a sailboat four years ago, we have done a two week family sailing trip each year on Lake Erie, which is one of the Great Lakes straddling the Canada–US border. Lake Erie is a huge body of water, approximately 250 miles long and 50 miles wide, providing an enormous area to explore. Being on your own, in the middle of a big lake, with young children and only yourselves to rely on, is an exhilarating and empowering experience. Many people curtail their traveling once children become a part of their lives, but if you put your mind to it, traveling can become even better when done as a family. This story is a series of daily journals I wrote during our first trip and is a modified version of the one that appears on my blog at blog.lifeisgrand.org.

Day 1 – Port Dover to Erie, Pennsylvania

After spending last night at our home marina of Port Dover loading and preparing the boat, we are up at 5am and throwing off the dock lines shortly after that. It is quite an exciting feeling knowing we are embarking on our first big journey on our new sailboat – the *Bella Blue*. We are planning on being away for about 18 days and our current plan is to travel across Lake Erie to the town of Erie, Pennsylvania then work our way westward up the US coast line to the town of Sandusky and the nearby islands. For the return journey we will either return along the US side, stopping at the harbours we missed on the out journey or we may cross over to the Canadian side via Pelee Island and explore some of the Canadian harbours. This decision will depend on weather conditions and our experiences along the way.

First, some background information. Our family, which includes me, my wife Ana and our two children Magnus, who is 5 and Stella, who is 3, purchased a 2005 Hunter 33 foot sailboat named *Bella Blue* in February of 2010. We had been looking for a sailboat for a couple years and finally the combination of extremely poor economic conditions in the US and a very favourable exchange rate yielded some fantastic bargains on boats. We were able to find a gorgeous sailboat that had been repossessed and was located in Port Annapolis, which is in the state of

Maryland on the eastern seaboard. Since we live in Paris, Ontario, which is a 40 minute drive from the town of Port Dover, snuggled away on the shore of Lake Erie, we are in a perfect location to own a boat. We have some previous sailing experience as I owned an older Hunter sailboat for about a year when I lived in Bahamas back in 1998. In fact, this is where Ana and I met, so we spent much of our initial time together sailing around the Bahamas. It's so much easier to find the love of your life when you own a boat in the Caribbean.

As we power out of the safety and security of our home harbour, I feel a chill of excitement running down my spine. The winds are strong, approximately 15 to 20 miles per hour and coming from the north, almost directly behind us, which is probably the most difficult point of sail. We pull out the sails, cut the motor and begin our journey with a nice cup of hot coffee for each of us sloshing around in the drink holders.

The first hour or two are excellent, but we need to pay strict attention to the sails to ensure we don't jibe accidentally, which could cause damage to the boat with these strong winds. A jibe is when the wind is behind you and you turn the stern of the boat through the eye of the wind in order to change direction, which causes the sail to flop from one side of the boat to the other and must be done in a controlled fashion, especially in heavy winds. We are moving at five knots, which is about six miles per hour but feels a lot faster on a sailboat with the wind rushing through your hair and the spray coming up on deck. I give Ana a turn at the helm so she can get a feel for the boat. She hasn't done as much sailing as me so isn't yet completely comfortable behind the wheel, but happily takes a turn. At this point the winds are strengthening and waves are getting larger. As we near Long Point the wind is really rocking and some of the larger waves are about five feet high. Ana begins wondering out loud whether we are prepared to continue with such strong winds and chop but I assure her that we will be fine and *Bella Blue* can easily handle these conditions. As we round Long Point and adjust our heading for Erie, the winds almost immediately die and we are left crawling at about two knots. After struggling slowly for a couple miles we decide to fire up the motor to give us some extra speed and we then enjoy a beautiful motor sail across Lake Erie all the way to the harbour entrance of Erie, Pennsylvania. The kids are natural boaters and enjoy the ride across, splitting their time between sitting in the cockpit with us and hanging around below in the cabin playing games and watching DVDs.

Erie has a huge protected harbour and probably a dozen marinas, so is a very popular boating destination. We pilot the boat into the harbour and eventually find Perry's Landing, which is one of the marinas having a video phone where you can clear US customs. Coincidentally, this is the same marina we had *Bella Blue* transported to back in April so it is comfortingly familiar, as we spent many hours here putting her back together and preparing her for the initial journey across the lake to Port Dover.

After clearing customs, we take *Bella Blue* over to the Bay Harbour Marina where we have booked a slip for the night. Our elapsed time since leaving Port Dover is about nine hours so it feels good to finally be at our first destination. We arrive to find a beautifully maintained, practically new marina with a lot of very large and very new boats. Upon docking, the marina manager greets us immediately and gives us the scoop on all we need to know. This includes telling us that the boat next to us, named *Marlin,* is a custom built fishing boat, and one of only two that were constructed. The other one is owned by Jimmy Buffet, the musical hero of sailors everywhere. I like how this trip is going.

After getting settled, we take the kids for a walk down to a local playground where they burn off a lot of the energy they stored up on the long boat ride across. We stop for a quick pee break at the Sloppy Duck, a local bar and restaurant, and the kids are thrilled to find a pond in front of it full of catfish and baby ducks, which keeps them entertained for half an hour.

We return to *Bella Blue* just in time for the arrival of our friend Andrew, who owns a 36 foot Sea Ray Sundancer power boat named *Endeavour,* and docks next to us in Dover. He also lives across from us in Paris so we are neighbours in almost every way possible. Thankfully we get along very well and enjoy similar hobbies, mainly restricted to boating and drinking.

We meet a number of people on the dock, mostly Americans, all of whom are super friendly and extremely hospitable. Every time we visit the US we are struck by how friendly people are. We are also usually shocked at the level of service you get everywhere. I think this is one big difference between the US and Canada; in the US people are very service oriented and take their jobs seriously. The service is nearly always superb and folks seem genuinely interested in doing a good job. In Canada…not so much.

After a long day, I wind up going to bed quite early (with a pounding headache...didn't drink enough water) and Ana stays up for a while visiting with Andrew, his friend Michelle and a couple other American friends who live nearby and stopped by for a visit.

Day 2 – Erie, Pennsylvania

We wake up to a beautiful day with temperatures expected to reach 30 degrees. We decide to make this a shopping day and hop on the free trolley that takes us downtown where we can connect to another public bus, which goes to the shopping malls. Upon reaching downtown we find a nice pub and realize the Netherlands/Brazil world cup soccer match has just started so we settle in for a few rounds of pre-noon $2 pints and enjoy the game. Ana wasn't too happy with Brazil losing but at least it was to a decent team, plus we just love Cloggies and their lovely orange uniforms (and skin, when tanned).

We eventually find a bus stop after walking eight blocks, and after a half hour wait, hop on to a bus which must have had a nuclear powered air conditioning system, as there were icicles forming on the bars and I swear I could see my breath. After several hours of shopping, walking across giant asphalt parking lots and having a terrible time finding a taxi, we are finally back to the boat with a huge load including groceries, clothes, and plenty of cheap American beer. We pack everything away then sit down for happy hour and agree that the US public transportation system is just as pathetic as the one in Canada and we vow that next time we will rent a car.

Day 3 – Erie, Pennsylvania to Conneault Harbour, PA

After a leisurely breakfast and a visit to the pristine showers and bathrooms at the marina office (our home marina is starting to look worse and worse by comparison) we head out on the lake and find beautiful winds of 12 to 15 knots. The only problem is that the winds are coming from the exact direction we need to go, so we start tacking as close to the wind as possible making wide runs of two to three miles, zigzagging our way into the wind. There seems to be a big fishing derby going on as there are probably a hundred powerboats out on the lake, all anchored out in deep water. After several hours of wonderful sailing, but limited progress towards our destination, we decide to head closer to shore to anchor and prepare some lunch. At this point, Andrew is calling on the radio and is shocked how little distance we had covered. Of course, power boaters with 700 horsepower of engine have a somewhat different perspective than sailboats with tiny diesel engines and sails that cannot send you directly into the wind no matter how well they are trimmed. In any case, he meets us for lunch and we have a nice barbeque, after which Andrew, Stella and I take his dingy into the beach to do some exploring. Poor Magnus fell asleep listening to Rob Zombie on my iPod so he misses the dingy trip and the post lunch swim, which was most refreshing.

After lunch, Andrew powers his way to Conneaut, Ohio to get us slips and scope out the situation, while we slowly make our way there under sail and power. We arrive many hours later to a blistering 32 degrees and a wooden dock so hot it scorches your feet. After docking, Ana goes down the office to get us registered and finds out that if we buy $15 tickets to tonight's steak dinner we don't have to pay for dockage!

Conneault itself is a working class marina, much like Port Dover but a little worse for wear. The people are rugged and friendly and definitely like to have a good time. The landscape is unique; directly east of the marina is a rail yard with huge piles of gravel and coal and plenty of large machinery scattered around. South of the marina is the town site, which sports a single giant windmill, in stark contrast to the nearby mountains of coal.

The marina is well set up and includes a full bar, a kids television room, a playground and a huge canopy with grills where everybody congregates to eat. The steak dinner is excellent, and partway through, one of the club members treats us to a tray full of Jello shooters. I am instantly transported back to my first year in university, which is the last time I've consumed vodka-infused Jello. They were as disgusting as I remember, but are easily washed down with Miller Lite and frozen daiquiris. As we make new friends around the picnic tables the kids have made friends of their own and one of them, Howie, has even taught Magnus and Stella his own personal version of the Scooby Doo song, which starts with the line, "Scooby Dooby Doo took a poo…" and gets even more disgusting after that.

The evening progresses as one might expect and I find myself with Ana sitting on Andrew's boat in the company of a few new friends who are charging through his onboard bottled beverages at an alarming rate. We retire around 2am and I actually remember to drink a litre of water and eat three Advil before bedtime, which always helps to sooth the next morning's hangover.

Day 4 – Conneaut Harbour

We wake up relatively early and head up to a local restaurant for a much needed fried breakfast. It is a classic American greasy spoon complete with hash, grits, and biscuits and gravy on the menu. We then take a walk through the town and find that a carnival has set up shop and will be opening at three in the afternoon. Being a huge fan of carnivals, Ana is very excited, as are the kids, but I am not equally enthusiastic as my memories of the carnival back at the Woolco mall parking lot in Saskatoon are equal measures of fist fights, drug dealing and being hit by vomit spewed from drunken teenagers on the Zipper ride.

We return to the carnival late in the afternoon and I am pleasantly surprised to find an extra grubby heavy metal cover band cranking out the likes of Warrant, Guns and Roses, Poison, Kiss and the ultimate - Faster Pussycat! The rest of the fair is as expected; crowded with teenage moms, tattooed and moustachioed muscle heads and skids of all sizes and colours. The kids and Ana enjoy a few rides, some of which seem to be on the brink of falling apart, then we grab an ice cream and we are out of there, back to the boats to enjoy the night's fireworks display. Yes, it is July 4th, and we are lucky enough to be in the USA to celebrate with them, so we crack open a bottle of wine, enjoy the show, then escape from the party and sneak off to bed, as we have a very early start tomorrow.

Day 5 – Conneaut Harbour to Mentor Harbour, OH

It's 4am and we are throwing off the dock lines and heading out into the darkness. This is our first experience with night sailing and it turns out to be a most tranquil experience. The winds are quite strong and directly in our face once again so we head out on a port tack and sail through the darkness, enjoying the sound of the water splashing on the hull and the wind whistling through the shrouds and rigging. Ana and I enjoy watching the sun rise over the east horizon then check on the kids below who are sleeping soundly. The kids have been incredibly comfortable on the boat and the limited amount of space has certainly not seemed to have limited their fun. They have not yet once complained about any of the long sailing days and seem to quite enjoy being down below playing games and hanging out. Stella likes to be in the cockpit sitting on one of the two built-in seats (which hang off the stern of the boat) watching the wake trailing behind. Any time the boat stops, Magnus is the first one to whip off his clothes and jump into the water for a swim.

Shortly after the kids wake up I cut the engine, allow the boat to coast to a halt, then get everybody out for a morning swim and bath. As we are several miles offshore we go the clothing optional route and have a skinny dip. The feeling of true freedom comes when you are able to swim naked off your own boat in the middle of a lake at 9 am on a Monday morning. Life is definitely good.

We arrive at Mentor Harbour around 2 pm to another scorcher – must be 33 degrees or more. There are two marinas available; one which is a member of the inter-lake yacht club that we belong to and offers a free night, and the other which is a paid marina and looks like it has a pool and restaurant. We cruise through a muddy channel that looks much too shallow to pass but manage to make it to the free marina at the end of the channel. We realize in an instant that this was a bad move; the dock was falling apart, there is nobody and nothing around and seems to be no electrical outlets available to power our air conditioner. We turn *Bella Blue* around and head back to the luxury marina. At a dockage rate of $1.75 a foot and the second night free, it is an easy decision. The marina turns out better than we could have hoped, as there is a beautiful pool and loads of kids around so we let Magnus and Stella loose in the kiddie pool then sit around the big pool on comfy loungers and enjoy a couple of drinks. We remain there relaxing for several hours, then return to *Bella Blue*, cook a nice dinner, and crash out.

Day 6 – Mentor Harbour

I receive a call from Andrew early in the morning with the sad news that he has been summoned back to work and will not be able to join us for the rest of the trip, which is too bad as he would have loved Mentor. We decided to spend another day as the forecasted high is again in the 30's and we need to pick up a few groceries. I spend a couple hours writing and chilling out before the rest of the gang gets up. Once we've had breakfast the kids and I head down to the pool and spend most of the day there. Ana takes off on her own to do the shopping, and by the end of the day we are fully re-provisioned and ready for our next leg of the journey, which we will begin at 4 am tomorrow.

Day 7 – Mentor Harbour to Kelly's Island, OH

Just heard a "Pahn Pahn, Pahn Pahn, Pahn Pahn" call on the radio from the Coast Guard in Cleveland. At 10:08 pm last night a 12 year old boy went missing and his last know location was in the water at Euclid Beach. They are asking all mariners to be on the lookout for him and to assist if possible. This is the first such call I've heard on the radio and it certainly reinforces the notion of paying strict attention to safety procedures on the boat. We heard a "Mayday" call a couple days ago from a boat taking on water but didn't hear if they found the boat or how it ended. The Pahn Pahn call is used when there is a potentially dangerous situation happening on the water somewhere, while the Mayday call is reserved for when potential loss of life is imminent.

Directly to the north a three mast tall ship just appeared – what a beauty! It is surprising to see such a wide variety of vessels on the lake, from tall ships to freighters to super yachts to 14 foot fishing boats. I guess that's why the Great Lakes are often called fresh water oceans.

We had a nice breeze until around 6 am when it turned directly into our face and slowed considerably. Up until then we'd been racing along nicely and actually hit 7.56 knots, which is the fastest we've done in Bella Blue. Since we're planning on covering a lot of miles today we decide to motor the rest of the way, which allows us to do over six knots and make pretty good time.

We stop at around 9 am for the morning swim and the lake is clear and much cooler out in the middle – about 26 degrees C. In some of the marinas the water temperature was as high as 33 degrees, which renders the boat air conditioning system much less effective since it relies on cool water. Speaking of that, when we bought this boat we had no idea how important an air conditioning system would be, without it we would have been melting this week. While we're underway and have the hatches open, we get quite a lot of air coming through which keeps it fairly cool, but as soon as you stop moving the cabin below turns into an oven.

We make landfall at Kelley's Island, Ohio around 4:30 in the afternoon and immediately head to the public dock for a swim. As I'm about to drop Magnus in the water, one of the other kids there mentions the abundance of water snakes that hang around the dock and swim in the water. Considering Magnus's morbid fear of snakes, we pull the plug on the dip and head back to the boat for cold beer and apple juice to help cool us down.

To end the day we decide to rent a golf cart for an hour and do a tour of the island. The island is not that large so an hour is plenty of time to tour around and see the interior forest and beaches. We stop for a quick walk on one of the beaches in the public park, which was just enough time for the kids to get covered in sand. After returning the golf cart we take the kids for an ice cream, walk back to the boat, make BBQ pizza for supper, enjoy the live band that is playing dockside at a pub and retire early to cap off our longest sailing day yet – 75 miles and 12 hours on the water.

Day 8 – Put-in-Bay and Islands Tour

We wake up at a blissfully late 6:30 am, make coffee, and then get the eggs and toast cooking. The marina we're staying at is called Portside Marina, and is located just steps away from the small downtown shopping area. The one thing we have noticed is that people here are not quite as friendly as what we've experienced in the other locations on our trip. But we've seen this over and over again in the places we've traveled to – the more touristy and popular a location, the less friendly the locals seem to be. I think it's partially due to them having to deal with all the bullshit that tourists and transients throw their way.

We spend the morning walking around town, visiting the shops, and tidying up the boat. At noon we take the island ferry over to Put-in-Bay, which is on Lower Bass Island, about eight miles from Kelly's. Most Canadians have never heard of this place, or even this area of Lake Erie. There's a series of half a dozen populated islands that are huge draws in the summertime to boaters and other non-boating tourists who reach the islands via high speed ferries. There is definitely a real Caribbean feel to the place, especially when the temperature is in the mid 30's.

We spend about four hours in Put-in-Bay, which is enough time to have a good walk around town and a great lunch. We also found a brand spanking new tiki bar that had been recently built, complete with timber frame construction, thatch roof, palm trees, swings at the bar and beautiful sand. Put-in-Bay has a reputation for being a hard partying place, but it seems that this does not hold during the week – on this Thursday the crowd was mainly older folks and families, and not a drunken twenty-something to be found anywhere.

We ferry back to Kelly's, make a delicious dinner and sit back for a movie. We have recently installed a 22 inch LED flat panel TV in the boat, which provides for excellent movie nights; although I'm yet to actually stay awake for an entire show.

Day 9 – Kelley's Island to Sandusky, Ohio

We wake up to a grey and rainy day, the first of the trip. It is actually quite a relief to get a break from the sun, though the temperature is still very warm. After breakfast on the boat we toss off the dock lines and start the short sail over to Sandusky, which is only ten miles to the south and on the mainland. Once we get offshore the wind really picks up, making for some great sailing. Ana takes over the helm for most of the way and has the boat doing over six knots on a mainly downwind course.

As we close in on Sandusky we pass by the Cedar Point peninsula, which has a giant amusement park at the point overlooking Lake Erie. We promised the kids a trip to Cedar Point since we began the trip so they are very excited to see the roller coasters and other rides. Sandusky has a huge harbour and the route in is quite congested with boats so requires more attention than normal, especially today with the strong wind. We take down the sails and motor into the harbour, eventually finding our way to the Sandusky Sailing Club, which offers a magnificent seven free nights to members of our yacht club. At the entrance of the marina stands a sign proudly declaring, "Sailboats Only!" the first of which we've seen, and the marina is indeed full of sailboats, but mostly older ones and few of any size. As we make our approach to the sea wall on the west side of the marina, Ana is busy readying the dock lines and fenders. As we approach the wall several of the local sailors have lined up on the dock to help with our lines and Ana launches into an unorthodox docking manoeuvre, never before attempted in these waters. As she winds up and hurls the coiled dock line to the waiting dock helpers she somehow manages to propel her body completely over the side of the boat, causing herself to travel further than the actual dock line. On the way overboard, she was able to snag one of the lifelines with a single finger (which would later turn a purple) then reposition herself and latch on with both hands, and hang there against the boat, dragging through the water, while the stunned bystanders stood speechless. Fortunately, one of them does speak up and reminds me that I have left the boat in reverse gear and am rapidly closing in on a boat behind me. I slam the shifter into forward gear, get into the clear, and then hop up on deck and give my waterlogged wife a lift back into the boat. By this time the dock line is now dragging in the water behind the boat, about to get wound up in the propeller, and the boat has turned and is heading directly towards the dock and the growing crowd there, wildly waving their hands and yelling advice. I leap back into the cockpit, smashing my toe in the process, ram it into reverse, and narrowly avoid a head-on collision with the concrete breakwater. Ana manages to hop onto land with the badly behaving line, and gets the boat safely tied down. I think she briefly considered telling the gobsmacked dock hands that we were visiting from Toledo…then reconsidered, and admitted we were Canadians, and part of the CVSS – Canadian Vaudeville Sailing Squadron.

After getting settled and shaking off the embarrassment, we attempt to take a walk downtown, but the rain picks up and washes us into the nearest building we could find, which turns out to be a Maritime museum. We happily enter and spend an hour or so learning about Sandusky's marine history and the history of sailing on Lake Erie. They have a large pirate display, which gets the children whipped into frenzies, and they speak Pirate to each other for the rest of the day.

After spending a few hours back at the boat, waiting for the weather to clear, we walk to downtown Sandusky and discover a big street festival with a live band and hundreds of people drinking Bud Light and other similar forms of tinned water. Yet again, it is a metal cover band and we are treated to all of my early 90's leather panted favourites. Ana takes the opportunity for some badly needed retail therapy and finds a junky thrift store, into which her and the kids disappear for thirty minutes and return with prizes. I was happy to wait outside as I had already found my prize during the walk – a dirty, small fish shop that served me the best fresh perch sandwich I've ever eaten.

We hang around downtown until night then walk back to the marina, but along the way partake in a highly organized firefly hunt. As it is well past dark, the fireflies are out in the thousands and we devise a technique whereby Stella rides on my shoulders and we run through the grass corralling the stray fireflies into Magnus's sticky grasp, where he easily captures the flickering creatures. A fine finish to another adventurous day!

Day 10 – Sandusky to Cedar Point

We awake early and hoof it back into town to check out a couple shops that were closed the evening before; namely, the West Marine boaters store, a small nautical antiques shop and the farmers market. All signs of the previous day's poor weather have vanished and it is another hot one.

Our trip takes longer than expected (once you own a boat it is impossible to spend less than an hour and $200 in a West Marine store) and we return to *Bella Blue* at noon, completely drenched with sweat after walking through the heat with a hundred pounds of groceries and boat stuff. We load up the boat and get everything in its place, then throw off the dock lines (nothing fancy this time) and head to Cedar Point. This will definitely be our shortest sailing day of the trip as our destination is only a mile or two across the bay. We enter the marina and head directly for the fuel dock. It has been ten days and, though the tank is not close to empty, it's time to gas up. She takes $60 worth of diesel – an incredibly meagre amount, considering the number of hours we've used the motor during the trip. I only wish Andrew was here with his boat beside me at the fuel pump, as his fill-ups are closer to a thousand bucks. It is a satisfying revenge for all the speed jokes he makes.

We get *Bella Blue* docked and have a quick look around – the marina is beautiful and very well organized. During check-in they gave us vouchers for reduced prices for the parks so we decide to get the full pass, which allows us to visit both the water park, called Soak City, and the amusement park with all the rides. We take the shuttle bus into Soak City and the kids are immediately in heaven. This is definitely the most elaborate water park I've ever been to and the kids wholeheartedly attack each ride they are tall enough to get into. The best part about the water park is that Ana and I can enjoy it too – unlike the kids rides at amusement parks, which are...well, lame. We spend the entire afternoon splashing around and it's not until 6pm that we dry off and head over to the amusement park.

The kids of course love it, and the only real excitement Ana and I get is when we're watching Magnus and Stella on the rocket ship ride, and notice Magnus leaning over way too far, then see him smash his front teeth into the steel bar that he is supposed to be holding on to. Now Magnus's previous experiences with pain have been very unhappy episodes, as he appears to experience painful sensations ten times worse than regular humans, but this one was special. On the first rotation of the ride he's holding his mouth and looks like he's about to cry. On the second rotation he is simply wiggling his tooth, which has been slightly loose for weeks, but has now clearly been knocked a bit looser. During the third and subsequent rotations he has his mouth closed and is intently running his tongue over his front teeth. He has clearly realized that this shot to the face has brought him one step closer to the Tooth

Fairy payout, which can then be easily used to purchase candy. I wish it was always this easy dealing with his wounds.

We return to *Bella Blue* by 9 pm and are amazed to look back and see the view to Cedar Point. The rides have all been lighted and the display is brilliant! There is clearly no other marina on Lake Erie with such magnificent night time views.

I check the weather forecast and it says the wind will be picking up and staying strong all night then turning into thunderstorms later on Sunday. Ana and I decide that it's the right time for our first sailing all-nighter so after doing several loads of laundry in the excellent marina facilities, we prepare the boat and cast off shortly before 1am.

Day 11 – Cedar Point to Cleveland, Ohio

The night view to Cedar Point leaving Sandusky is awesome and very peaceful now that the rides are closed and all the people are gone. We navigate our way out of the channel using the flashing red and green buoys, which are much easier to see at night than during the day.

We proceed out into the open lake, deploy the sails and are happy to find that the wind is strong and coming directly from the south-east, which is perfect for our heading. We trim the sails, get the GPS coordinates set up, turn on the autopilot, then sit back and enjoy the ride. Ana goes down below to try and get some sleep, which is constantly interrupted by various events – Stella needing milk, Magnus getting kicked by Stella in bed and wanting to move, things crashing around in the boat because of the heeling, and me calling for more coffee! She eventually does get some sleep then relieves me at the helm at about 4am.

This is the fastest sailing we've done yet – for a total distance of 60 miles we average 5.65 knots with a maximum of 7.67 knots and the entire trip takes just over eight hours. The night sailing is very nice but it does take a toll on the sleep quality.

Our arrival in Cleveland is exciting as this is the first big city we've boated to. The harbour entrance is massive and the inner channel is very easy to navigate. By now the kids are awake and surprised to see that we've already arrived at our destination. To top it off, at least six tall ships are moored downtown – likely part of some sort of exhibition or festival. Once the kids spot the pirate ships in port they are immediately intrigued.

We arrive at the Forest City Yacht Club and they immediately arrange a slip for us. After tying up the boat, I retire for a much needed hour long nap to recharge the batteries, and leave my poor wife to deal with the energetic kiddies who have had a wonderful, long sleep. After I wake up, we get organized and head over to the yacht clubhouse where we meet some very nice people who give us the lowdown on local transport options, which are pretty much limited to taxi. Luckily, one of the members, Lynn, offers us a ride downtown, which we accept, and she whisks us over to the Cleveland downtown waterfront.

Once there, we split up into two teams. Team A, consisting of Ana, Stella and Magnus, will hit the science centre gift shop to select one toy for each of the kids, and then take in the Omnimax movie about the ocean. Team B, which consists of me and my big hair and leather pants, will take in the Rock and Roll Hall of Fame. In the interest of brevity, let's just say that both groups were wildly successful with their chosen activities, except when Ana fell asleep during the movie.

We return to the boat via taxi cab, have a great dinner and are completely done for the day.

Day 12 – Cleveland to Mentor Harbour

We are up at 4am and have a steady, strong wind blowing from the south east. The weather forecast reports scattered showers but so far we haven't had any rain. We head out into the lake and about five miles into our trip, a big gust of wind pushes us to a new all time speed record for *Bella Blue* – a scorching 8.11 knots! It seems that the fastest point of sail for us is a broad reach (this is when the wind is coming from behind the boat – not directly behind, but off to one side 20 degrees or so). It's a lot of fun sailing the boat when the winds are strong, as it forces you to really pay attention and stay focused. Mistakes made in strong winds can be costly.

As we near Mentor, the rain catches up with us and we get hit with a squall. Luckily I could see the rain coming up behind us, which gave me time to pull in the jib and get my rain gear on. Magnus sees me out in the cockpit and decides that I could use some help so he gets his rain jacket on and joins me. I put him to work tightening up some lines and keeping a lookout for other boats, as the rain has reduced visibility substantially. I am constantly impressed with how well the kids have taken to the boat; it seems very natural to them and they enjoy being on the water. They are going to grow up to be excellent sailors.

Since the run was only about 25 miles and our speed averaged over six knots, we arrive early in Mentor and have most of the day left, so decide to rent a car to do some local exploring. We get the car and drive to two of the places we missed on the water – Chagrin River and Grand River. We stop at Pickle Bill's on Grand River, a place that's been mentioned to us several times. In fact, we've heard that three out of four babies born in the Lake Erie region were conceived after, or even during a visit to Pickle Bill's by their future parents. Luckily for Magnus and Stella and their potential future inheritance, the bar is closed on Mondays, though we are able to go inside and have a look around. At the head of the bar is a life sized female mannequin straddling the bar top, as if to suggest that you, as a patron, may be taking a similar position later on if you dare to enter. Hanging about the gigantic bar are full sized sharks, fish netting, many other full sized mannequins including pirates, buccaneers, circus freaks, and other assorted creatures. The restaurant extends out into the river with a dock-up bar and room for lots of boats, making me wonder if there is a higher incident of "total loss" insurance claims for vessels in this particular area.

We cruise around in the car, checking out some bookstores, clothing stores, take the kids (and Ana) to McDonalds for lunch, and stop at a going-out-of-business sale at a video store and buy 24 DVD's for about three bucks each – sure to provide plenty of hours of in-boat entertainment.

We eventually make it back to the boat, take the kids for a swim at the pool, prepare a nice dinner, and then chill out for the rest of the night.

Day 13 – Mentor Harbour

We decide to again take advantage of the free second night at the Mentor Harbour Yacht Club and spend one more day before heading to Erie early the next morning. Ana takes the car to do some grocery shopping and I stay with the kids at the boat for a while, then later visit the playground. The rest of the afternoon is spent hanging out at the pool, after which, we return to the boat and the kids enjoy their movie supply in their cabin while Ana and I have a relaxing evening drink (and

I a cigar) sitting on the back of the boat enjoying the quiet marina and the opportunity to do absolutely nothing. This doesn't happen to us very often so we truly appreciate it.

Day 14 – Mentor Harbour to Erie, Pennsylvania

We are up at 3am for an early start on the 75 mile trip back to Erie. The forecast is for strong north winds early in the day, then dying out towards noon so we want to use the wind while it's there. As usual, the first few hours are excellent sailing with ten knot winds, but they start to die around 7am. I fire up the engine and we continue on motor-sailing, making about six knots, which should put us into Erie sometime around 2:30 in the afternoon.

We've been thinking of where to go from here. One idea was to continue up the lake and visit Dunkirk, which is probably about 20 miles or so past Erie. But now we're thinking we might head back to Port Dover a bit earlier and spend a couple nights on the boat in the marina like a regular weekend and save eastern Lake Erie for a future trip. After all the sailing we have done on this adventure we are much more comfortable with the boat, and in particular night sailing, which makes three or four day long weekend trips over to the US very achievable.

We stop and anchor around 2 pm for a late lunch and a swim - feels like heaven! At 4 pm we arrive in Erie at the Commodore Perry Yacht Club after a total of 71 miles. The last time we were here we stayed at the marina next door, and couldn't help but notice that the Perry's had a lovely swimming pool, which came in very handy today as it was in the low 30's again. We sit by the pool for a couple hours and enjoy the sunshine and a couple cold beverages then head back to the boat for a Mexican fajita supper and the third attempt at getting through the same movie. Yes, one gets a bit tired after a 13 hour sailing day.

Just before bedtime, Magnus pleads for me to pull out his front tooth. Since the kiddie rollercoaster incident, his front tooth has become progressively less connected and is now wiggling freely. I've tried pulling it with my fingers but that is not working so he is now begging for me to use the pliers in the toolbox to yank it out. I pulled out his last two, so I do have the stomach for it, but I'm not entirely sure it's ready so I've asked him to wiggle it as much as possible and we'll try to extract it tomorrow. We'll be sure to do it in front of Ana as she was completely spooked out and actually shrieking the last time I cranked one out.

Day 15 and beyond – Erie, Pennsylvania to Port Dover, Ontario

We awake at a leisurely 7:30 to yet another beautiful, sunny day. We have decided that we will head back to Dover today sometime before noon, so we have a quick breakfast and get the kids over to the pool for a nice swim before we leave. In the two weeks we have been gone, Magnus has learned to use a mask, snorkel, and fins, and is now diving for pennies in the deep end of the pool. As I watch him dive I have future visions of us spear fishing spiny lobsters in the Caribbean as the girls cook them up on board.

As the kids are playing in the pool and running around the deck a lady who is also at the pool comes over and says, "Your children talk very loud, have you ever had their hearing checked?"

I said, "Yes, we've already had them diagnosed – apparently they are half Portuguese, which explains the high volume."

I don't think she gets the joke; she must not have any friends of the Portuguese or Italian persuasion, all of whom, in my experience, love to yell instead of talk. We pack up our high volume spawn, stop for a free waste tank pump out and are headed out of Erie harbour and soon on the open water pointed due north for Long Point.

The trip across seems to take a very long time, probably because of the anticipation of getting home. We eventually reach Long Point and stop for a quick swim and lunch before continuing on the last leg to Port Dover, which is about 20 miles. It is around 7 pm when we finally pull into our familiar old home slip and it does feel pretty good to be on Canadian soil, or at least water. Ana calls customs on the phone and they clear us with no issues. The dock is very quiet, with hardly anybody around so we have a calm night on board and finally manage to see the rest of *The Matador* on the fourth attempt.

We spend the next day and a half doing some work on the boat, visiting dock friends and walking around Port Dover checking out the shops. We finally arrive back at our house on Saturday afternoon and Magnus immediately goes next door to show his neighbour friend Lilly his loose tooth. The aggressive wiggling breaks the last few strands and the tooth pops out! He is thrilled to discover that he can still whistle even without a primary frontal ivory, so he is happy indeed.

We are all decidedly happy to be home, especially after such a successful adventure. We feel much more confident with *Bella Blue* and are overjoyed that the kids have taken so well to sailing.

There will be plenty more trips to come.

****

The Hunt for Kalik

The first overseas trip we did with our new baby Magnus was to the Turks & Caicos. It was a test of how we would be able to manage our traveling ways with a child, and I'd say we did quite well. But the primary theme of the story is my love for the Bahamian beer called Kalik. I've maintained a beer page on our website www.lifeisgrand.org where I do humorous reviews of world beers, and it has been the most clicked on page of our site for many years! Seems a lot of people are fond of beer.

As the wheels of the Boeing 737 struck the asphalt and spun to life with a puff of blue smoke, two thoughts occurred to me. First, we were finally back in the Caribbean, evidenced by emerald blue ocean staring at me from across the dusty dry strip of land separating the runway from the sea. Second, I needed to find Kalik. In case you were unaware, Kalik, brewed in the Bahamas, is the best beer in the world and my brand of choice. Kalik is adventures. Kalik is suntanned bodies and memories. Kalik is slumming along the shoreline looking for conch shells. Kalik is beer, but more than beer, it is a state of carefree bliss. Kalik is the sound of rattling cow bells amongst a thousand drumming, beating, sweating, rhythmic black bodies on a humid Caribbean night.

In short, I was thirsty. And my skin was already squandering the precious little moisture the dry Canadian prairie climate allowed it.

The island onto which we had just landed was Providenciales, of the Turks & Caicos chain. These islands are located just south of the Bahamas and north of the Dominican Republic, home of Presidente, another fine beer, though not the target of this particular mission. This was to be my wife Ana's and my first overseas vacation with our new little son Magnus. At the ripened age of seven months, he was already jetting off to the Caribbean for a dirty weekend.

The scene at the airport was similar to other Caribbean airports – unintelligible patois, white teeth, stunned tourists. After some sweaty pacing in the sun we found a taxi driver to take us to the hotel. That first taxi ride in a new country is where you always pay your ignorance tax. You know you will be charged at least twice as much as you should be, but the sooner you dish out, suck up your pride and forget about it, the sooner you can begin to figure the place out. We piled our gear in the back of the van, gave him the name of the hotel, then glued our asses into the hot vinyl of the seats, trying hard not to let the sweaty baby slip from our grasp. Extensive government funded research shows that squirmy babies have a 150% greater chance of escaping their parent's grasp while vacationing in the Caribbean, and a 200% greater chance of being left crying in a crib while the parents are enjoying a cocktail and sunset on the balcony. As the van took off and we began the sweltering ride, Ana's wandering finger found conclusive proof that the Caribbean heat softens babies' gums and promotes dental activity; Magnus's first tooth!

"Hey buddy," I said to the taxi driver, "in our culture it's customary for a taxi driver to give a free fare if his passengers find their baby's first tooth during the ride!"

"Uh huh, yeah mon," he replied glumly. I didn't think he was going for it; perhaps my attempt at humour was premature. Enough subtleties – it was time to embark on my hunt.

"Hey, can you get Kalik beer here?" I asked innocently.

"Whah dat?" he asked.

"Bahamain beer," I explained.

"You in de Toiks, mon," he kindly pointed out. I decided to take this line of questioning no further. After spending years in the Caribbean, I knew it was sometimes better to give in right at the start and avoid frustration.

"Oh yeah? Thanks man," expressing my gratitude for his insight.

We were soon at our hotel, called the Turtle Cove Inn, where we got checked in and up to our rooms within five minutes, a minor miracle in this land of leisure. On the way up to our room I noticed a sign for a liquor store across from the hotel lobby.

"Ana my dear, I shall return shortly with a case of beautiful cold Kalik to stoke up this sweet little bar fridge," I pronounced, and in one swift motion deposited the sweaty baby onto the bed and stuffed some moist beer money into my pocket.

I walked out of the room and into the open air corridor. Here, the walk turned into a shuffle, which in turn transformed into a jog by the time I reached the stairs. The eighteen steps posed no difficulty as I took them six at a time, gaining momentum, then hit the ground at full speed and sprinted around the pool, hurdling over the sun tanning Speedoed Quebecois in their lounge chairs, through a small grove of palm trees, not stopping to check for falling coconuts, around the side of the hotel and into the short corridor, which opened into the blessed liquor store. Applying full brakes, I skidded to a halt barely in time, scaring the living shit out the dude at the counter, who appeared to be sleeping standing up. "It all in de knees mon," a friend from Barbados once told me, "we Caribbean men, we learn to lock de knees, den you can sleep while you look like you woikin." Great skill, that one.

I frantically slid open the beer cooler and scanned the shelves. The first beer I saw was Miller Light, what the hell? Next came Presidente, ohh, that's good, I'll have to get some of those later, after the Kalik. Wait, where is the Kalik?? There were no goddamn cold Kaliks in the cooler, just a couple local brands! *Ok, don't panic*, I thought to myself, *I'll just buy a warm case and put them in our fridge and let them cool for a bit*. Eyes shift rapidly to the cases of beer stacked against the wall. The familiar blue Kalik label was not jumping out at me and the rapid scan confirmed my fears. No Kalik.

"Hey, do you guys have any Kalik? You know, Bahamian beer?" I asked the guy behind the counter, who was now fully conscious.

"No mon, no Kalik," he answered, offering no alternatives.

"But you normally have it? You're just out of stock?" I pleaded, hardly trying to mask my disappointment.

"No mon. Well, sometimes, but it rare," he carefully explained.

Rare? Rare?? Four leaved clovers are rare. Two headed dogs are rare. Passenger pigeons are friggin rare. How can beer be rare?

"What do you mean rare?" I had to ask.

"We don't get it offen," he told me.

"But it's available on the island?" I continued, trying to stay calm.

"Yeah mon," he concluded, offering no clues as to the whereabouts of this apparently endangered beverage.

"Okay. Well, then I guess I'll take six Miller, just to tide me over for now." I was actually very thirsty and since the price of the Miller Light (not to mention the alcohol content) was comparable to bottled water, I went for that option. *This will just make that first Kalik taste all the more spectacular*, I thought. I hoped.

I returned to the room and explained the sad situation to my understanding wife, who was now using towel grips to manoeuvre the sweaty baby around on the bed. "Don't worry," she said pointing her finger out the balcony window, "they probably have Kalik at the hotel bar, it's just over there."

Minutes later, Ana, me and young Magnus, in his hot new sunglasses and hat, were on the deck of the hotel bar, overlooking the beautiful yachts in the marina and enjoying the rays of the hot sun. With what was to become a ritualistic interrogation I would soon perfect, I asked the approaching waitress, "Do you have Kalik beer? You know Kalik, right? It's made in the Bahamas."

"No mon, no Kalik," she reported.

"But how can that be? The Bahamas is so close I can practically see one of the islands from here. The web sites I read said Kalik was available all over the Turks & Caicos. How can it be?" I desperately questioned. Was I starting to sound pathetic?

"No Kalik, mon," she said apologetically, "but I tink dey got Kalik at the supermarkets." *Well, at least I can always go there to get some if none of these bars have it*, I thought, trying to calm my feelings of angst. I then decided that I wasn't going to let the rareness of Kalik get me down and instead ordered up a couple of Coronas for Ana and I, with which we toasted our own happiness and fortune to be able to visit such a wonderful place. But on the inside, beneath the smiles and glee, I had begun plotting my next move in the hunt for Kalik.

Day 2 arrives with no Kalik hangover. The previous nights plan to find Kalik failed, but we did find a lovely Tropical Chicken Salad at a harbour side restaurant called Tiki Hut. To make things worse, our server was a Bahamian who claimed to be a Kalik lover but didn't have a clue where to find it, though she did say it was available from time to time in certain places. The only real success of that episode was the discovery of a delicious local brew, called Turks Head Light, which helped to get me through this time of trouble.

I would follow this routine over the next couple of days. See a restaurant or bar. Go into said establishment. Ask for Kalik. Get looks of dim recognition, but no solid leads. Much talk of the existence of Kalik, but no proof. Despite becoming increasingly disappointed and gradually more tempted to abandon my quest, I didn't let this sour our vacation. We adventured around the island, on and off the track well traveled, one afternoon finding ourselves all alone on a mile long pristine beach with our beautiful little baby, eyes lit up, enjoying the pleasures of the warm Caribbean sea and flavour of the warm Caribbean sand for the first time. Another afternoon, we happened upon a local conch shack called Boogaloos, which produced a magnificent conch salad; an almost spiritual mingling of hot goat peppers, fresh onions, crunchy conch and tangy citrus juices. The perfect beverage to accompany such a meal would have been a Kalik, but I settled for Turks Head lager, which was much, much better than nothing at all.

On our last day, I seemed to get a break. As we were driving across the dry landscape one morning on the way to the beach, we passed a huge supermarket, parking lot packed with cars, people carrying out groceries and crates of beer – surely, the best place to find Kalik. I walked into the massive store and immediately found the beer section, which was a full aisle teeming with boxes of brews. *Finally*, I thought, *my search is over.* Why on earth didn't I find this place earlier? I can taste that sweet beer already, let me at it!

I charged down the aisle, rapidly scanning the shelves, left and right, up and down, looking, wanting, needing, finally reaching the end of the line and finding....nothing. I panicked, thinking I must have somehow missed it, so I turned and slowly walked back down the cursed alley of ales, analyzing each bottle as I passed. Turks Head, Heineken, Guinness, Miller, Corona. OK, those are pretty standard export beers, I rationalized. Next came Samuel Adams, Carib, Sol, Presidente, what the hell? It got worse. I was then faced with obscure Japanese beers, Spanish beers, French beers, and Haitian beers. Haitian beers?? They seemed to stock every type of beer ever made, from every part of the globe, lagers to bitters to stouts. Every beer you could imagine except the one beer I was in pursuit of; Kalik. It was then I felt a wave of sweet surrender wash over my body as I realized it was not meant to be. I was not going to find Kalik, and as I accepted this fact, I was overcome by a strangely comforting sense of detachment, and I could feel my spirit floating up and out of my body, and from overhead watching myself reach out and pick up a case of Presidente beer, walk up to the checkout, lay down some bills, and exit the building, then get into the car and drive away.

At last, I was at peace. We spent our final day on a perfect beach, with perfect weather, and as the end of the day approached I recognized my failed mission was actually an opportunity...to set off on another hunt for Kalik somewhere in the beautiful Caribbean next winter!

####

About the author:

Kris lives with his family Ana, Magnus and Stella in Paris, Ontario. He finds peace early in the morning, with a hot cup of coffee, listening to great music, experimenting with words, sometimes on a sailboat, sometimes at home, sometimes elsewhere in this big, beautiful world.

Connect with Kris online:

Website: http://www.lifeisgrand.org

Blog: http://blog.lifeisgrand.org/

Twitter: https://twitter.com/kristoforolson

Facebook: https://www.facebook.com/kristofor.olson.3

Made in the USA
Columbia, SC
28 May 2024

35965972R00153